Praise for *Vox Popular: The Surprising Life of Language in the Media*

"In our times, film and television show America talking in a more realistic way every year, and it's high time someone wrote a book on language and society that puts *Modern Family, Boyz n the Hood*, and much else front and center as useful sources of discussion on how America talks and why. Robin Queen has done the job." – *John H. McWhorter, Columbia University*

"Robin Queen's *Vox Popular* manages to do many things at once, and with finesse: it introduces the study of language in its social context in a way that will be accessible to non-linguists; it establishes an approachable, achievable methodology for the study of language in the media that is theoretically sound; and it provides a treasure-trove of material gathered over many years that will be invaluable for anyone teaching these subjects. There are years of work distilled into a readable, useful whole about one of the least studied and most promising areas of research: the role that mediated language plays in constructing social identities, from Donald Duck to *Breaking Bad* and beyond." – *Rosina Lippi-Green, author of* **English with an Accent: Language, Ideology and Discrimination in the U.S.**

"Not only an important contribution to media studies but the kind of book that makes you want to design a new course specifically in order to use it as a text. A pleasure to read!" – *Barbara Johnstone, Carnegie Mellon University*

"*Vox Popular* convincingly shows that in our media-saturated world, linguistics and cultural studies need each other. Students and faculty in both fields will learn a great deal from this insightful and engrossing text." – *Mary Bucholtz, University of California, Santa Barbara*

Vox Popular

The Surprising Life of
Language in the Media

Robin Queen

WILEY Blackwell

This edition first published 2015
© 2015 John Wiley & Sons, Inc.

Registered Office
John Wiley & Sons, Ltd, The Atrium, Southern Gate, Chichester,
West Sussex, PO19 8SQ, UK

Editorial Offices
350 Main Street, Malden, MA 02148-5020, USA
9600 Garsington Road, Oxford, OX4 2DQ, UK
The Atrium, Southern Gate, Chichester, West Sussex, PO19 8SQ, UK

For details of our global editorial offices, for customer services, and for information about how
to apply for permission to reuse the copyright material in this book please see our
website at www.wiley.com/wiley-blackwell.

Library of Congress Cataloging-in-Publication Data

Queen, Robin M. (Robin Michelle), 1966– author.
  Vox popular : the surprising life of language in the media / Robin Queen. – First edition.
    p. cm.
  Includes bibliographical references and index.
    ISBN 978-0-470-65991-5 (hardback) – ISBN 978-0-470-65992-2 (paper) 1. Mass media and
language. 2. Popular culture–Social aspects. 3. Language and languages–Variation. I. Title.
  P96.L34Q84 2015
  302.2301′4–dc23

                                2014030903

A catalogue record for this book is available from the British Library.

Cover image © bulentgultek / iStockphoto

Set in 10/12.5pt Galliard by SPi Publisher Services, Pondicherry, India

Printed in Singapore by C.O.S. Printers Pte Ltd

1 2015

Contents

Preface and Acknowledgments

I grew up in a household full of televisions, and my childhood was one marked especially by the rhythm of the television schedule. I got ready for school watching *Sesame Street, Looney Tunes*, and, if my mom got up before we kids did, *The Today Show* or *Good Morning America*. I did my homework in the afternoons to ABC's *Afterschool Special, H.R. Pufnstuf*, and reruns of *The Dick Van Dyke Show*. I tolerated my parents watching the evening news before primetime began at 7 pm, with each evening a buffet of half-hour sitcoms and hour-long dramas. I grew up in the Central Time Zone of the United States, with its primetime schedule running from 7 pm to 10 pm, a timing that imprinted on me so strongly that I have never gotten used to the Eastern Time Zone primetime schedule of 8 pm to 11 pm, even though I've lived in the Eastern Time Zone for most of my adult life. The effects of television on my life were wide-ranging.

My childhood experience of television included noticing language. The Ewings on the television show *Dallas* spoke like we did, but Christine Cagney and Mary Beth Lacey from *Cagney and Lacey* most surely did not. Some kids used Spanish and taught it to the adults on *Sesame Street*. My father could imitate Donald Duck's odd speech (which I found out later came from forcing air from your cheeks) but could never teach me how to do it. My sister and her friends thought it was hilarious to speak in Smurf (though thankfully not for very long).

Things have changed significantly since then and the television schedule no longer structures the day quite like it used to. Audiovisual media, especially what we have traditionally called "television" and "film," are available pretty much on demand at any time of day or night using pretty much any device on which you might want to consume them. Whole seasons of a television series can be viewed in a weekend, and you can watch your favorite film on your phone while you travel. Something that hasn't changed all that much, though, is how language gets used in these venues.

The vampires on *True Blood* sound as (inauthentically) Southern as the *Beverly Hillbillies* did, and the imagined language of the West permeates *Breaking Bad* just as distinctly as it did *Gunsmoke*.

This book represents my attempt to pay homage to two of my favorite things: language, especially language variation; and media, especially television and film. It's been curious to me for a long time that two things that seem to me so obviously connected to one another have not frequently been paired together in scholarly research. Linguists tend to see the media as somehow not "real" while media studies people tend to see language as not "interesting" (or at least not as interesting as many of the other elements of TV and film). Perhaps because of my fascination with both of them, I have long seen language as fundamental to the workings of audiovisual media and audiovisual media as a fascinating source of information about language. To be sure, I come to this book as a linguist and not as a media studies scholar and that orientation will be clear throughout the book. Still, I'd like to believe that the discussions you'll find in this book will tell you as much about audiovisual media as they will about language.

The book is written for people like me who love language and who love watching television and movies. It's also written for people unlike me who may not have thought about any of this from the perspective of scholarship, and especially those who may not be familiar with thinking about language like linguists do. I have tried as much as possible to use media sources that are current, but of course almost as soon as this book was finished, new and interesting media products appeared. By the time you are reading these words, many of the examples will undoubtedly seem like they came from long ago. I hope that the general points of the book will help you see past that inevitable fact and that you'll be able to take the discussions here and apply them to whatever new and intriguing sources have come along in the meantime.

In the course of writing this book I learned firsthand that the old adage about it taking a village to raise a child holds true for books as well. I never could have imagined the many twists and turns my path through this book would take but now, coming to the end of this journey, I can absolutely say that it was only possible because of the treasured village of people who helped me along the way. My sincerest thanks go to all the friends, colleagues, and students who have been so generous with their time, energy, and expertise. Particular thanks go out to: Jannis Androutsopoulos, Marlyse Baptista, Rusty Barrett, Erika Beck, Pam Beddor, Andries Coetzee, Lisa Del Torto, Monika Dressler, Jennifer Glen, Scott Glen, Phil Hallman, Hayley Heaton, Amy Hemmeter, Barbara Johnstone, Deborah Keller-Cohen, Nate LeFave, Susan Lin, Rob McIntyre, Barbra Meek, Kelly Murnighan,

Kris Brown, Carmel O'Shannessy, Rachel Oakford, Carly Skinder, Sarah Thomason, Stephen Tyndall, and Jeanne Weaver. Thanks especially to Kevin McGowan for the excellent idea to use *Vox Popular* as the title.

Particular thanks are owed to Lauren Squires, who helped me refine the thinking in this book in numerous ways, and to Anne Curzan, who gave me confidence in the project when I wasn't sure it was merited and who read every word of the manuscript at a time when she was in the middle of her own pressing projects. Thanks are really hardly sufficient for either of them.

Writing this book showed me the merits of working with an academic coach, and I'm sure that I would not have reached this point without the coaching help offered by Jo Van Every. I am also greatly appreciative of Laura Esterman, who helped me understand the publishing side of writing books and who dropped everything to edit this manuscript in record time. I had an expert editorial team at Wiley Blackwell, especially Danielle Descouteaux, who saw this project as something worth pursuing, Julia Kirk, who provided just the right blend of encouragement and reminders for keeping the project moving, and Janet Moth, who copy-edited the manuscript.

Much love and gratitude are due the various members of my family who have always encouraged me even in what seemed to them frivolous pursuits, and the merry band of dogs, cats, chickens, and sheep who have kept me sane and made me laugh.

It's nearly impossible to put into words all the ways I am grateful to Susan Garrett, my best critic and biggest fan, who didn't know what she was signing up for all those years ago when she read through my dissertation but who has made every major piece I've written better and, most importantly, whose optimism and sustaining love make every day so very worth living.

A Note on the Linguistic Conventions Used in *Vox Popular*

Like many disciplines, linguistics has special symbols and conventions for representation. Unlike many disciplines, the representations used by linguists to capture facets of language compete with the systems, especially spelling and punctuation, that non-linguists use to do the same thing. This can make reading linguistic data somewhat confusing. To mitigate that confusion, I have used the conventional systems of spelling and punctuation as much as possible because most readers will already be familiar with those systems. This includes some seemingly standard ways of representing accents and dialects (for instance spelling < they > as < dey > for speakers who pronounce it that way).

Still, there are quite a few instances where the conventions of linguistics have been necessary in order to better capture the details of the language use. While it really isn't possible to capture everything that might be relevant about language in a way that is unequivocally "true" to the way the language was produced, many of the conventions used by linguists make it possible to come closer than is often possible with standard spelling and punctuation.

Below is a list of conventions that I use in this book:

- Single quotation marks indicate words and phrases that are being mentioned as linguistic data rather than used specifically within a sentence.
- Double quotation marks indicate quoted speech and "scare quotes" (which are used in academic writing to call critical attention to the word in question). I have also used double quotes around a word that sounds like a word being transcribed phonetically or phonemically. For instance, [toyn] has the same vowel as "coin."

- Italics mark keywords and titles.
- < > mark conventional spelling in the body of the text.
- / / indicate phonemic transcription.
- [ ] are used for a phonetic transcription.

I have provided transcribed data from a variety of television shows and films. Transcriptions are generally marked by Courier font and depart from scripts in capturing details of interaction and pronunciation. I have maintained conventional spelling for the most part to make the transcripts accessible. Some basic conventions that are used to capture elements not captured with conventional spelling are listed below.

Vocal Details

Specific voice quality	<xxxx> (e.g. breathy, falsetto, etc.) follows speech
Falling pitch	.
Rising pitch	?
Emphasis	!
Loudness	ALL CAPS
Softness	*italics*
Truncated sound	' (example: las')
False start	% (example: gar%street)
Reported speech	" "
Long pause	[N] where N = seconds
Medium pause	[..]
Short pause	,
Lengthened segment	: at lengthened segment. Can be multiple
Nonstandard stress	′V
Laughter	@
Exhalation	[hhh]

Turn-Taking

Speaker identity/turn start	:
Latched turn	=
Continued turn	-

Overlapping speech   [ ]
Co-constructed utterance   [[ ]]

Transcriber Notes

Unintelligible speech   ( )
Uncertain   (xxxx)
Noise   (clanking dishes)
Transcriber comment   < >
Phonetic transcription   <[ ]>
Spelling notation   << >>
Visual action   [ ]

Finally, linguists typically use a special alphabet to have an unambiguous correspondence between one sound and one symbol used to represent that sound. Often, these symbols, especially the consonants, correspond to the Latin alphabet we use to represent English. But, unfortunately, not always. Below is the set of phonetic symbols I use when necessary to pinpoint particular sounds. These are the symbols that do not occur in the Latin alphabet or that represent different sounds than the ones you might expect. Unless noted with underlining, the relevant sound is the first vowel or consonant.

Vowels

Symbol	Example
i	geese
ɪ	give
e	gave
ɛ	get
æ	gap
ə	sof<u>a</u> (this vowel is called the **Schwa**)
ɑ	got
ɔ	cough (in many dialects of American English, ɑ and ɔ sound the same)
ʌ	gut
o	goat
ʊ	good
u	goose

Symbol	Example

The following vowels are diphthongs, which means
two vowels acting together as one

αy	tide
oy	toy
αw	cow

Consonants

Symbol	Example
θ	<u>th</u>ing
ð	<u>th</u>at
ɾ	rat (note when /ɾ/ comes after a vowel in non-rhotic varieties, it will be marked as V:)
ʃ	<u>sh</u>ore
ʒ	gara<u>g</u>e
ɳ	si<u>ng</u>
ʔ	Sound that occurs between syllable of 'uh oh'. This is called a glottal stop

Keywords Found in Each Chapter

Chapter 1: Language in a Mediated World

- Categoricity
- Characterization
- Gradience
- Language
- Plot development
- Type
- Typification
- Variation

Chapter 2: Exploring Language and Language Variation

- Accusative
- Alveolar ridge
- Antecedent
- Auxiliary verb
- Bound morpheme
- Case
- Clause
- Derivational morpheme
- Diachrony
- Dialect, Accent
- Free morpheme
- Grammar
- Inflectional morpheme
- Intensifier

- Interference
- Lexicon
- Morphemes
- Morphology
- Nominative
- Package of variation
- Phonology
- Pragmatics
- Rhotic
- Semantics
- Sociolinguistics
- Synchrony
- Syntax
- Terms of address
- Velum
- Word

Chapter 3: Studying Language Variation in the Media

- Coding
- Collocate
- Concordance
- Conversational analysis
- Conversational repair
- Critical discourse analysis
- Data
- Discourse analysis
- Epistemology
- Experimental approach
- Intercoder reliability
- Metalinguistic
- Methodology
- Methods
- Ontology
- Qualitative
- Quantitative
- Transcription
- Triangulation

Chapter 4: Dimensions of Variation

- Ad-libbing
- Categorical
- Cluster
- Formal
- Global
- Informal
- Linguicism
- Local
- Modality
- Multimodal
- Planned
- Private
- Public
- Scalar
- Spoken
- Standard
- Standardization
- Written

Chapter 5: Making Language Variation Meaningful

- Cognitive schemas
- Convention
- Icon
- Ideologies about language
- Ideology
- Imagined communities
- Index
- Indexical meaning
- Indexicality
- Indirect indexicality
- Linguistic sign
- Metalinguistic
- Metapragmatic
- Order of indexicality
- Power
- Reference
- Signified
- Signifier

- Social meaning
- Symbol

Chapter 6: Language Variation and Characterization

- Archetype
- Authentication
- Authenticity
- Characterization
- Diffused
- Focused
- Identification
- Identity
- Linguistic indicator
- Linguistic marker
- Linguistic stereotype
- Norm
- Prototype
- Relational identity
- Social personae
- Stance
- Stereotype
- Trait indexicality
- Type indexicality
- Typification

Chapter 7: Language as Narrative Action

- Authority
- Citation
- Code-shifting
- Context
- Felicity
- Performance
- Performative verbs
- Performativity
- Plot device
- Poetic function of language
- Speech Act Theory
- Taboo words

Chapter 8: Connecting to the Audience

- Addressee
- Audience design
- Auditor
- Communities of practice
- Double voicing
- Eavesdropper
- Enregisterment
- Genre
- Gestalt
- Intertextuality
- Metalanguage
- Overhearer
- Parasocial activity
- Referee design
- Register
- Strategic inauthenticity
- Style
- Styling
- Stylization
- Transatlantic accent

Chapter 1

Language in a Mediated World

Mad Men in a *Modern Family* World

On November 7, 2012, the political commentator Matthew Dowd said that the GOP had become "a *Mad Men* party in a *Modern Family* world." His comment was meant to partially explain the reelection of Barack Obama; however, when I heard it I was struck by his use of two popular television shows as the metaphorical representation for that morning's political reality. The fact that his comment was repeated frequently and posted to social media venues like Facebook and Twitter illustrates its resonance. What he seemed to mean with the first part was that the GOP was living in, and appealing to, a past in which the leaders of the party were the same kinds of white, upper-class, men in their thirties, forties, and fifties depicted as the main characters in the series *Mad Men* (2007–2015), a show set in a 1960s Manhattan advertising agency and renowned for its realistic connection to a specific time and place but as seen through an early twenty-first-century set of eyes. The show also captures the start of the transition in the United States from post-World War II sensibilities about the homogeneity of political and social life to a seemingly messier engagement with heterogeneity.

Dowd contrasts the world of *Mad Men* with the one that is presumably more centrally located in 2012, namely the diverse suburban California world inhabited by the extended family depicted in *Modern Family* (2009–). On *Modern Family*, the social hierarchies are transparently unstable, shifting as scenes and relationships change. It is never entirely clear who, if anyone, is "in charge," and as Gina Bellafante (2013) notes about the show, it "[mainstreams] the various and sweeping changes in domestic life."

Vox Popular: The Surprising Life of Language in the Media, First Edition. Robin Queen.
© 2015 John Wiley & Sons, Inc. Published 2015 by John Wiley & Sons, Inc.

Modern Family captures the contemporary outcomes of many of the nascent changes caught by *Mad Men*. Through its lens, the focus of attention shifts from a political, public, and domestic life that was idealized as homogenous to one that celebrates its diversity.

Of further interest in this analogy is the fact that *Mad Men* is a modern testament to historical detail and to capturing a feel of a time, while also critiquing that very time and many of the values and personal qualities the characters of the show hold as dear and inevitable. It's by design that the kings of *Mad Men* are womanizers and that the few people of color who populate their world rise no higher in the social hierarchy than the hired help. On the other hand, *Modern Family* presents an idealized view of the modern suburban United States and captures a feel of the early part of the twenty-first century. The show attempts to portray the messiness of difference. At the same time, the show celebrates the power of things that are shared, like family connections, shared histories, love. Like *Mad Men*, *Modern Family* is visually of its time, with a deep embedding of electronic forms of communication and "mockumentary" moments in which characters let the audience in on their true feelings even if they don't actually share those feelings with the other characters.

While neither show is specifically about language (and, in fact, few media products ever are), language is of course an inextricable component of both shows and helps to sustain the general settings, the internal consistency of the characters, and the unfolding of both the broad and the narrow narrative arcs. Language can function this way primarily because of what linguists refer to as *variation*, by which they broadly mean alternative ways of using grammar, of pronouncing vowels and consonants, of structuring conversations, and of selecting particular words over other similar words. The *Mad Men* and their families are mostly not the New Yorkers depicted in films like the *Midnight Cowboy* (1969) or shows like *All in the Family* (1971–1979) – audiovisual products set in roughly the same time period in the Manhattan of the 1960s and 1970s. They are not Taxi Drivers or George Jeffersons. They speak in ways that provide consistency for their characters as "masters of their own destiny." They use Standard American English and the general linguistic style that modern audiences associate with aristocrats and the Golden Age of film and television. They use a formal style no matter the situations in which they find themselves. As John McWhorter (2009) writes:

> More generally, however, the writers at *Mad Men* seem to have an idea that in the early sixties, people spoke more "properly" than they do now. And they did, in formal and public settings. Until the late sixties, there was a sense that language was to be cosseted and dressed up in public in the same

way that one wore deodorant. Think of the old gesture of clearing your throat before Making a Speech, the speech having been carefully written out and practiced, as opposed to today when we prefer looser "talks."

This same style is interestingly echoed in *Modern Family* in the character of Manny, the half-grown son of the one non-native English speaker in the cast of characters. Manny's speech style is extremely formal in virtually all settings and contrasts directly with the much more casual style of most of the other characters. Each of the characters is a recognizable *type* and their language supports their *typification*: for example, the spacey, shallow teenage girl; the brainy, nerdy teenage girl; the sexy Colombian wife and mother; the geeky, gadget-obsessed white dad who tries too hard to be cool; the flamboyant gay uncle; and, yes, even a gruff, old, white master of the universe in the family's patriarch. While all the characters save the non-native speaker of English use more or less Standard English, just like the characters in *Mad Men*, it is a Standard English that relies on variation to help distinguish the characters from one another. The older teenage daughter peppers her lines with 'like'; the goofy younger son says 'dude,' as does his trying-to-stay-hip father. One of the gay uncles uses extremely precise color terminology, and both uncles are masters of snark.

Even though *Modern Family* and *Mad Men* differ in fundamental ways, their similarities as contemporary media products make them available as metaphorical reference points. While Matthew Dowd's quote was a comment on politics, it also serves as a useful illustration of why I've written this book. People use media broadly as a way of understanding, organizing, and categorizing their experiences. Matthew Dowd could have made his critique, as many others did, based on some of the actual political events and players, but doing so would have missed the nuance and creativity that the juxtaposition between *Mad Men* and *Modern Family* specifically highlighted. For as much as the facts of our actual lives influence our perceptions and understandings, the facts of our stories do the same. As I'll show throughout this book, language has an important place as part of the package we use for those perceptions and understandings.

Why Does a Linguist Care about *Mad Men* or *Modern Family*?

Before moving too deeply into the substance of language within the mass media, it's important to understand the specific perspective of this book and me as its author. *Language* is a topic in which many different kinds of people, including many different kinds of scholars, take keen interest. While ostensibly talking about the "same" issue when we focus on "language," in fact linguists, including me, have a particular way of thinking about language and of posing questions related to language. A linguist is someone focused on the broad understanding of language as a characteristic of the human species, an understanding that is oriented fundamentally around the question, "What do you know when you know a language?"

Answering that question leads us in various directions, and linguists explore lots of different things about language – from the details of the sounds of language, how speakers of languages create words and sentences, how language changes over time and what constrains that change, how meaning works, how writing is related to speech, how children acquire language, how adults acquire new languages, how language comes to be understood as a resource for social information, what things languages have in common, and in what ways languages differ. Regardless of the wide variety of questions and conversations about language that linguists find intriguing, virtually all of them are united by an interest in what it is about human beings that makes us language users. Linguists also tend to agree that even though all humans are predisposed toward becoming users of language, one critical ingredient must trigger that process. In order to become language users we require some kind of linguistic input, and the primary mechanism by which we get the input is through interaction with other people.

Social interaction is not only the source of our language input, though; it is also one of the major functions facilitated by language. As we interact with one another, we constantly monitor both our own speech and that of the people we're interacting with, sometimes shifting our language to be more like that of those we're interacting with and sometimes shifting it to be more distinct. For instance, if you notice someone you really like using a word that you are unfamiliar with, you are likely to find ways to use it in your own speech once you have determined what the word means.[1] In this way, you add to your own vocabulary and indicate to your conversational partner that you want to be somehow more connected to her. As you use the new word in interactions with new people, the process repeats itself. If the new folks also know your original conversational partner, then they may connect the two of you via your similar use of language. They may also notice that the two of you are using a word that other people don't. In other words, even as you are linguistically similar to one another, you differ from people who don't use that word.

The use of a single word is obviously highly simplified as an illustration of the role of language for social interaction. Language turns out to be infinitely more complex than just a series of words, and it can vary across sounds, words, and sentence constructions. In a more direct connection to social interaction, language can also vary in areas like how it's used to produce stories, indicate whose turn it is to speak, and say hello and good-bye, to name a few. We'll delve into these details further in Chapter 2, where we'll see that language variation is often tied to characteristics of speakers such as where they are from, who they are, and their underlying motivations and experiences. For right now, it's important to see the inherent connection between social interaction and language variation.

Language is just as important to setting up a story and making that story believable as are the visual, audio, and other special effects that may be used. For instance, language mediates between my own conceptual world and yours. In other words, language is the mechanism by which you gain access to my thoughts and by which I can make my thoughts (or at least parts of them) available to you. Like language, the mass media provide a set of channels that connect different conceptual worlds. This connection can be related to the "real" world as we see in informational media, which curate, package, and deliver specific representations of the world we live in. And of course it can also be related to the conceptual worlds generated through imagination and creativity, the worlds that are the main focus of this book.

Language and media share other characteristics as well. One of the curious ones is that their workings are typically rather hidden from their users. For instance, "the media" consist of regular people, just like the audience does, and thus are not really separate from the audience. The people who produce the media rely on many of the same social, cultural, and political contexts to make sense of their experience as the audience does. They draw on many of the same stylistic and linguistic repertoires to make their art and stories accessible to others. In other words, "the media" don't do things independently of the communities of which they are a part. They exist in those communities in the same way that schools and churches and ice cream shops are parts of communities. The media represent institutions and as such have their own particular systematic structures that affect how they engage and are engaged by the people who use them. Claudia Bubel (2006, 58), for instance, writes the following about the process of producing a television show:

> Once these ideas are realised as scripted dialogue, verbal interactions between actors/characters are shot by the camera team, with the camera focusing in on the face of the speaking or listening actor/character and sometimes all of the conversationalists. The filmed material is then edited in a joint effort by cutters, directors, and producers. . . . All of this process is relevant in the design of utterances for the overhearers so that the

co-construction of meaning in screen-to-face discourse is a joint effort of the audience in front of the screen, the actors, the directors, the screen-writer, the story editors, the producers, the camera team and the cutters involved in the editing process.

This very collective process of constructing a media product is part of what makes exploring language variation in the media so fascinating and also explains why it differs so significantly from the capture of everyday language (such as we see in many homemade videos on YouTube, for instance). Like "the media," language is a highly structured system – or really a system of systems, but its rules are not always transparently available to its users and it does not lend itself entirely easily to change. All human beings are users of language, and yet we frequently have a very poor sense of how language really works, tending to focus mostly on "words" and what they mean. We think of language as primarily a mecha-nism of communication, and, while it is certainly that, there is much more to it than most of us realize.

Another characteristic that media and language have in common is that their users have many opinions about them. The media are frequently the culprit when other kinds of social anxieties arise. During politically charged times, the media are blamed for being partial to one side or another. Similarly, language is often a focus of deep concern and seen as an emblem of societal decay. As Jim and Lesley Milroy have discussed it (Milroy and Milroy 1999), language becomes the focus of moral debates when anxieties about morality more generally arise. It connects, for instance, to questions of being a good citizen when immigration becomes of social concern or to questions of standards when technologies, such as the Internet, bring anx-ieties about social change occurring too rapidly. To return to one of the media products that began this chapter, we can look at a scene from *Modern Family* in which an area of current linguistic change is the focus of a scene.

This scene illustrates how language may be simultaneously part of the overall contextualization of the story, including the contextualization of the characters themselves, and also can be a mechanism of moving the plot forward. The scene involves the mother, Claire, who can be described as a "helicopter par-ent"; Haley, Claire's daughter, who is a stereotypical teen-aged American girl, and an unnamed friend of Haley's. This scene is a flashback scene tied to an earlier discussion in the episode of issues different members of the family want to avoid. Claire wants to avoid having to drive Haley around and this flashback scene explains why. Driving together is often the scene of arguments.

In this scene, Haley is in the back seat with her friend, talking ani-matedly about clothes, and Claire is listening in as she drives. (You can find a list of the some of the conventions linguists use, and that are being used in this book, on page **00**. These conventions capture various components of spoken language that are not usually written out formally.)

Example 1.1   *Modern Family*, "Fears," Season 1, Episode 16, Christopher Lloyd and Steven Levitan (creators), ABC, March 2, 2010

```
 1  Haley:     And then I'm like "There's no way I'm
                wearing that" and she was like "If you
                don't wear it then you can't play."
 2  [Claire    shakes her head as she listens]
 3  Claire:    Like! [turns toward the girls while still
                driving]
 4  Haley:     And I was like "That's fine by me."
 5  Claire:    Honey, like!
 6  Haley:     And she was like "If you don't play
                then "=
 7  Claire:         = Like!
 8  Haley:     Mom! Stop!
 9  Claire:    Stop saying like all the time
10  Haley:     [You're embarrassing me! Sto::::p<screams
                incoherently>
11  Claire:    [Like like like like<screams incoherently>
```

This scene illustrates a juxtaposition of characters primarily linked to age. Haley is using a newish form of the word 'like' in which 'like' together with a form of 'to be' can be used as a verb of quotation.[2] 'Be like' is the focus of frequent commentary outside the media world and is especially associated with teenage girls even though it is used with more or less equal frequency among males and females and across the age spectrum, including among speakers as old as 80 and as young as 3 (D'Arcy 2007).

This scene, however, captures a fairly typical dynamic in which an adult is bothered by a younger person's language use. The scene thus exemplifies something familiar and recognizable for the audience. First, it illustrates why Claire would want Haley to earn her driver's license. Claire doesn't wish to continue driving Haley around because she's worried about arguments erupting. The fact that the example argument Claire thinks of has to do specifically with language is notable, especially because this source of disagreement appears to need no further contextualization or clarification. Claire's dislike of the use of quotative 'be like' is assumed to be clear, recognizable, and largely independent of any broader context.

Second, within the context of the show as a whole, the encounter over 'be like' captures the broader tensions between Claire and Haley in which Claire continually seeks to change her daughter into a more mature, thoughtful person and Haley resists that change, finding her mother intrusive and embarrassing. The scene provides further support of Haley's characterization as a stereotypically teenaged girl with shallow interests and concerns, who is portrayed as not very intelligent. Haley's character is in many ways the quintessential Valley Girl, and character bios of her that are available in various places, including the show's Internet home page, frequently characterize her as a Valley Girl (and always characterize her as a stereotypical teenager girl). This characterization of Haley runs throughout the show as Haley is regularly presented as something of an airhead and juxtaposed with her sister, Alex, a nerdy, smart, but not very popular girl. It is difficult to imagine a more iconic indication of a shallow, non-school-oriented teenage girl in the United States in the early part of the twenty-first century than the use of 'be like.'

Food for Thought

Think of three or four characters who appear in one of your favorite movies or one of your favorite television series. Write a character bio about each of those characters that includes something about how they use language. Then, compare your bios to those that are available online for the same characters.

Beyond being part of characterization, language can also be an integral part of moving the plot forward, either because it is used to explain or narrate something that has happened outside the narrative, such as when a character tells part of her back story in order to explain something about her actions, or someone divulges his inner thoughts while he was involved in doing something and that narration changes the course of the action.

Sometimes, the very form of language itself is the action, such as in the following scene from the film *Love Actually* (2003). This film explores various aspects of love through several different stories about people who will turn out at the end of the film to be either casually or coincidentally related to one another. The vignette in Example 1.2 involves a young man, Colin, who is generally inept at courting young women, and so he decides to exploit his Britishness by going to the United States to try and pick up women there, drawing on his understanding of the prestige his British accent will afford him. He ends up in a bar in a small town in Wisconsin in the middle of the winter.

Example 1.2 *Love Actually*, Richard Curtis (dir.), 2003, Universal Pictures

```
 1  [Colin comes into the bar.]
 2  Bartend:  Can I help you?
 3  Colin:    Yes. I'd like a Budweiser please. King of
                Beers.
 4  [woman slowly looks up from her drink]
 5  Bartend:  One Bud comin' up.
 6  Stacey:   Oh My God. Are you from England?
 7  Colin:    Yes. [smiling]
 8  Stacey:   Oh [hhh]. That is so cute [removing coat
                hood] [..] Hi, I'm Stacie.
 9  [They shake hands and each giggle]
10  Stacey:   Jeannie?
11  Jeannie:  [at jukebox, turns around] Yeah?
12  Stacey:   This is [..]
13  [cut to Colin]
14  Colin:    Colin. [shakes Jeannie's hand] Frissle.
                [removes knit cap]
15  Jeannie:  Cute name. Jeannie.
16  Stacey:   He's from England.
17  Colin:    Yep, Basildon. <noticeable British-
                accented first vowel [basɪldn̩>
```

```
18 Jeannie:  Oh. <rising falling pitch>
19 Stacey:   Oh. <breathy>
20 Jeannie:  Wait til Carol Anne gets here. [looks
             at Stacey] She's crazy about English
             guys.
21 Stacey:   Uh-huh.
```

In this scene, the basic characterization is established and the individual characters are set up. The two dialects of English – American English and British English – are central to the overall contextualization and setting of the interaction and are fundamental to the various characters. In this sense, the accents are a property of the characters, just like the clothes the characters are wearing and the general setting in a bar are central to the overall context. Who these characters are is tied to how they speak, and how they speak helps create them as recognizable and believable characters. The young women for example use a distinctive style of American English, indicative of people who are geographically and socially somewhat provincial. They also represent very clear images of young women who spend their leisure time in bars hoping to create romantic liaisons with desirable men.

As the scene continues, it becomes clear that language is also fulfilling a different function. Rather than being used only to establish the context, it becomes the vehicle of the actual plot development.

```
1 [A few minutes later. Colin, Stacey, Jeannie, and
   Carol Anne at a table laughing. There are lots of
   empty beer bottles on table.]
2 Stacey:      That is so funny. @@@@ Wha% whaddya
               call that? [points to beer bottle]
```

3	Colin:	A bottle. <with glottal stop at the<<tt>>>
4	All three:	Bottle. <mimic Colin's pronunciation>
5	Carol Anne:	What about this? [grabs a straw]
6	Colin:	Straw. @@@@@< [str ɔ] >
7	All three:	Straw. <unsuccessfully try to mimic Colin's pronunciation>
8	Jeannie:	What about this? [points to the table]
9	Colin:	Table.
10	Jeannie:	Table. <falling pitch>
11	Stacey:	<disappointed>Oh.
12	Jeannie:	<disappointed>It's the same.
13	[1 sec. pause]	
14	Carol Anne:	Where are you staying?
15	Colin:	I don't actually know. Guess I'll just check into a motel like they do in the movies.
16	Stacey:	Oh my god, oh my god, that is so cute.

As we see from the continuation of the bar scene, the juxtapositions of British and American English pronunciation are central to the plot and Colin is able to do what he set out from England to do: pursue young women by making use of the prestige of his Britishness, even though his fundamental awkwardness has prevented him from being successful in Britain where he has no such capital to work with. In the bar, the narrative moves to the characters having a lot of fun together as they exoticize (and sexualize) their linguistic differences. This is particularly evident in lines 4 and 7 where the women try to mimic Colin's pronunciation and then show disappointment in lines 10–12 when it turns out that the British and American pronunciations of "table" are the same. Still, Colin ends up being invited back to stay with the girls and eventually returns to England, triumphantly involved with the fourth roommate, Harriet. This scene highlights the two major functions language variation plays in the context of the mass media, *characterization* and *plot development*. On the one hand, the characters are partly created through the juxtaposition of the variety of English they use, and on the other, the specific differences between those varieties provides a central mechanism for advancing the narrative plot.

Food for Thought

Watch an episode of a television series that you know reasonably well. Explain as clearly as you can what the plot of the episode is and what specific actions, conversations, or other elements move the plot from one stage to another. How many different plot lines are there in the episode? How exactly does each plot move from beginning to end? How does this episode fit the overarching plot of this season of the series? What about the plot of the series as a whole? How are the different layers of plot related to one another and how does the audience know they are related?

It's exactly these two functions of language within the context of the mass media that make the mass media interesting for people who are interested more broadly in language from a linguistic perspective. Although linguists have traditionally been fairly skeptical of the narrative media as a source of interesting information about language variation (Chambers 1998; Labov 2000), scenes like this one illustrate just how intriguing and analytically rich an examination of language in the media can be.

Narrative Media as a Site for Linguistic Exploration

Narrative media as I envision them for this book involve people who are representing someone other than themselves, usually someone fictional or historical. This differs from informational media in that information-oriented media typically have people representing themselves (or at least some version of themselves) in particular kinds of situations (cooking, talking to a host, delivering the news, and so on) (see the following for further discussion of this distinction: Thompson 2003; Kolker 2009; Cullen 2014). I assume narrative media to be tied largely to fictionalized content, though there is no clear-cut line for unambiguously distinguishing fiction and non-fiction or imagination and information. For instance, virtual online communities, such as *Second Life* (2003), or multiplayer video games, such as *World of Warcraft* (2004), have non-fictional as well as fictional components. Reality television presents another genre of popular representation that is difficult to clearly delineate as fictional or non-fictional. Like a documentary, reality television frames a narrative in particular ways and for particular purposes, but the people and events being represented are fundamentally representations of themselves. Like more canonical fictional television, though, the situations in which reality television characters find themselves are often scripted for them and they may be encouraged by the show's producers and directors to highlight similarities and differences with other characters.

Media is a massive construct, made up of various kinds of technologies, products, people, and activities. A medium is a channel through which information, entertainment, communication, and so on can flow. At some level, of course, language itself is fundamentally a medium, an intermediary between my thoughts and yours. In the more conventional sense, and in the sense being used here, media act as an intermediary, or a channel, between particular content and its audience. For instance, broadcast media are a channel through which content is transmitted electronically to an audience that is not in the same place as the content. Print media, on the other hand, are a channel in which content is presented via some kind of material object such as a book. Finally, news media refers to channels through which specific content – news – is delivered. These can include both print and broadcast channels. In this book, I am interested in the broader spectrum of commercial media, namely, those media that create information and entertainment products to be delivered to a public. Commercial media are financed either directly by that public (for instance, via taxes or subscriptions) or by advertisers who hope to use the media product as a vehicle for connecting advertised products and services to the public.

Canonically, most people mean "mass media" when they speak of "the media." Examples of mass media include broadcast, print, and electronic forms of content distribution that are available simultaneously to a broad range of recipients, regardless of those recipients' geographic or temporal location. Non-mass forms of media are those forms that are not designed or intended for a broad and largely unknown audience and which are not focused on some kind of commercial appeal. These include products like home movies, telephone calls, and texting.

The distinction between mass and non-mass is largely idealized and gradient rather than specific and categorical. The gradience is apparent in the changing nature of the meaning of "mass" from being primarily about mass delivery of a media product at a specific point in time, such as when a movie opens in theaters or a television show is broadcast, to being a system in which the distribution of media products is independent of time so that an individual viewer may access the product when s/he wishes. This change to the distribution mechanisms makes it less likely that many people are watching the product at the same time even though it is available to them all at the same time (and at virtually all times). The notion of *gradience*, as compared to *categoricity*, recurs throughout this book and is applicable to a wide range of conceptual distinctions concerning media as well as language.

A second distinction worth bearing in mind with respect to the media is the one between media products that are informational as compared to imaginative. Informational media are largely those media that are representing actual events, people, or situations, such as the news media, sports broadcasts, awards broadcasts, documentary films, and game shows. In contrast, imaginative media emerge from the media producer's imagination and are largely fictional in nature. These types of media include novels, situation comedies on television, non-documentary films, and so on. Of course, the difference between informative and imaginative is not a strict distinction, and there are many ways in which the functions of both broad types are shared. For instance, both can be centrally connected to the commercial nature of entertainment. Further, it's easy to imagine cases where the two types blend together. For instance, several types of reality television programming combine aspects of informational and imaginative orientations and that combination is part of their specific appeal. Still, in a reality program, as compared to a situation comedy, the people being depicted are portraying some version of themselves rather than characters created out of whole cloth for the purpose of the show. In this book, I will primarily discuss language variation in the context of imaginative mass media.

A third distinction worth considering is between scripted and unscripted (or edited and unedited) mass media. As with the distinctions between information/imagination and mass/personal, the distinction between scripted and unscripted serves to define two edges of a continuum. The distinction matters because of the complex relationships between the writer, director, actor, and character involved in producing scripted, performed language. At some level, characters are not themselves animators of language because they are always the product of an author's, an actor's, a director's, and an audience's imagination. As Richardson (2010, 3) writes,

> [Television] repeatedly displays people talking, showing audiences how characters behave in the varying circumstances of their narratives. These stories, and the talk they give rise to, mediate between the familiar and the extraordinary, and engage the imaginative powers of their receivers as well as their creators.

In addition to the different set of participants involved in producing and receiving media, the evolution of technologies of production and distribution also plays an important role when thinking about the place of language in the mass media (Cullen 2014). At some level, the story of language in the mass media goes back at least to the medieval period when the majority of the population couldn't read, but when works of imagination nonetheless relied on language variation to do some of the work of plot development and characterization. Very early works of fiction, such as *Don Quixote* (1605, 1615), the *Inferno*, and *The Canterbury Tales* (both fourteenth century), for instance, relied on the vernacular, rather than Latin, to represent their respective stories. Further, the characters Don Quixote and his trusty sidekick, Sancho Panza, speak differently from one another, with Don Quixote using the chivalrous language of knights and Sancho Panza speaking as an uneducated peasant. Similarly, Chaucer made use of regional dialects in his famous *Canterbury Tales* to differentiate the characters in particular ways. Language variation was part and parcel for some of the earliest forms of mass media and has remained so through various technological advances such as recording sound, linking sound and image, and electronically broadcasting to a wide audience via radio waves, physical cables, or satellite, and doing so in both analog and digital formats.

As Bauman (2011, 39) notes, media forms always carry some of their contextual history with them, and that contextual history matters for thinking about language variation. The representation of language variation and the role of language variation for character and plot development are linked to the contextual histories of the media channels.

Some of the most interesting historical moments for language variation in the narrative mass media occur at those points of transition facilitated by

Table 1.1   Critical points for language in narrative mass media

Medium	Date range of adoption
Novels and narrative poems	As early as the fourteenth century (*Canterbury Tales, Inferno, Don Quixote*)
Early sound recordings	Late nineteenth century
Silent films	Late nineteenth century–mid 1930s
Radio broadcasts	1920s
"Talkies"	1927 (*The Jazz Singer*)
Television	Late 1930s, commercial viability by late 1940s
Internet and digital media	Late 1980s–early 1990s

technological change. For instance, the transition from stage performance to audio-recorded performance brought with it an introduction from an actor who would go on to animate the recorded narrative, often using a different vocal persona (generally his own – recorded actors were typically male). This introduction did the work of framing the narrative for the listening audience and setting up language variation to mark stylistic shifts (Bauman 2011, 27). Similarly, the transition from recording performance on discs to electronic broadcasting changed the audience experience from one of listening to disconnected performances to one of following characters and plots in a serial fashion. This transition linked authenticity and authority, especially in language, to the experience of consuming mass media products. That transition also heralded the channeling of media products through networks as commercial endeavors, which simultaneously linked the audience to advertisers via those products. That relationship further focused questions of authenticity and authority. Finally, the transition from audio-only-oriented media, such as radio, and visual-only media, such as silent films, to the synchronization of sound and image made the experience of mass media products much more similar to the experience of everyday communication than it had been. Imagine sitting in a theater and hearing language come from the screen for the very first time. It's almost impossible to imagine given how awash we are today in audiovisual media. And, yet, there was a time where silence gave way to speech.

Food for Thought

How do you experience and use different media channels? What devices do you use for different media experiences? What media channels do you use by yourself? Which ones do you experience with friends? Are there any that you engage with without multitasking? Are there any that you always use at the same time? How has your experience of the media changed over time and do you find the changes overall positive or negative?

The ability to sync the audio and the visual channels made it possible to hear dialogue (in the case of film) and see radio (in the case of television).

The technical ability to synchronize sound with the moving image proved to be a game-changer in the history of film precisely in the area of

Figure 1.1 Publicity Poster for *Blackmail* (1929), the first "talkie" by Alfred Hitchcock. Note the comment on the left: "See and hear our mother tongue as it should be spoken."

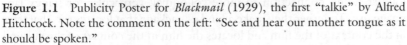

language as you can see in the movie poster for *Blackmail* shown in Figure 1.1. One of the earliest, and most profound, effects was a new ordering of the actors and studios comprising the silent film industry. As the film *Singin' in the Rain* (1952) highlights, the connection between the visual image of the actor and that actor's actual voice suddenly became paramount (see Taylor 2009). Michael Rogin (1996, 81) writes of *The Jazz Singer* (1927), widely considered to be the first successful commercial film to synchronize dialogue with dramatic action,

> The second sound interval is even more startling. When the grown Jack Robin (formerly Jakie Rabinowitz) sings "Dirty Hands, Dirty Face" at Coffee Dan's, for the first time in feature films a voice issues forth from a mouth. Jack then breaks free of both the intertitles that have carried the dialogue and the musical accompaniment that has carried the sound, and speaks his own words. "Wait a minute. Wait a minute. You ain't heard nothin' yet," says Al Jolson, repeating the lines he'd already made famous in vaudeville. These first words of feature movie speech, a kind of performative, announce – you ain't heard nothin' yet – the birth of sound movies and the death of silent film. The vaudeville performer, Al Jolson, has killed silent movies.

The Jazz Singer highlights three important points with regard to language and language variation in the mass media. First, we have in that first line of synchronized dialogue the symbolic moment that categorically shifts one form of mass media production to another. Second, we see the contextual history noted above in which a vaudeville star (Al Jolson) brings his live performance persona to life in the fictional character Jack Robin specifically by uttering a bit of speech made famous, and hence recognizable, in live performances by Al Jolson. Finally, and of special interest for this book, we have the actual form of that first line. Those eleven words include examples of linguistic variation that many people consider "bad" grammar, grammar that is available to be ridiculed and its speakers to be shamed – the word 'ain't', two negatives, and the "dropped g" in 'nothin'.'

Why did the various producers of the film use that particular line, said in that particular way, as the very first line of synchronized dialogue in a film? As we'll see again and again in this book, the reasons are complex and point to the cultural tensions embedded in linguistic difference. On the one hand, those three elements of "bad" grammar each retain a long-standing connection to more colloquial, vernacular, or slangy language use. Together they make a kind of package that locates the character in the context of the film and locates the film in the context of the cultural and historical moment of which it was a part. On the other hand, those three elements transcended that moment to link to many of the same tensions we deal with today, such as struggles over equality and struggles over the place of religion, class, and ethnicity in our cultural lives. The power in that line didn't, and doesn't, really come from the content embedded in it. Rather, it comes largely from its difference from we might call Standard English.

Unlike film, television arrived on the media scene as a vehicle for porting existing radio programming to an audiovisual medium. Whereas the ability to synchronize audio and video brought language variation more centrally into focus in the case of film, being able to broadcast synchronized audio and video to a large audience displaced in space was the key technological advance for television. For early television, this meant especially being able to broadcast live programming across space. It also meant that, rather than the concerns about the fit of the voice to the persona of the actor that animated the transition to "talkies" in film, the concern for television was much more about whether the visual image matched the persona created by the voice. This concern, for instance, led to an actor shift for the situation comedy *Amos 'n' Andy* (1951–1953), the first television situation comedy (Kolker 2009). In the radio program, the characters were animated by white actors performing as if they were black. For the television program, some aspects of the problematic nature of this kind of performance were recognized and black actors were hired to animate the characters (of course, the stereotypical and biased representation didn't change all that much in terms of the situations the characters found themselves in).

Another area in which narrative television differs from film is in the nature of serialization (Thompson 2003). While television broadcasts include a variety of live and non-narrative productions, such as sports events, lifestyle programming, awards programming, and news, as well as feature-length films and single-time productions, a hallmark of television is in fact its serial nature in which either the same basic set of characters comes together in more or less similar sets of circumstances (as in *Mad Men* and *Modern Family*) or in which more or less the same set of circumstances is shown over and over (as in the *Twilight Zone* [1959–1964] or *American Horror Story* [2011–]). The bulk of narrative television programming consists of the former type of show – serialized encounters among groups of semi-stable characters. This means that language variation plays a different role in television than in film.

Finally, in addition to the technological changes that have resulted in the narrative audiovisual landscape we experience today, the various funding models, and the changes to them, have been important (Cullen 2014). For television, control over funding shifted from sponsored producers of programming (*Kraft Television*; *Texaco Star Theatre*; *Goodyear Playhouse*) to the networks airing the programming. The quiz show scandal of the late 1950s and televised news programming, especially the McCarthy hearings, effectively shifted control for the development of television programming away from corporate sponsors and to networks, which saw themselves as more capable of managing the relationship between media products and the audience (Kolker 2009, 189). The networks then sold corporate sponsors time during programming in which to advertise their products. This model was challenged beginning in the late 1970s when subscription television became more widely available. The subscription model of funding has enhanced the move to niche programming and also to content that does not have to answer to corporate sponsors or federal regulators (Archive of American Television 2013). Both of these changes, which also affect the non-subscription-based networks, have meant changes to how language variation is used in the context of both plot and character development in television series, as we'll discuss more in Chapters 6 and 7.

For film, the transition of funding models differed in that the early period of film (from the turn of the century through about the 1950s) was one in which most of the financial power was concentrated in the hands of studios. Actors, writers, and producers were more or less employees of studios and were told by studio executives which films they would be involved in. Studios also owned the rights to film distribution in that they owned most of the theaters in which their products were shown. Studios thereby controlled both the process and the product (Kolker 2009, ch. 6). A legal challenge in the late 1940s to this perceived monopoly meant that studios lost their ability to own both the production and distribution rights and thus also their ability to keep certain films – for instance, independent films or films that pushed social and cultural boundaries – from being shown in theaters. The weakening of the studios also meant that the participants in film production could manage their careers more as free agents and were no longer bound to their studio employers. These changes had the effect of bringing more diversity to the kinds of products that were produced and thus also increased the possibilities for different kinds of linguistic variation to be woven into those products. This diversity is particularly apparent in the rise of the independent film movement, from the success of the only X-rated film to ever win an Oscar, *Midnight Cowboy* (1969), to the fantastical, magical realism caught in the voice of a 6-year-old using the English of the Louisiana Bayou in *Beasts of the Southern Wild* (2012).

Language Variation in the Narrative Media

All language in the media is primarily performed, or representational, in that it does not present "real-life," face-to-face conversation. The majority of studies that have used media data for thinking about linguistic variation have focused on print and broadcast news media or other forms of largely unscripted media such as talk shows, sportscasts, and broadcasts of live events. The fact that the vast majority of the scholarship on language variation in the mass media is drawn from unscripted media sources can largely be explained by the assumption that the language of scripted, imagined media is somehow less authentic than either unscripted language in the media or real-life communication (see Coupland 2007 for a discussion of authenticity in the media).

However, we can consider the scripted media to be fundamentally interesting precisely because of the ways in which they are of the culture of which they are a part, even as they play a role in shaping that culture.

The primary difference between the scripted media and other sources of information about sociocultural life is that what appears in the media derives from imagination and thus represents a highly edited version of social and cultural life. Thus, the scripted media offer a fairly contained, and edited, microcosm of the places from which their players come. In this sense, they are no more and no less "real" than the unscripted media.

The idea of language variation is built directly into the production and reception of media products, particularly narrative or imagined products. If it weren't the case that viewers expect some degree of variability, all characters in all kinds of programming would speak more or less the same way. But that is not how media products are produced or how we as audience members experience them. We want female characters to sound like females; children to sound like children; non-human aliens to sound different from humans. If the connection between the voice and the actor can be decoupled, such as in animation, then the actors animating the characters need not embody the broad demographic characteristics of the characters themselves – as many people know, the character Bart Simpson, a pre-adolescent boy, is voiced by Nancy Cartwright, a middle-aged woman. If voice and body can't be decoupled, then we also want the actor to look like we expect the character to look.

Things get interesting when characters who should sound a particular way based on who they are don't. For instance, in the film *Pocahontas* (1995), the title character would likely speak with a non-native English accent; however, in the film, she speaks with a fairly unmarked Standard American English accent.

Food for Thought

Imagine a story that you might want to tell. How would you use language to construct part of the context of the story and the characters?

Language and variation in language are as intrinsic to our experience of media products as costume, scenery, and musical score. As Spitulnik (1996) has explained, one of the real benefits of looking at the media, and especially the place of language in it, lies in the ways that media give (and reflect) the linguistic values of a given cultural moment. Those linguistic values can be found in representations of events that have actually

happened, such as in news reports or documentary films; in live representations of events, such as in talk shows or live sports broadcasts; and in
representations of fictional narratives, such as in much of our movie and
television culture. Spitulnik further notes that media products provide
fodder for socialization, for discussion and critique, for cultural reflection,
and for the broad circulation of culturally relevant/salient ideas, terms,
and beliefs. This fodder emerges through the processes that use language
to delineate social identities (the subject of Chapter 6) and its availability
to facilitate interaction between producers and consumers (the subject of
Chapter 8). Fictional narrative requires the creation of interrelationships
between a plot, characters, and a particular (fictional or factual) time and
place in which events unfold. As we'll see throughout the book, those
interrelationships are inextricably bound to the knowledge of language and
language variation that media producers and consumers bring to the
experience of interpreting fictional narrative, knowledge that we'll explore
in a lot more detail in Chapters 2–4.

For the most part, this book focuses on language variation that occurs
in the context of fictional representation. Further, although there are
many different channels for the delivery of fictional content, this book
takes the fairly narrow representational context of fiction that is delivered
via synchronized video and audio. Thus, this book focuses primarily on
fictional television and film products rather than similarly interesting
sources such as novels, radio dramas and podcasts, gaming situations,
online communities, and so on. However, I hope that by constraining the
kinds of data that we explore here, the concepts and methods of analysis
will prove highly portable to those other areas as well.

This focus is not intended to afford a particular primacy to the language of the narrative audiovisual media or to suggest that narrative
audiovisual media represent the key exemplars of language variation.
Rather, it takes advantage of the unique properties of narrative audiovisual media as stories that, once created, can be repeatedly rehearsed and
performed. Language in the narrative media differs from other forms of
language in its paths of circulation and its relative polish once produced,
and yet it shares with other forms of language an utter dependence on an
audience and interaction. Narrative audiovisual media involve linguistic
events that highlight the intention of the writers, actors, directors, and
producers to entertain and engage the audience. Narrative audiovisual
media also depend on predictable, recognizable forms of language that
combine with the skills and styles of the people involved in the production, and the response of the audience, to form multilayered representations of social life.

Notes

1   Robert LePage and Andre Tabouret-Keller (1985) have talked about this kind of move as an "act of identity." This move also forms the basis of an idea promoted by Howard Giles and his colleagues that people increasingly act similarly to one another unless something intervenes to cause them not to do so (Giles and Ogay 2007).
2   This change has been noted as early as the late nineteenth century; however, it has become more prevalent since about 1970 in most varieties of English. Further, *like* is undergoing several changes that won't be discussed here, but see D'Arcy (2007) for some discussion.

References

Archive of American Television. 2013. TV History. Retrieved January 10, 2014, from http://www.emmytvlegends.org/resources/tv-history.

Bauman, Richard. 2011. The Remediation of Storytelling: Narrative Performance on Early Commercial Sound Recordings. In *Telling Stories: Language, Narrative and Social Life*, ed. D. Schiffrin, a. de Fina, and A. Nylund, 23–42. Washington, D.C.: Georgetown University Press.

Bellafante, Gina. 2013. When the Law Says a Parent Isn't a Parent. *New York Times*.

Blackmail. n.d. Retrieved April 15, 2014, from http://www.hitchcockwiki.com/wiki/Blackmail_(1929).

Bubel, Claudia. 2006. The Linguistic Construction of Character Relations in TV Drama: Doing Friendship in *Sex and the City*. Dissertation. Ludwigshafen am Rhein: Universität des Saarlandes.

Chambers, J.K. 1998. TV Makes People Sound the Same. In *Language Myths*, ed. L. Bauer and P. Trudgill, 123–131. London: Penguin.

Coupland, N. 2007. *Style: Language Variation and Identity*. Cambridge: Cambridge University Press.

Cullen, Jim. 2014. *A Short History of the Modern Media*. Malden, MA: Wiley Blackwell.

D'Arcy, Alexandra. 2007. Like and Language Ideology: Disentangling Fact from Fiction. *American Speech* 82(4): 386–419.

Giles, Howard, and Tania Ogay. 2007. Communication Accommodation Theory. In *Explaining Communication: Contemporary Theories and Exemplars*, ed. B. Whaley and W. Samter, 325–344. Hillsdale: Lawrence Erlbaum.

Kolker, Robert. 2009. *Media Studies: An Introduction*. Malden, MA: Wiley-Blackwell.

Labov, William. 2000. *Principles of Linguistic Change: External factors*. Oxford: Basil Blackwell.

LePage, R.B., and Andre Tabouret-Keller. 1985. *Acts of Identity: Creole-Based Approaches to Language and Ethnicity*. Cambridge: Cambridge University Press.

McWhorter, John. 2009. Mad Men in a Good Place: How Did People Sound in 1963? *New Republic Blog*. Retrieved July 11, 2014, from http://www.newrepublic.com.

Milroy, James, and Lesley Milroy. 1999. *Authority in Language: Investigating Standard English*. London: Routledge.

Richardson, Kay. 2010. *Television Dramatic Dialogue: A Sociolinguistic Study*. New York: Oxford University Press.

Rogin, Michael. 1996. *Blackface, White Noise: Jewish Immigrants in the Hollywood Melting Pot*. Berkeley: University of California Press.

Spitulnik, Debra. 1996. The Social Circulation of Media Discourse and the Mediation of Communities. *Journal of Linguistic Anthropology* 6(2): 161–187.

Taylor, Jessica. 2009. "Speaking Shadows": A History of the Voice in the Transition from Silent to Sound Film in the United States. *Journal of Linguistic Anthropology* 19(1): 1–20.

Thompson, Kristin. 2003. *Storytelling in Film and Television*. Cambridge, MA: Harvard University Press.

Chapter 2
Exploring Language and Language Variation

Introduction

In the previous chapter, I noted that the most basic question for linguists concerns what we know when we know a language. This is a relatively simple question, but the more you think about it, the more complex you realize the question is to answer. If you were to make a list of all the things you know because you know English, what would it include? Most people would probably think of vocabulary and rules of grammar. They'd have in mind the rules that go along mostly with formal writing, including issues like spelling (for instance, which 'there,' 'they're,' or 'their' to use); comma placement (for instance, 'time to eat Grandpa' versus 'time to eat, Grandpa,' to use an example that circulates on social media fairly regularly); and matters of general style (for instance, avoiding the passive voice). When linguists think about the rules of grammar, we are typically thinking of grammar in a different sense. For a linguist, one way of answering the question of what you know when you know a language is to say that you know a *grammar*, by which a linguist will mean everything from the sounds that make up the language through the ways that you create sentences to the conventions for saying 'hello' and 'goodbye.' To know a grammar linguistically could also include knowing the rules that people learn in school with one important caveat. It is not at all necessary to know school grammar in order to know the linguistic grammar of a language. For thinking about language variation, though, it is necessary to understand the differences between school grammars and linguistic grammars.

Vox Popular: The Surprising Life of Language in the Media, First Edition. Robin Queen.
© 2015 John Wiley & Sons, Inc. Published 2015 by John Wiley & Sons, Inc.

One interesting difference between school grammar and linguistic grammar is that we learn or acquire the linguistic grammar more or less organically as we interact with other speakers. While some aspects of this grammar might be deliberately taught, for the most part they are not. Assuming there is no cognitive disability affecting them, children acquire the linguistic grammar of their community regardless of any formal instruction and in the face of notoriously messy input. (If you've ever transcribed some face-to-face conversation, you'll know how messy it is. If you haven't ever transcribed such conversation, give it a try, making sure to transcribe every 'um,' pause, and false start you find.) Children's more or less flawless acquisition of language in the face of messy input represents one of the foundational empirical arguments behind the idea that language is something tied to us as a species, an idea most associated with the linguist Noam Chomsky. School grammar, on the other hand, is largely learned through specific instruction. Children have to be formally taught or formally study on their own how to read and write, how to use conventional punctuation, and how to vary their written and spoken styles.

You can think of this chapter as providing the basis for thinking about what linguistic elements exist in our language repertoires. These elements include invariant pieces as well as pieces that can vary. For instance, think about the different ways in which the indefinite article 'a' can be pronounced. You can say it so that it rhymes with "hay" or so that it rhymes with "d'uh." The choice to say one or the other depends on a host of factors (most of which we don't think about consciously but which nonetheless influence which choice we make). Chapter 4 explores the basis for thinking about the factors that influence those choices. These two pieces, the elements in the repertoires and the factors influencing the choice on how to use them, are central to understanding what we know when we know a language and for this reason are of interest to many linguists. They are also critical for understanding the role of language variation within the narrative media. Although language as it's used in the narrative media tends to be much less varied and perhaps even closer to school grammar than regular face-to-face conversation, it nonetheless draws from the same repertoires and is affected by the same factors surrounding the choices for varying the elements in the repertoires.

This chapter starts with what is perhaps the most obvious form of language variation, namely, that between different languages, and then moves through various ways that English as a specific language can vary. The chapter shows that much of the variation language users produce and experience is not random but, rather, structured systematically. From this foundational point, three additional points arise that will be central for the rest of the book. First, language variation is both a natural and normal component of human language and is governed by the rules of the (linguistic) grammar along with the social nature of language. Second, people evaluate variation in particular, often very predictable, ways, and that evaluation provides the basis upon which social effects may be achieved by variation. Third, variation occurs across time as well as within a specific time, across and within geographic and social space, and across and within individuals.

Languages and Dialects

Even though there are lots of ways in which languages are fundamentally very similar to one another, they are typically perceived to be fundamentally different, something we recognize in the very fact that languages have specific names that distinguish them from one another. What do we actually mean when we reference "Turkish" or "Tagalog" or "Tzotzil"? We don't usually spend much time thinking about how we know that Turkish is different from Tzotzil. It just seems obvious that they are different languages. But how can we figure out where the boundaries between them lie? What makes them different, and are they really as different as they seem at first glance?

People who use what gets labeled "Turkish" produce sounds, words, and sentences that are so different from what the people using "Tagalog" produce that they can't even begin to understand one another. These elements make up the codes "Turkish" and "Tagalog." Things get even more complicated when you add to those basic elements other aspects of the language, such as norms for using language when we interact, the histories of people who have used "Turkish" or "Tagalog," literary and other traditions in which language is mediated, and the connections that may exist between the languages and the cultures in which they are embedded. It isn't enough to just identify differences in the grammar in order to decide what repertoires are "languages." Differences in the grammar are a reasonable place to begin, though.

Language systems can vary at pretty much any level, from something as small as a single sound to something as large as whole grammatical structures. Often, variation in language occurs in clusters, what we might call a *package of variation*. In the case of many systems that we call languages, the package involves all parts of the grammar. For instance, the package of elements that are found in Turkish differs quite a bit from those found in

Tagalog. Turkish has a wider range of consonants and vowels than Tagalog does, and in Turkish the vowels in a word harmonize with one another, which means that some of the vowels change to be more like other vowels in the words. Beyond the sounds, Tagalog sentences typically start with verbs while Turkish sentences typically end with verbs (and both of these differ from English in that English verbs tend to come between the subject and the object of the sentence). In Turkish, most of the words are formed by adding a series of suffixes to a stem whereas Tagalog uses suffixes, pre-fixes, infixes (elements that go in the middle of a stem), and circumfixes (elements that go around the stem) to make words.

For some pairs of codes, the packages of features don't differ nearly as much as they do for Turkish and Tagalog. For instance, if we think about English as it's used in New York City and English as it's used in Chicago, it's immediately clear that most of the elements in both packages are pretty much the same, with some relatively minor differences in the sounds and the vocabulary.[1] When the packages seem to be pretty similar, with minor differences that don't inhibit people from understanding each other, the codes are often considered by linguists and non-linguists to be dialects.

A curious fact about these bundles is that there are no straightforward criteria for determining whether or not some particular bundle is a *language* or a *dialect*. That's because the relative differences and similar-ities in the grammar present only part of the picture. The other part involves criteria outside the elements in the bundle, including especially what people believe about the package of features. There is a famous saying in linguistics (generally attributed to Max Weinreich) that a lan-guage is a dialect with an army and a navy. This saying highlights the com-plex calculus involved in deciding which codes constitute languages and which dialects, and captures the relationship of labels like "language" and "dialect" to intricate social, political, and economic dynamics among people. The saying also points out that knowing what a language is goes beyond aspects of the sounds, words, and sentences. Knowing what a language is includes knowing something about the social context in which those sounds, words, and sentences are used and evaluated.

Two broad criteria hinted at above present guideposts for thinking about which codes constitute languages and which constitute dialects. First, we can think in terms of mutual intelligibility. Speakers of different languages generally don't understand one another without altering some aspects of their speech or switching to a mutually shared language. Second, we can think in terms of cultural histories. Speakers of different languages generally assume that they have different cultural histories. This means that in cases where people can understand each other (despite some differences in the sounds, words, and sentences) and where they assume some degree of a shared cultural history, they will also generally assume that the codes they are using are dialects of the same language. Thus, we end up American English, British English, Australian English, as well as Southern American English, Cockney, New York English, and so on. In cases where people can't understand each other and don't believe they have a significantly shared cultural history, they will tend to believe that they are using different languages, and so we get Turkish, Tagalog, and Tzotzil (along with approximately 7,000 others).

Of course, human life and language are not as simple as our two guideposts might suggest, and having guideposts doesn't necessarily make the task of deciding what is a language and what isn't straightforward. For instance, there are plenty of cases in which people can generally understand each other but perceive themselves to have a significantly different cultural history. This is the case with Serbian and Croatian, which are written in different scripts but whose sounds, words, and sentences aren't different enough to be mutually unintelligible. However, since their speakers maintain that they are different languages, at some level they are. Similarly, you can have cases where the sounds, words, and sentences aren't mutually intelligible but in which the sense of a shared cultural history is so strong that people believe they are using dialects of the same language. This is the case with many of the dialects of Chinese as well as the dialects of Arabic.

And finally come the cases in which the sounds, words, and sentences are somewhat mutually (un)intelligible, and there is the sense of a partially shared cultural history. In those cases, people may disagree about whether this or that code is a language or a dialect. For instance, Frisian falls into this kind of situation relative to Dutch and to some degree German. So does the variety known in the United States by linguists as African American English (AAE) or African American Vernacular English (AAVE).[2]

However we determine whether a code is a language or a dialect, once the determination is made, it can lead people to make all kinds of interesting assumptions. For instance, we may start to link speaking a particular language with being a citizen of a particular nation, or we may start to assume that people who look a certain way or have a certain name will speak a particular language or dialect.

It gets even more complicated than that. Individual people may speak more than one language (in fact, the majority of people in the world do), and multiple languages may coexist in communities. In the United States (and in the UK, Australia, and New Zealand), it is common to find communities of monolingual English speakers, so much so that people in these places often assume that being monolingual is the common state of affairs in human communities. However, when we look across the world, we find that monolingualism is more the exception than the rule and that most of the world's communities play host to several languages at once. Further, even in places that assume monolingualism as the norm, speakers often use multiple dialects.

Food for Thought

Think about contexts you know from your own life and what languages are spoken and when. Do you have occasion to use particular dialects? Is it clear in your experience which codes are languages and which are dialects?

The greater the general variability between two codes, the more likely that speakers will come to think of those codes as different languages. That likelihood only increases as cultural distances increase. Different languages provide one way to divide a very large group of people (say, the global human population) into somewhat smaller groups, while dialects provide a means for further subdivision within those groups. Here's a simplified example of how these divisions based on language might work. At the broadest level of analysis, all humans are language users, and that distinguishes us from other mammals. At the next level, many, but by no means all, humans are users of Turkish. Yet a different, but still relatively large, group of humans are speakers of Tagalog, and yet a third are speakers of Tzotzil. Among Turkish speakers, people are further divided based on regional and social geography. People in eastern Turkey speak Turkish differently than those in western Turkey and differently again from Turkish speakers living in some parts of Europe, even though they can all understand each other. People who are very religious speak differently from those who aren't, while people who live in rural areas speak differently from those in urban areas. And even within urban areas, people who are wealthy speak Turkish differently than those who are not. Distinctions based on social and regional geography constitute another layer, one largely tied to dialects. While it may not be entirely satisfying to think in terms of groups like this, particularly since the boundaries between groups of people based on any particular set of criteria are likely to be permeable, such groupings link bundles of linguistic characteristics to a wide variety of types/groups of people.

One further component of language variation that is useful to have on the table is *accent*. Linguists and non-linguists alike sometimes conflate accent with dialect. However, "accent" generally refers to variation that is wholly or primarily in the sound system, whereas dialects capture linguistic bundles that involve other elements of the grammar in addition to sounds. Within communities in which a dialect is used, let's say the southern United States, individual speakers will vary on which elements of the dialect they use, with some using a whole range of elements that include all areas of the grammar and others using only the particular sounds that distinguish this variety from other varieties of American English. Thus, we can speak of both a southern American dialect and a southern American accent, where accent comprises a subset of the features found in the dialect.

A second way that accent gets used is to refer to the general outcome of using a language that isn't one's native language. When people learn new languages, especially once they've matured out of childhood, they almost always experience some influence of their native language on the language they are learning (often referred to as *interference*). This is what frequently gets called a "foreign accent" and is what people are referring to when they talk about someone having a Spanish or Chinese accent. While it may be the case that this kind of accent is primarily about using sounds that differ from the way a native speaker uses them, a foreign accent may also involve aspects of grammar. As with the distinction between languages and dialects, the distinction between what people call an accent and what they call a dialect is generally based on grounds other than strictly linguistic ones. Nonetheless, languages, dialects, and accents can each provide the basic raw material for speakers to do all kinds of interesting things with language, including within contexts such as the narrative mass media.

Within narrative mass media, as is true outside of them, too, language variation often serves to constitute difference and sameness. The more demographically different characters are from each other, the more different the codes they use will likely be. Conversely, characters who are more alike demographically (and sometimes more like the presumed demographics of the audience) will use similar codes. For instance, in films that have a mix of human and humanoid (but non-human) characters, the humanoid beings may speak languages that were constructed from the author's (or playwright's) imagination. A good example of this is a film like *Avatar* (2009) in which the Na'avi were both non-human and users of a language made up solely for the purpose of the film itself. In that sense it isn't a "real" language, but one that was constructed in order to help reinforce the large-scale differences between the Na'avi and the humans trying to interact with them. As the protagonist changes over time from being oriented toward his (human) employers to being more oriented to his Na'avi friends, he speaks more and more Na'avi. Thus, the variation in the protagonist's speech signals shifting alliances and plot trajectories within the film.

Sometimes, of course, films that are primarily in one language will also make use of distinctions between languages to illustrate differences between characters or between situations. *The Godfather Part II* (1974), for instance, is primarily in English; however, scenes that show Vito Corleone's early life in Sicily are in Italian with English subtitles. One of the ways that viewers are keyed into these scenes as flashbacks is, in fact, with the switch to Italian. Illustrating difference using different languages is only the tip of the iceberg, however, and most films rely on more subtle linguistic distinctions – distinctions based primarily on dialect and accent – to help constitute various axes of difference and similarity.

In the *Godfather Part II* (in fact in the entire trilogy), even the scenes that are entirely in English involve some degree of variation. Vito Corleone speaks with Italian-accented English, while his sons speak English that is recognizably drawn from the native English used on the streets of Little Italy in New York. The sons speak slightly differently from one another, too, with the youngest son Michael having the least pronounced accent, a characteristic that reinforces his early lack of interest in the family business, organized crime, and his orientation toward a world outside of Little Italy and New York City. Further, Michael's wife, Kay, doesn't sound like she's from New York at all (and she isn't; she's from New Hampshire), a characteristic that reinforces a host of differences between her and the other Corleone wives. In this case, subtle differences in accent among the characters are linked to subtle differences in character traits, motives, and overall plot trajectories. This linkage is something we will explore in great detail in later chapters of the book, but before doing so it will be helpful to start by considering what exactly is involved when we talk about bundles of linguistic features that make up the grammar. Because even though codes often appear to differ significantly from one another, all languages and dialects share some basic fundamental building blocks.

The Components of a Grammar

As discussed above, by the time they enter school, children have acquired most of the grammar of their language or languages. What exactly have they acquired? Most obviously, they have acquired a vocabulary, what linguists call the *lexicon*. The relationship between different items in the lexicon, such as those items that are about content ("nouns," "verbs") and those that are about more formal or logical connections (i.e., logical operators like 'and,' 'but,' 'or,' 'not' or prepositions like 'up,' 'on,' or 'by'), is called *semantics*. Most broadly, word meaning involves the lexicon and the semantics.

In addition to the basics of meaning, children have also acquired the sound system of their language (*phonology*), the mechanisms for creating words (*morphology*), and the rules and constraints for forming sentences (*syntax*). These elements make up what we might think of as the raw material of the grammar because it's these elements that will generally influence the degree to which people perceive codes to be similar or different from one another.

In addition to these basic building blocks of the system, children have also started to understand that different people may speak differently or the same people may speak differently in different situations (*sociolinguistics*) and that different contexts may require different forms of language (*pragmatics*). With these components (simplified here somewhat), children (and adults) are able to interpret nuances of meaning that go beyond the lexicon and the semantics. Chapter 5 will focus on these additional kinds of meaning in much more detail. Here, the most important aspect of this type of meaning involves recognizing that there is more to understanding a language than understanding the basic building blocks and that the knowledge that we have when we know a language includes our knowledge of different ways of using that language.

Each of the components of language individually represents a complex area of inquiry, and, of course, each component is intricately bound to all the others.

Table 2.1 captures elements that we find in every known human language, and one of the quests for many linguists is to figure out elements within each of these systems that are themselves shared across all human languages. So, for instance, phonologists try to understand what properties the sound systems of all the world's languages share, while semanticists try

Table 2.1   The basic components of human languages

Lexicon	Mental dictionary
Phonology	System of sounds
Morphology	System of creating and composing words
Syntax	System of creating sentences
Semantics	System of connecting sounds and words (creating meaning)
Pragmatics	System of connecting words and sentences to contexts of speaking
Variation (sociolinguistics)	System(s) for altering the other components, often in response to aspects of the social dynamics of speaking

figure out what kinds of meaning relationships occur regardless of the language spoken. Although we are focusing in this book primarily on variation in language, it turns out that variation is not a free for all, and principled constraints govern how much languages vary from one another and in what ways they vary from one another.

All the Systems Work as a System

What we see by looking at the elements in Table 2.1 is that grammar consists of multiple parts, each of which works as a system and which together also function as a system. In order to get a sense of how all these systems work together, we can examine the case of a single suffix in English, the suffix < ing>, such as in the word 'running.' < ing > engages all areas of the grammar, from the phonology (sound system) through to the pragmatics and sociolinguistics (systems of variation).

   <ing > can be pronounced in one of two major ways. If you say the suffix by itself and pay attention to where your tongue is when you get to the end of the word, you'll notice that the back of your tongue is touching the very back of the roof of your mouth, generally at the point where your hard palate ends and the softer, squishy part of the oral tract begins (that soft squishy bit is called your *velum*).

   In Figure 2.1, which shows a mid-sagittal section of the oral tract, with a stylized nose at the top left and lips at the left center, you see what the

Figure 2.1 Mid-sagittal section of a velar nasal consonant. The back of the tongue is raised to the palate.

oral tract (your mouth) looks like when you make the last sound of <ing>. The tongue is the blob-like structure pretty much in the middle of the image. You'll notice that the tongue in the image is touching the roof of the mouth right at the back. You'll also notice that the little flap at the very back of the roof of the mouth (the velum) is down, allowing air into the nasal cavity (the large white space). The placement of the tongue gives you the sound at the end of the <ing> and the velum down gives you the nasal quality of the consonant. When you combine this sound with the vowel, you get <ing>.

There is also the pronunciation that people sometimes call "dropping the g." If you say a word with <ing> in it and practice "dropping the g" (something virtually all English speakers do sometimes), what you'll notice is that now your tongue is in an entirely different position. Now, rather than that last sound being made with the back of your tongue at the back of your mouth, it's being made with the tip of your tongue at the front of your mouth. Your tongue is probably located just behind your teeth on a bony ridge known as the *alveolar ridge*. You can see this in Figure 2.2, which in tandem with Figure 2.1 illustrates the primary difference involved with articulating an [ING] and an [IN]. Note that in both cases, the consonant is nasal, which means that the air goes through your nose. You can see this on the mid-sagittal sections, where you see a clear path (shown in white) from the nose to the bottom of the frame (and going to the lungs).

Figure 2.2   Mid-sagittal section of an alveolar nasal consonant. The tip of the tongue is raised to the alveolar ridge.

If you go back and forth saying 'running' and 'runnin' and pay attention to your tongue at the end of each, you can get a real awareness of the shifts between these two sounds. You'll also probably notice that there isn't really a "g" sound present in the "running" form of the word. Even though we spell the word with a < g>, there's only a nasal sound at the end of the word, no actual "g" sound. So, when you pronounce 'runnin,' you aren't really dropping a < g>, you're simply changing where you put your tongue for that final sound.

This distinction is part of the sound system of English, both in terms of the details of articulation and the particular sounds involved. Another thing, for instance, that you might have noticed between the two different version of [RUNNING] is that the vowel in the suffix is a little bit different depending on whether you're doing the back of the mouth or the front of the mouth version. That difference is linked to how you are anticipating the following sound; in a sense, you have mentally prepared to use one of the two variants, and the vowel you produce already anticipates the consonant that will follow. These are part of the knowledge of the sound system of English that any child (or adult) acquiring English will have. You can find all the vowels and consonants found in American English on page **00**. The list serves as a useful reference for the various discussions about sounds that will occur throughout the rest of the book.

<ing > follows other rules, too. As shown in Table 2.1, the rules that govern the creation of words from smaller units of meaning (for instance, stems, suffixes, and prefixes) are called morphology and units of meaning themselves are called *morphemes*. The term morpheme differs from the somewhat more ambiguous term *word* in being precisely about the smallest units of meaning in the lexicon (mental dictionary). If you think about prefixes and suffixes in English, you'll quickly notice that even though they have a kind of meaning, they can't occur (for the most part) unless they attach to some kind of stem. They are what are known as bound morphemes, which means that they can't occur in isolation, only in combination. You can't just say < ing > and have it actually mean something specific. In English, stems (such as nouns), verbs, and adjectives can occur by themselves, and for this reason they are called *free*. Words in English are combinations of bound and free morphemes. Unlike morphemes, though, words may have several different units of meaning in them. For instance, the word 'cats' is made up of two distinct meaningful elements: 'cat' and '-s'. The '-s' simply indicates that the stem it attaches to is plural. 'Cat' is free, and '-s' is bound.

There's another distinction that matters for <ing>. Among morphemes that aren't stems, there's a distinction between those that change something about the meaning of the stem and those that provide some kind of information about the relationship of the stem to other elements of the sentence. The first type of morpheme is called a *derivational morpheme*. When a derivational morpheme connects to its stem, it changes the meaning of the stem. So, for instance, compare "run" and "rerun." When you add 're-' to the verb 'run,' it means to "run again." Or, if you look at "space" and "cyberspace," you see that the addition of 'cyber-' changes the general meaning of space to a specific kind of space, namely, space that occurs via some kind of electronic medium.

These are different from <ing>. When you think about <ing>, you notice that if you attach it to a verb, it doesn't really change the nature of the verb in the way that derivational morphemes change the nature of their stems. Instead, it gives you some information about the grammatical properties of the stem in the context of use. In the case of <ing>, it creates the present participle of the verb. In English, the present participle can do a few things; one of them is to indicate that an action is ongoing (or continuous). In the sentence 'Sue is running,' the <ing> indicates that Sue is doing something (running) presently and is continuing to do it. Compare the meanings of "Sue is running" to "Sue runs" or "Sue ran" or "Sue has run." Each of these gives different grammatical information about when the running took place, but, unlike the 'rerun' example above, the basic meaning of the verb remains unchanged. Suffixes that provide additional information (often grammatical in nature) but that don't change the basic meaning of the stem are called *inflectional*.[3]

Now you've seen two ways in which the grammar of English works. First, you've seen how the sound system is at work, and second, you've seen how the morphology, or the system for creating words, works on the example of <ing>. The suffix is also influenced by the syntax of English, which refers to the order in which the parts of a sentence occur and to the hierarchical relationships between those parts. In terms of the order of the elements, in the sentence "Sue is running," the participle ("running") occurs as part of a verb phrase ("is running"), and the participle always occurs after a form of the verb "to be." While it doesn't necessarily always come directly after "to be" (e.g., "is quickly running"), it never comes before it. This is one of the rules of the syntax of English and why you don't hear speakers of English say things like "Sue has running" or "Sue running is" (unless they are Yoda, of course).

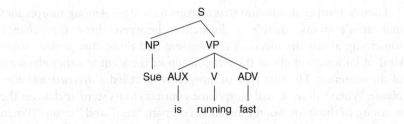

Figure 2.3   Schematic tree diagram drawing of "Sue is running fast."

If we add the adverb 'fast' to the end of the sentence 'Sue is running,' we start to get a sense of some of the internal structure, or system, for putting words together into bigger units like sentences. Clearly, 'fast' modifies the verb phrase 'is running' rather than 'Sue' directly. Most linguists tend to think that we can represent this interpretation (that 'fast' describes the action of the sentence rather than the subject of the sentence) such that words combine into units that themselves combine into larger units. If we were going to do a schematic drawing of this relationship, we might draw it something like it looks in Figure 2.3 (there are other ways to draw this, too, but this will work for right now).

In the tree in Figure 2.3, you see that 'fast' is part of the larger phrase marked by the term "VP" (which stands for "verb phrase"), while 'Sue' is part of a different phrase, the noun phrase "NP". (The term "AUX" means the *auxiliary*, or helping, verb). From this schematic drawing, you can see that words combine into units (like verb phrases) that themselves combine into larger units (like sentences). This drawing shows that syntactic units are not created simply by a linear string of words, but rather also include an internal structure that is organized by smaller units building into larger ones.

Now the basic system with < ing > is in place in terms of the phonology (sounds), the morphology (making the participle), and the syntax (the ordering and hierarchy of the participle relative to other elements of the sentence). We also see that using the '-in' or '-ing' form doesn't change the meaning of the participle. 'Runnin' and 'running' denote pretty much the same action. And yet additional meaning can be associated with one or the other form. That meaning is tied to what the form means within its context of use, which connects to both pragmatics and socio-linguistics.

Example 2.1 from the TV show we saw in Chapter 1, *Modern Family* (2009–), illustrates the pragmatic meaning of < ing >.

Example 2.1 *Modern Family*, "Dude Ranch," Season 3, Episode 1, Christopher Lloyd and Steven Levitan (creators), ABC, September 21, 2011

Phil: I've been practicing like crazy all my cowboy skills [...] shootin', ropin', pancake eatin'. Why? Because sometimes I feel like Jay doesn't respect me as a man.

Phil, one of the main characters in the show, is married to Claire and the father of Haley, both of whom appear in the example discussed in Chapter 1. As a character, he is what we might call a nice guy nerd archetype. (We'll talk more about archetypes in Chapter 6.) Jay is Phil's father-in-law, and, unlike Phil, generally reflects what we might call the tough guy archetype. Phil's concerns over Jay's assessments of his masculinity are an ongoing topic of conversation throughout the show.

By calculating each character's relative use of -in and -ing in the first five episodes of the first season, I found that Phil typically uses the -ing variant on the show, using -in only 16 percent of the time. Jay, on the other hand, is more of an -in user, using it 65 percent of the time. Thus, the three words 'shootin,' 'ropin,' and 'pancake eatin' represent something of a departure for Phil. The reasons why reveal something about the system of varying these two pronunciations.

One of the clear meanings in Phil's use in Example 2.1 is tied to different associations with masculinity as well as some other meanings. As Kathryn Campbell-Kibler has pointed out in a series of publications (2008, 2009, 2011), -ing is linked to a constellation of factors broadly captured by "educated" and "articulate," while -in is linked to a set of factors largely captured by "informal," "friendly," and "masculine." Another association for -in is with southern and western varieties of American English, and characters in the narrative media who are supposed to be from the south and from the rural west often categorically use the -in variant (and not only in the participle but also in gerunds and in compounds using 'thing' like 'something,' 'nothing,' 'anything,' and 'everything').

Food for Thought

Try recording an actual conversation, or one from one of your favorite TV shows or movies. Listen for how different people/characters use <ing>. Do some people use more -ing and some more -in? Does anything special seem to determine when one or the other occurs?

<ing> gives us a nice example of the complex ways that linguistic variation can occur. Not only is it tied to every facet of the grammar of English, it can further be tied to region, to gender, to formality, and to education. In the discussion on <ing> above, we examined how one English suffix can illustrate all the components that make up a language. In the section below, we'll examine how one subsystem of the grammar can vary.

Systems of Variation

Consider the sentence 'John and me went to the store.' This type of sentence often elicits a correction, whereas other versions of the sentence, such as 'John and myself went to the store' or 'She gave a dollar to John and I' don't. In fact, the latter two sentences are often found specifically in formal situations used by speakers who are trying to speak "properly." Understanding what's going on in those sentences depends on an understanding of an area of syntax called *case*.

In many languages, the nouns in sentences get marked grammatically as subjects, objects, indirect objects, possessives, and a host of other relationships. If you know German, for instance, then you know that in a sentence like 'The boy saw the dog,' you mark 'the boy' as *nominative* (which means the subject) and 'the dog' as *accusative* (which means the object). You mark them on the definite article 'the.' (In German, a nominative, masculine noun gets the definite article 'der' while the accusative masculine nouns gets the definite article 'den.' Thus, 'The boy saw the dog' shows up as 'Der Junge sah den Hund'). English also has subjects and objects, of course, but in English, we mostly don't mark nouns grammatically by the case role they fulfill in a sentence. English relies instead more on the order of the words (the syntax) to tell the listener what the object and what the subject are. It's a kind of neat puzzle, really. Sentences (or *clauses*, which are groups of words that together form a coherent, often multiword concept) have internal relations that can be analyzed. How do you know what the subject of a sentence is in English? In general it's the noun (or noun phrase) that comes before the main verb. The noun or noun phrase that comes after the main verb is the object. In the sentence 'The boy saw the dog,' this relationship is pretty clear, and if you switch the order of the noun phrases, you get a different meaning (whatever comes before the verb "saw" did the seeing). In German, though, because the definite article overtly tells you which noun is the subject and which is the object, reversing the order of the nouns "the boy" and "the dog" doesn't change the meaning of the sentence. 'Der Junge sah den Hund' means the same thing as 'Den Hund sah der Junge.'

With that explanation of case in mind, let's look at the personal pronouns of English, which are the only nominal forms in English that still get overtly marked for case. In the pronominal system of English, we make distinctions based on person (first, second, third), based on number (singular, plural), and based on case (roughly, subject, object, possessive, reflexive) to have a full system that looks like Table 2.2.

The pronoun in 'John and me went to the store' is marked as an object ('me') but occurs in the subject position. The pronoun that's marked as nominative (or subject) is of course 'I.' So the "correct" version of that

Table 2.2   The pronominal system of English

	Subject	*Object*	*Possessive*	*Reflexive*
First				
Singular	I	Me	Mine	Myself
Plural	We	Us	Ours	Ourselves
Second				
Singular	You	You	Yours	Yourself
Plural	You (you guys, y'all, youse)	You (you guys, y'all, youse)	Yours (you guys', y'all's, yous')	Yourselves
Third				
Singular	She/he/it/ (they)	Her/him/it/ (they)	Hers/his/its/ (their)	Herself/himself/ itself/ (themself)
Plural	They	Them	Theirs	Themselves
Interrogative	Who	Whom	Whose	

Note: Items that appear in parentheses vary in different varieties of English.

sentence is 'John and I went to the store.' What about 'She gave a dollar to John and I'? Here, the same general issue is in play, namely, which case-marked personal pronoun is "correct." However, in this case, the pronoun marked as nominative 'I' is in an object position (here the object of the preposition 'to,' which is one way that English speakers mark indirect objects). In this case, we'd normally expect the pronoun to be 'me.'

What about in 'John and myself went to the store'? Again, the issue is the case marking for the pronoun. 'Myself' is reflexive, meaning the speaker is referring to themself rather to someone else. But it's also an object of the verb. Reflexive nouns work because their *antecedent* (the noun to which they refer) has usually already been named as the subject. In the sentence, 'I gave myself a haircut,' 'myself' refers to the same person as 'I' refers to. In 'John and myself went to the store,' there is no subject noun that is the same as the reflexive. The "correct" form of that sentence should be 'John and I went to the store.'

In all three of the example sentences involving John and me, the first person pronoun being used is not the one that carries the case marking expected for the role being fulfilled in the sentence. Either an object pronoun is being used as a subject or a subject pronoun is being used as an object.[4] Yet, even though the three sentences 'John and me went to the store,' 'She gave a dollar to John and I,' and 'John and myself went to the store' all have the same basic issue – using the "wrong" case-marked pronoun – they are typically evaluated, and used, differently. If you listen to people making formal speeches, for instance, you will undoubtedly notice a high percentage of the first person subject and object pronouns being the reflexive. This is because even though it's "wrong," it has come to be interpreted as marking a kind of formality, something we'll discuss in Chapter 4 in more detail.

We can see a parody of exactly this process in the following example from the film *Austin Powers: International Man of Mystery* (1997).

Example 2.2   *Austin Powers*, Jay Roach (dir.), 1997, Capella International

```
1  Dealer:   I'm sorry sir
2  AP:       Well [.] I won't lie to you. Cards are
             not my bag baby. <Loudness increase> Allow
             myself to introduce [.] myself. My name is
             Ritchie Cunningham [.] [looks to companion]
             And this is my wife Oprah.
3  #2:       My name is number two. This is my Italian
             confidential secretary. Her name is Alotta
             [..] Alotta Fagina.
4  [Austin Powers' face sinks]
```

In this example, Austin Powers is trying to find information about Dr. Evil's plan to take over the world, so he and his companion have gone under cover in a Las Vegas casino, where associates of Dr. Evil are believed to be gambling. *Austin Powers: International Man of Mystery* is a well-known parody of many spy thrillers, but particularly the James Bond films (as an interesting note of film trivia, the name of #2's companion is supposed to be a joking reference to Pussy Galore, a character in the James Bond film *Goldfinger*, 1964). James Bond, of course, has a persona that is suave, sophisticated, and highly cultured. This is exactly the group of people who are likely to use the reflexive in subject or object positions. In line 2, this usage is parodied when Austin Powers uses 'myself' instead of the canonical 'me' associated with the Bond phrase, "Allow me to introduce myself. My name is Bond. James Bond." Here, Austin Powers introduces himself as a fictional television character Ritchie Cunningham of the television series *Happy Days* (1974–1984). The layers of irony are too involved to disentangle here; however, playing with the reflexive pronoun illustrates both the variability itself and the awareness that in some senses its placement as a subject is "wrong," an awareness captured in the lengthy pause that occurs between 'introduce' and 'myself.'

The third person singular pronoun presents another fascinating puzzle of variation within the pronoun system. Traditionally, English is considered to have three singular third person pronouns. In Table 2.2, however, you'll notice that forms of 'they' appear in the singular, third person row. This is because there are cases when the gender of the antecedent noun is unknown, irrelevant, or simply not specified. In those cases, we need a generic pronoun. However, the three singular third person pronouns don't lend themselves well to being generic. 'He' and 'she' are marked for sex/gender and 'it' is used for non-human, non-pet nouns. While most grammar books specify 'he' or 'he and she' to fulfill the generic singular role, most English speakers instead use 'they' as a generic singular third person pronoun, as in "Each student should bring their books to class." You may have seen an example of this usage a page or so back and wondered about it (see Hill and Mannheim [1992] for a discussion of how the pronominal system in fact predicts exactly this usage).

Singular 'they' has a long and venerable history of both being used and being sanctioned. For our purposes, we can see it as one of the variable elements that provide a resource for speakers generally but also for the narrative mass media more specifically. For instance, in Example 2.3, from the film *Chasing Amy* (1997), we see Alyssa use generic 'they' (as well as some other generic pronouns) to avoid admitting to her friends that she is dating a man. The film is an exploration of a romantic relationship between Alyssa, a young, out, and proud lesbian, and Holden, a comic book author. The film was released in 1997 at a time when the politics of lesbian, gay, bisexual, transsexual (LGBT) life were under heated discussion in the United States. Thus, while Holden was not generally "traditional," the social context of the film was very much one in which a relationship between a straight man and a lesbian was potentially problematic for both of them.

Example 2.3   *Chasing Amy*, Kevin Smith (dir.), 1997, Too Askew Production, Inc.

```
 1 G1:      Yeah, Alyssa, who you shackin' up with?
 2 Alyssa:  Shacking up with? Please. [..] [squirms
            around] I'm so in love.
 3 All:     Aw::
 4 Alyssa:  I know, I know. I feel like such a goon
            but I can't help it we have such a great
            time together.
 5 G2:      Who is it?
 6 Alyssa:  Someone you guys don't know.
 7 G3:      That chick you left the restaurant with
            that night
 8 Alyssa:  They're not from around here.
 9 G4:      Don't even tell me you met 'er down the
            shore
10 G1:      Ew [.] a bridge and tunnel Jersey dyke=
11 G4:      =With huge hair and acid wash jeans.
12 All:     @@@@@@@@
13 Alyssa:  For your information, they don't have big
            hair or wear acid wash. They're from my
            home town.
```

```
14  [Women look at each other, questioning]
15  G2:      Why're you playing the pronoun game?
16  Alyssa:  What? What are you talkin' about? I'm not
                  either.
17  G2:      You are. I met someone. We have a great
                  time. They're from my home town. Doesn't
                  this tube of wonderful have a name?
18  [..]
19  Alyssa:  Holden.
20  [Faces fall]
```

In this example, 'they' is being used specifically to obscure the gender of the antecedent due to Alyssa's fear that her friends will reject her (as they indeed do) for dating a man (lines 8 and 13). This strategy of obscuring the gender by using the singular 'they' shows another component of the social nature of language variation.

Line 6 in the example involves another place where the pronoun system varies. Alyssa refers to her friends as 'you guys.' It turns out that the second person plural pronouns also exhibit some intriguing variation. If you look back at the pronoun chart, you notice that unlike the first and third person pronouns, there is no traditional distinction between the singular and plural forms of the second person pronouns, except in the reflexive where we find 'yourself' (sg.) and 'yourselves' (pl.). This was not always the case in English, and through the Early Modern English period, there was a singular/plural distinction in the second person, with 'thou' being the singular and 'ye' being the plural form. Early Modern English also had a case distinction in the second person pronouns, with 'thou' being the subject form and 'thee' being the object form of the singular. For the plural, 'ye' was the subject form and 'you' was the object form. In addition to this, English also had a distinction between formal and informal *terms of address*, such that 'you' was used in situations of formal address and 'thou' was used in situations of informal address (this is much like the French system of using 'tu' in informal contexts and 'vous' in formal contexts). The particulars of this system are fairly complex and involve dimensions of power and solidarity in addition to formality. For our purposes right now, the important information is that over time, English lost both the case distinction (something that was going on generally and that contributes to the interchangeability of the first person pronouns we discussed above) and the formal/informal distinction, with 'thou' eventually being mostly lost (it's still retained in some dialects of English) and 'you' coming in as the main term of address in the second person for both the singular and the plural.

This is an interesting case in which a plural form of the pronoun came to take on singular meaning (just like it does with singular 'they'), and, as a result, it's not possible phonologically or syntactically to distinguish the singular and plural forms of the second person from one another.

While that presents a fascinating story, it left English speakers in a tricky situation because sometimes, of course, it is important to distinguish between 'you' in the singular and 'you' in the plural. Just as English speakers created a solution to the generic singular third person, they have also created a solution to the lack of a singular/plural distinction in the second person. Unlike the use of the singular 'they,' which is found among the majority of speakers of English, the solution to the singular/plural 'you' was solved dialect by dialect. There are currently many different forms of a plural second person, and the major ones that are found in American English occur in the pronoun chart above. While 'y'all' is broadly linked to southern varieties of American English and AAVE, some of the others, especially 'you'uns' and 'youse,' are also indicative of variation across social space as these forms are more commonly used by people in the working classes than in the upper classes.

The form that shows the least restriction in terms of both geography and social distribution is 'you guys,' the form we see in line 6 in the *Chasing Amy* example above, which is set in New Jersey (where 'youse' is also found). In a fascinating study of the rise of 'you guys' as a generic plural second person in the United States, Theresa Heyd (2010) illustrates that in the television show *Friends* (1994–2004), 'you guys' occurs in roughly equal measure with the bare plural 'you.'

In addition, she shows that 'you guys' increases modestly over the ten-year period of the show and that it is significantly more frequent in *Friends* than it is in other (written) genres over the same time period, such as in news magazines like *Time*. Heyd argues that 'you guys' helps reinforce the friendly, colloquial nature of the show. Thus, much like we saw in the case of <ing>, here, the use of an overtly marked plural second person helps construct laid-back characters and a specific ambiance for the show.

Food for Thought

Using the same conversation that you used before (or if you didn't like that conversation, record a new one), go through and note how the pronouns are being used. Do you find examples of forms of the first person in the "wrong" place? Ways of marking the plural second person? Singular 'they'? Why do these different forms occur where they do? What do they seem to mean within the context in which they occur?

One of the central insights of the discipline of sociolinguistics, particularly as practiced by the linguist William Labov and his followers, is that ongoing changes in any language can be tracked by following (or at least paying attention to) the variation among speakers of that language. Thus, by watching how speakers use aspects of the pronoun system and comparing their use over time, we can start to understand something about how English has changed and is continuing to change. This is especially clear with the second person pronoun, where a series of changes first caused English to lose the plural/singular distinction and then more recently saw new plural forms arise to reinstitute the distinction. We can see this change in both real-life language and in the language found in the narrative mass media, as illustrated in all the cases discussed above.

Language Change

Although we may think about language as something relatively stable, particularly when we consider the written language, in fact, languages are constantly changing. If you've ever looked at *Beowulf* or Chaucer's *Canterbury Tales*, you'll have seen immediately that, although they are written in "English," in many ways the English they were written in differs from the English this book is written in. In the case of *Beowulf*, the differences are nearly as great as if it had been written in an entirely different language.

Language change is about shifts to grammar over time across a group of individuals or within individuals across their lifespan. Some important questions about language change include how it gets started, how it happens without anyone really noticing (most of the time), how it moves through different groups of speakers, and how speakers evaluate the change as it happens. For instance, one change that is currently happening in English concerns the word 'like,' as we saw in the *Modern Family* scene we looked at in the first chapter. That particular change is occurring in many varieties of English in the world, and yet in many places, the United States included, it is evaluated as something negative and as a way young women in particular come to appear unintelligent. This very dynamic is evident in the *Modern Family* scene, as discussed in Example 1.1.

The media can thus be a useful source of information about these kinds of changes, and particularly about the questions of how variation is evaluated and how it moves through groups of speakers. While the cases of < ing > and most of the pronoun discussion that we looked at above caught a moment in time (what is often called *synchrony*), we can also look at language variation across time (what is often called *diachrony*). Heyd's study of the plural 'you guys' does this to some degree in comparing *Friends* to other, non-narrative genres and contexts, and shows that 'you guys' is much more frequent in *Friends* than in those other sources.

Sali Tagliamonte and Chris Roberts (2005) do something similar in their comparison of *intensifiers* in the *Friends* corpus and in other corpora of spoken English. In their study, they want to know whether the relative frequency of different intensifiers on *Friends* indicates changes to the system of intensifiers more broadly. They find that the *Friends* data do indicate such a change. Intensifiers are linguistic elements that don't add to the general content of an utterance but serve to enhance and strengthen the force of the terms they modify. Common intensifiers in English include 'so,' 'very,' 'really,' 'totally,' and so on. Tagliamonte and Roberts look at three specific elements of intensifiers in the *Friends* data. First they look at the overall distribution of all the intensifiers and compare them to the distributions in other corpora of spoken English. Table 2.3 shows the findings for *Friends*.

The *Friends* corpus shows a different frequency ordering of intensifiers relative to other corpora, with "so" being more frequent. Tagliamonte and Roberts argue that this indicates that 'so' is the newest intensifier, and that it is on track to supplant both 'really' and 'very,' something supported by the general historical record as well.

Table 2.3   Frequency of intensifiers by lexical item in the Friends Corpus

'so'	832	(44.1%)
'really'	464	(24.6%)
'very'	269	(14.2%)
'pretty'	115	(6.1%)
'totally'	53	(2.8%)
All other intensifiers	153	(8.1%)
Total	*1,886*	

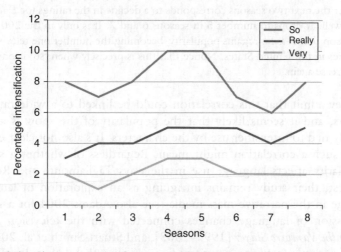

Figure 2.4   Change in intensifier use over eight seasons of the television series *Friends* (1994–2004, David Crane and Marta Kauffman [creators], NBC). Copyright 2005, the American Dialect Society. All rights reserved. Republished by permission of the copyright holder, and the present publisher, Duke University Press.

The second element they look at is whether the intensifier use differs among the male and female characters because in many studies that look at changes to the language, gender turns out to be strongly correlated with both new, incoming forms and older, conservative forms, with women being more likely to use incoming forms. In the *Friends* data, they found that the female characters were significantly more likely to use 'so' relative to the male characters (and in proportion with 'really' and 'very'). Finally, they also looked at whether the use of 'so' increased over the eight-year span of the show they examined, the results of which are shown in Figure 2.4 (Tagliamonte and Roberts 2005, 291).

Figure 2.4 shows that the use of 'so' relative to other intensifiers increases during seasons 4 and 5. Tagliamonte and Roberts (2005, 295) argue that this increase coincides with the general popularity of the show:

> Televised media material is subjected to relentless scrutiny by corporate marketing firms, which measure and quantify the amount of audience attention. Consideration of the Nielsen ratings for seasons 1–8 provides an interesting perspective. The height of 'so' use was seasons 4 and 5, and season 5 was the very year that *Friends* rose to become the number 2 television series in the United States. The popularity of *Friends* actually declines dramatically almost immediately thereafter. Interestingly, the drop in use of 'so' over the next two seasons corresponds to a decline in the ratings for *Friends* as well. It drops to number 5 in seasons 6 and 7. It is only in the 2001–2 season that *Friends* regains popularity, becoming the number one television series in the United States. Notice that this is precisely when 'so' is on the increase again.

They admit that this correlation could be linked to a wide range of factors, and it seems likely that the popularity of the show is at best weakly tied to intensifier use by the characters. It's also not clear exactly what such a correlation might mean. Regardless of whether a show's popularity affects language use in the ways Tagliamonte and Roberts suggest, their study remains intriguing as an exploration of language change in the narrative mass media (see also Adams 2004 for a similar discussion of language changes connected with the television series, *Buffy the Vampire Slayer* [1997–2003], and Stuart-Smith et al. 2013 for a discussion of change connected to viewing the drama *EastEnders*, 1985–).

Food for Thought

Texting (and other electronic forms of communication) is an area where people believe there is a lot of language change going on. Examine some of your own electronic conversations for different ways that language is being used. What does 'lol' seem to do? How is punctuation being used? What other strategies do you notice? Do any of these seem like actual changes to you or are they mostly about variation in spelling and punctuation?

Another nice example of tracking language change through the media is the case of the /r/ sound in the United States. Varieties of English distinguish themselves in many different ways, but one of the fairly consistent ways is whether or not they are what linguists call *rhotic*. Rhotic means whether speakers of the variety of English pronounce the /r/ sound before consonants and at the ends of words or not. Thus, for example, some varieties of English don't have an actual /r/ sound at the end of a word like 'car' or between the vowel and the final consonant in a word like 'large.' Those that don't are called non-rhotic and those that do are called rhotic. Many varieties of American English are rhotic, while many varieties of British English are not. Importantly for thinking through questions of language change, the "standard" variety of American English is rhotic, while the "standard" variety of British English is not. Similarly, across the globe where English is the native language of a population, that English will vary on whether it is rhotic or not, with the majority being non-rhotic. This is historically linked to migration patterns of English speakers from the British Isles. Historically in Britain, the southern varieties were typically non-rhotic while the more northern varieties (Scots English and Irish English in particular) were typically rhotic. As these English speakers migrated to different parts of the world during periods of colonialism, the variety they brought with them typically seeded itself in the places they landed.

Rhoticity was a variable linguistic ingredient that went into the stew of American English. In the United States, speakers of non-rhotic varieties settled in the eastern seaboard, while rhotic users settled the inland areas. In those communities that were settled by rhotic speakers, there was prestige associated with rhoticity and vice versa. This is why the English used in Pennsylvania and Maryland was historically rhotic, while that used in the northeast and the far south, particularly the Carolinas and Virginia, were non-rhotic. As non-rhotic speakers moved west, they came into contact with rhotic speakers. The result of this contact was general convergence with the rhotic speakers such that the varieties of American English spoken west of the Mississippi are generally all rhotic.[5]

In the United States, /r/-lessness was seen as more prestigious through the 1930s and was generally associated with coastal New England and the coastal south. /r/-fullness as found in the midwest and west was seen as less prestigious, something that is clearly reflected in the films of the thirties and early forties. For instance, in the film *Philadelphia Story* (1940), there is a clear class distinction drawn between Jimmy Stewart's midwestern Macaulay Connor and Katharine Hepburn's Philadelphian Tracy Lord, and it is reflected in part through Connor's rhotic pronunciations and Lord's non-rhotic ones.

By the end of the 1940s, the use of non-rhotic variants in films set in historically non-rhotic parts of the country had shifted almost entirely from being used by upper-class and lower-class characters to being used primarily by lower-class characters.

Food for Thought

Watch an older movie, like *Gone with the Wind* (1939), and note whether the speakers are rhotic or not. Compare that to a more recent film set in the southern United States, say *The Help* (2011) (which we'll look at in some of our subsequent chapters) and compare the characters' use of /r/ across the two films.

This shift in how characters use rhoticity corresponds to shifts in the non-media world of the same, as William Labov famously demonstrated by looking at rhoticity among employees in department stores in New York City that largely served upper-, middle-, or lower-class customers (Labov 1972). Labov found that employees in the higher-class store used more rhotic variants (in the utterance 'the fourth floor'), and those in the lower class store used fewer rhotic variants, with employees at the middle-class store more or less in the middle. He argued that this was evidence of language change in progress. That change continues to progress today as more and more speakers in traditionally non-rhotic areas produce increasingly more rhotic forms. In the coastal south, this shift is nearly completed, and most speakers under the age of 50 are rhotic. In the northeastern United States, rhoticity has become a variant that intertwines region and social class, something that is reflected in media products that do the same – for instance, in 1997's *Good Will Hunting*, in which the main character's non-rhotic Boston accent is juxtaposed with that of many of the students and faculty he encounters as a janitor at Harvard University, who in the film are all rhotic.[6]

The four cases we've just discussed –<ing>, personal pronouns, intensifiers, and rhoticity – illustrate different aspects of variation, including variation across time. Some of the variation, for instance, the reflexive pronouns and intensifiers, occurs among most speakers of American English, while rhoticity and the second person plural pronouns are tied to more geographically specific areas. <ing> is particularly interesting in this regard because it occurs in virtually all varieties of American English but is especially prevalent in the narrative media among characters who are supposed to be southern or western, particularly western characters who are also in Westerns (as a film/television genre).

We've seen how variation is both directly implicated in the grammar and also serves as a resource for speakers (and characters). In the case of Phil in the *Modern Family* example, the -in pronunciation links directly to his attempts to appear more masculine for his father-in-law. In the case of Alyssa from the film *Chasing Amy*, the use of the singular third person pronoun 'they' obscured the gender of the pronominal antecedent, Hayden, and in the case of Austin Powers, the first person reflexive made it possible for him to parody a certain kind of formality and control. Further, in the cases of intensifiers and rhoticity, the variation over time that we find in real-life communities appears in narrative mass media. With these examples, the basic toolkit for thinking about the components of language and language variation are in place. In the next chapter, we explore some of the dimensions affecting the choices about using elements of this toolkit.

Notes

1   Of course, people still care a lot about the differences even when they are minor. Try asking for a 'pop' in NYC or a 'soda' in Chicago and see what happens.

2   Discussions about the status of African American English, also known by a variety of other names, including the name most commonly used in the news media, Ebonics, are longstanding and complex. For details about the variety itself as well as discussions about its relative status, see Green (2003). For the rest of the book, I will refer to this variety as AAVE.

3   Just to keep things interesting, there is another <ing> in English that is used to form gerunds. For instance, in the sentence, 'Running is strenuous,' <ing> attaches to the verb stem to turn the stem into a noun. Since this <ing> changes the part of speech from a verb to a noun, it is derivational rather than inflectional. We know that these are different morphemes because they have slightly different histories and are related historically to different early Germanic stems.

4   In general this shifting of which form is used is found primarily in places where the pronouns are conjoined to another noun. Except for very young children, few speakers of American English, for instance, will use 'me' or 'myself' when it's the only subject, as in 'Me went to the store.'

5   Non-rhotic varieties are still found in Louisiana and parts of east Texas, and speakers of AAVE in most areas of the country (except the west coast) are non-rhotic, as are varieties such as Chicano English that have been influenced by AAVE.

6   Some very high-class accents in Boston, such as those associated with Boston Brahmins, are non-rhotic still today; however, characters like this do not appear in *Good Will Hunting*.

References

Adams, M. 2004. *Slayer Slang: A Buffy the Vampire Slayer Lexicon.* New York: Oxford University Press.

Campbell-Kibler, Kathryn. 2008. I'll be the Judge of that: Diversity in Social Perceptions of (ING). *Language in Society* 37(5): 637–659.

Campbell-Kibler, Kathryn. 2009. The Nature of Sociolinguistic Perceptions. *Language Variation and Change* 21(1): 135–156.

Campbell-Kibler, Kathryn. 2011. The Sociolinguistic Variant as a Carrier of Social Meaning. *Language Variation and Change* 22(3): 423–441.

Green, Lisa. 2003. *African American English: A Linguistic Introduction.* Cambridge: Cambridge University Press.

Heyd, Theresa. 2010. How You Guys Doin'? Staged Orality and Emerging Plural Address in the Television Series Friends. *American Speech* 85(1): 33–66.

Hill, Jane, and Bruce Mannheim. 1992. Language and World View. *Annual Review of Anthropology* 21: 381–406.

Labov, William. 1972. The Social Stratification of /r/ in New York City Department Stores. In *Sociolinguistic Patterns*, ed. W. Labov, 43–69. Philadelphia: University of Pennsylvania Press.

Stuart-Smith, Jane, Gwilym Pryce, Claire Timmins, and Barrie Gunter. 2013. Television Can Also Be a Factor in Language Change: Evidence from an Urban Dialect. *Language* 89(3): 501–536.

Tagliamonte, S., and C. Roberts. 2005. So Weird; So Cool; So Innovative: The Use of Intensifiers in the Television Series Friends. *American Speech* 80(3): 280–300.

Chapter 3

Studying Language Variation in the Media

Introduction

Every time I start a project that deals with the media I have to think about the best methods for turning what I see and hear on the screen into data that can be analyzed. In working with data from the mass media, I've worked with print media, film, television, and electronically mediated data. Each time I've first figured out what kind of question I wanted to answer. The easiest way to get started is always with brainstorming. My own interest typically turns to questions concerning how the characters are created and constituted as real; what kinds of beliefs about language must be in place to produce the outcomes I find; and how the media facilitate the circulation and diffusion of linguistic forms, including those that may be changing.

Answering those questions, or any other questions, depends largely on the tools and methods available. Those tools and methods form the backbone of this chapter, which focuses on several of the major ways that researchers working with media data have analyzed those data once they've noticed something interesting and formulated a question or set of questions about that interesting tidbit. Thus, this chapter is primarily intended as a general introduction to methods of analysis for pre-existing data sources such as those found in the narrative mass media. It progresses from the very early stages of thinking about narrative media as *data*, to *transcribing* and *coding* the data to prepare for analysis, and then to using different *methods* and approaches for conducting the analysis.

Vox Popular: The Surprising Life of Language in the Media, First Edition. Robin Queen.
© 2015 John Wiley & Sons, Inc. Published 2015 by John Wiley & Sons, Inc.

Formulating a Research Question

Deciding what you want to know by virtue of doing an exploration of language variation in the mass media represents the first step in the research process. Research generally can be thought of as engaging in a very particular kind of conversation, one that may have been going on for decades or one that may be forging what appears to be entirely new territory. Like all conversations, scholarly conversations typically progress as different people take their turn at holding the floor. Within a scholarly conversation, the means of holding the floor generally include developing questions that are linked to the ongoing conversation in some way and then providing an answer. Most often, each contribution to the conversation is intended to further or deepen the general understanding of some particular phenomenon. Scholars achieve such enriched understanding by pointing to relevant holes in the scholarly record, by showing how a theoretical premise does or doesn't predict particular outcomes, by correcting what they perceive as errors in the description or interpretation of data, and/or by showing how phenomena that were previously considered distinct may in fact be integrally connected and vice versa. In order to accomplish any of these, scholars typically start with a general idea about the phenomena that develops into a specific question or thesis that they then seek to answer through empirical or theoretical exploration, most often both.

While it might seem obvious that you can't start looking for answers until you have a clearly formulated question, in reality, a lot of research, maybe even the majority, begins with only a very vague sense of the question the research will address. Over time and through studying the existing scholarly record on the topic, a researcher continually refines this early idea into a question that becomes answerable. That answerable question then gets presented as the driving force behind the research project. For instance, Richard Bauman (2011, 23) presents his research question as exploring how oral storytelling was adapted to the emerging technology of sound recording in the late nineteenth century in the article on early vocal recordings that I discussed in Chapter 1. Similarly, Sali Tagliamonte and Chris Roberts (2005, 281) explain that an interest in understanding whether the language found in popular culture could be a useful source of data animated their study of *Friends* (1994–2004) (discussed in Chapter 2).

Once you have determined broadly what you want to explore and more narrowly what specific question or set of related questions you want to answer, the next general step is to engage in the process of turning the

Food for Thought

Go through some of the articles used for this book (or other scholarly articles to which you have access) and find the research question that drives the article. Where is it generally located? What form does it take? How generally is it stated? How does the author locate it in the scholarly conversation?

narrative media into a source of data that can then be analyzed. These two steps, determining your question and creating data that you can analyze, often occur in tandem and sometimes even occur in reverse order, with the creation of the data preceding the development of the research question, especially the narrowing of a general interest into a specific question to be addressed.

Turning Narrative Media into Data

Most commonly, data for linguistic research are gathered in the service of answering a particular research question. Thus, the data are, in a sense, specifically created as part of the research process. Even data gathered in the context of ethnographic fieldwork, which are less mediated by the research process than are data drawn from interviews, experimental protocols, or surveys, are preserved explicitly for the purpose of addressing a research question. The opposite is the case for data drawn from the mass media. Language variation in the mass media becomes data long after it has been preserved. Thus, selecting data for analysis from the media is in many ways more serendipitous and therefore requires careful consideration in terms of motivating the relative representativeness and specific selection.

The bulk of the existing literature using data from fictional media draws on a final product, namely, the commercially released film, television program, book, or other media product. Before the late 1990s, it was much more difficult than it has been subsequently to preserve audiovisual media data for the purposes of analysis. Since the late 1990s, however, a range of technologies and new consumer markets has made it much easier to obtain media programming. For instance, it is a relatively trivial matter to obtain the entire run of a given television series and much programming can be found at any time or place via streaming technologies available through the Internet. Similarly, many different types of information about specific performed media outlets can be found relatively simply and quickly online. Thus, a researcher might use a full run of a television series (Adams 2004; Tagliamonte and Roberts 2005; Heyd 2010), the entire oeuvre of a single actor (Bell 2011), or a single season of a television series (Mandala 2008; Richardson 2010). Alternatively, a corpus of materials could be collected and then a specific set of criteria developed for selecting data for analysis. In my own study of dubbing practices (Queen 2004), I used this type of method to select data involving the dubbing of AAVE, and Bucholtz and Lopez (2011) use it for their analysis of linguistic minstrelsy in Hollywood films.

Turning language from the mass media into data typically involves some kind of transcription, and scholars must decide how much detail to transcribe. Generally speaking, most researchers engaged in qualitative research do not transcribe the entire set of performed language data being analyzed, while those working to quantify and statistically model their data do. Thus, an important early consideration for working with performed media involves the decision of how much of the data requires transcription, and this decision will largely be tied to the research method and the question(s) being addressed. Fans have already transcribed many performed media products, which can be a useful starting point for turning the final media product into an analyzable set of data. For instance, Bednarek (2011) discusses a searchable, fan-generated database of dialogue in eighty-six episodes of the series *Lost*. Similarly, the transcriptions used in Tagliamonte and Roberts (2005), Quaglio (2009), and Heyd (2010) were based on transcriptions of *Friends* available online.

Analytic Orientation

The process of turning language in the mass media into data that can be analyzed begins with considering what it means to think of language in the mass media as data rather than as entertainment. Most of us engage with the media to gain information or be entertained or, probably most commonly, both. Focusing on language in the mass media as a source of data shifts that orientation to being about making the mass media available for systematic and critical exploration and reflection, with the hope of enhancing broad understandings of some particular phenomena based on the mass media as a source of evidence. As an example, when I began the *Days of Our Lives* (*DOOL*; 1965–) project (Queen 2012), I was primarily interested in understanding more about different models of masculinity and how they are represented in the media.

Although the process of doing research often involves shifts in thinking and analytic focus, and that is something any researcher should be willing to embrace, it is nonetheless typically a good idea to decide on a general analytic orientation very early in the process of turning mass media products into data. This may begin by developing a very specific kind of question that you'd like to explore, as discussed above. For instance, you might want to know how frequently different characters in a television series use terms of endearment (e.g., terms like "honey," "sweetheart," and so on). On the other hand, your general interest might be much more vague. You might, for instance, have noticed something curious going on in the plot development of a film and want to explore how language is tied to that development. In general, regardless of how vague or specific your question(s) are at the beginning, it's important to recognize and bear in mind that different kinds of questions require rather different orientations to analysis, and those orientations in turn constrain what it is possible to say about any given piece of data. Part of what distinguishes research from anecdote is that research takes a systematic approach to formulating questions, analyzing data, and arriving at conclusions. It does so as part of a larger tradition of thought linked to disciplinary knowledge. In other words, research answers questions in relation to questions other people have asked about the same or similar phenomena.

When you do any kind of research, you necessarily confront long-standing traditions about the nature of knowledge and how to develop it. These traditions typically provide the boundaries between academic disciplines and help unite people who may be working on different kinds of questions and problems by setting up shared assumptions concerning the generation of knowledge. These assumptions typically include traditions concerning the nature of the object being studied (*ontology*); what we can actually know about the object being studied and how we can be certain we know it (*epistemology*); and, finally, how we go about uncovering knowledge about that object (*methodology*). The majority of this chapter is linked to the last of these three, methodology, as I hope to illustrate some of the different ways that researchers interested in language variation have approached working with fictional media data.

However, deciding on a methodology often depends critically on the ontological and epistemological starting points a researcher brings to the task of doing analysis. Unfortunately, it is often the case that these starting points are left unspecified or simply assumed as shared between the researcher and the audience, though that may not always be the case. Given the ubiquity of both human language and fictional mass media, it is inevitable that researchers will come to the "same" data with vastly different understandings and assumptions about those data and what it is possible to know about them. Thus, it's important to be as clear as you can be about what you assume about the nature of what you are studying and what you believe it is possible to know. For instance, I approached the DOOL data with the assumption that the language I was interested in was not particularly different in kind from the language used outside the context of DOOL. I also assumed that it was possible to discover patterns worth further discussion by counting the number of times particular phenomena (like the use of particular kinds of commands) occurred.

Methodologically, two major approaches to data collection and analysis are found across the academic disciplines: *quantitative* and *qualitative* approaches. While these methods can be equally rigorous, systematic, and informative, they differ in some fundamental ways, as illustrated in Table 3.1.

As you see from Table 3.1, one of the primary distinctions between the two methods emerges from whether the data remain in their original form or are converted in some sense into a numerical quantity, through direct counting, measurement, index scoring, or ratio building. The other differences represented in the table generally fall out either directly or indirectly from this difference. Naturally, it is important to understand that these characteristics are meant to illustrate general differences between these types of methods rather than categorical procedural differences. Qualitative work, for instance, may well begin with specific hypotheses, while quantitative work may involve induction as well as deduction. Although these differences may not strictly distinguish these two broad approaches, the fact that the two differ in some fundamental ways should not be ignored. Each approach brings with it different strengths and costs, and the kinds of questions that can be answered in one approach are typically not answerable with the other.

Table 3.1   Broad parameters of qualitative and quantitative methods

Qualitative methods	Quantitative methods
Raw data	Numerical data based on raw data
Texts, images, objects, and activities	Frequencies, distributions, and probabilities
Descriptive	Model
Interpretive	Measured
Less generalizable	More generalizable
Highly contextual	Decontextualized
Inductive	Deductive
Observation-driven	Hypothesis-driven
More focus on meaning	More focus on form and function

The constraints on the kinds of questions one can address using either a quantitative or qualitative approach explain why many studies, especially of language variation, use both types of methods, often relying on qualitative methods to both develop and help explain quantitative findings while using quantitative findings to make predictions about and illustrate general patterns that occur in the data. We'll look at quantitative and qualitative approaches in more detail later in the chapter.

Food for Thought

Given a piece of transcription (take one of the transcripts that occurs in Chapters 1 and 2), formulate a quantitative question and a qualitative question based on them. In order to answer your question, what else might you need to know? What additional data would you need? How would you get it?

Once you have broadly determined your analytic orientation, the next step involves turning the audiovisual stream from the media into data that can be used and manipulated through the process of analysis.

Transcribing Your Data

When you do a transcription, you are shifting an audio or audiovisual representation into a written one. You should think about this as a type of translation in that the norms of the written language differ considerably from those of spoken language (as we saw in Chapter 2). For data coming from the fictional media, this can prove to be especially complicated because the audio or audiovisual output is itself usually a representation of something that was initially written. As noted above, one potential starting point is to obtain a written record that someone else has produced, such as the published script or fan-generated transcription. Another, probably more common, starting point is for you to transcribe the output yourself. With either approach, you should plan to redo the transcriptions as your analytic focus and understanding of the data sharpens.

The primary issues with transcribing data involve consideration for exactly what you should capture given the range of features and characteristics it is possible to capture. You can use a more phonetically oriented approach, a more orthographically oriented approach, or a hybrid approach.

For the most part in this book, I'm using a hybrid approach. This means I capture the relevant phenomena I want to talk about but do not try to accurately capture a full range of the spoken or visual output. It's not possible to fully re-create a written record of exactly what is present in the raw data, and in many ways that's a good thing. Transcription is one of the places where you are able to narrow the analytic focus by virtue of the very decisions you make. There are of course pros and cons to any decision you make about transcription, and it isn't possible to create a fully neutral transcription. Your own knowledge of what (and who) you are transcribing always comes into play, and, as Mary Bucholtz (2000) points out, this in itself can be an interesting vantage for analysis. The most important point to keep in mind is that all transcription is perspectival, and you want to be as aware as you can be of the various pros and cons associated with the choices you make. You also want to transcribe with the questions you are trying to address in mind and attempt to capture only those characteristics that will help you address those questions.

Most generally, I start the transcription process by trying to capture what is said in a more or less standard written form. Then, I typically go back through the transcript several times, altering it and retranscribing as I make decisions about what exactly I want to analyze. For example, in the paper I wrote about the daytime drama, *Days of Our Lives* (Queen 2012), I first decided that I would capture (via video recording; this was before DVR after all) two weeks' worth of data. This amounted to ten hours of data (*DOOL* broadcasts Monday–Friday for one hour each day). The very first thing I did with those data was transcribe them in as simple a manner as possible. I transcribed each episode in a fairly standard form of written English, noting the name of the character speaking and what they said.

Example 3.1a   *Days of Our Lives*, Episode 7271, NBC, April 25, 1994

```
Bo:       Please tell me why does Hope not wanna commit
          to me?
Billie:   Because she's still upset that you committed
          to me in Rome. That we conceived a child
          together.
Bo:       Yeah she was upset about that, but why is it
          still an issue? I mean we're divorced we've
          moved past this. Why can't she?
Billie:   O.k. from a woman's point of view when the man
          you love gives his heart to another woman the
          hurt never goes away
```

Bo: Right and you have experienced that hurt. I'm
           sorry. I I shouldn't be askin' you for advice
           on this.
Billie: No no Bo please. I I want to be your friend go
           ahead ask.
Bo: What the heck is goin' on with Hope? I mean
           ever since that night when she had
           the accident she's been distant and unlike
           herself
Billie: O.k. like how? Give me an example
Bo: Oh, I'll give you several. Let's see. Today
           I saw her with DiMera. They were acting very
           friendly
Billie: Hope and Stefano? Are you sure?
Bo: I am very sure I mean she's been having
           memories of bein' with him when she was Gina
           and I found this picture of the two of them
           together and they look like a couple. She was
           sittin' on his lap. Isn't that a sickening
           thought?

One thing I did in that initial transcription that differs from standard forms of written English was to capture things like speech errors, false starts, and hesitation output like "um" or "uh." (One of the interesting differences between data from the fictional media and data from face-to-face conversation is that these features are far less frequent in fictional media. On the other hand, because they are rare, they can be more meaningful when they occur, so it can be important to capture them.) Transcribing these features takes special attention since we typically don't pay a lot of attention to these features as we interpret language in real time and may not notice them at all unless we are paying attention to capturing everything that is said.

You can think about this level of transcription as the most basic, or the rough draft. The next step is to go through and capture more detail. The

Food for Thought

Select a scene or two from a film or television show and transcribe the scene.

details you include will be specific to your own project, and for that reason you'll have to determine what exactly you want to include and develop a general protocol for what you have included. This will include noting the conventions you have chosen for representing various elements of the raw output. You can find a list of conventions that many linguists use on page **x** above.

Here's what the scene above looked like once I did another pass through the transcription, paying more attention to various elements that I was interested in analyzing further.

Example 3.1b   *Days of Our Lives*, Episode 7271, NBC, April 25, 1994

```
 1  Bo:       Please [.] tell me [.] why does Hope not
               wanna commit to me?=
 2  Billie:                       =Because she's still
               upset that you committed to me in Rome.
               that we conceived a child together.=
 3  Bo:        =Yeah [..] she was upset about that [..]
               but why is it still an issue? I mean,
               we're divorced, we've moved past this,
               why can't she?
 4  Billie:    O.k. from a woman's point of view [..]
               when the man you love gives his heart to
               another woman [..] the hurt never goes
               away=
 5  Bo:           =Right [.] and you have experienced
               that hurt. I'm sorry [.] I I shouldn't be
               askin you for advice on this.=
 6  Billie:                       =No no Bo, please, I
               I wanna be your friend […] go ahead, ask.
 7  Bo:        What the heck is goin on with Hope?
               I mean ever since that night when she had
               the accident, she's been distant
               and unlike herself=
 8  Billie:                        =O.k. like how? [..] give me an
               example=
 9  Bo:        =Oh, I'll give you several [..] let's see.
               Today I saw her with DiMera. They were
               acting very friendly=
10  Billie:                        =Hope and Stefano? [.] are you
               sure?
```

```
11  Bo:        I am very sure I mean she's been having
               memories of bein with him when she was
               Gina and I found this picture of the two
               of them together and they look like a
               couple. She was sittin on his lap. Isn't
               that a sickening thought?
```

Comparing transcripts 3.1a and 3.1b reveals some interesting and potentially important differences. While 3.1a captured aspects of the characters' pronunciation, especially of forms involving < ing > and a few other forms like 'gonna,' it contained no information about the pause structure or about how the interaction took place as far as different speaker turns was considered. Transcript 3.1b captures that information, something that became relevant in the analysis as I explored how the characters created a sense of solidarity through this interaction based on the rapid turn-taking style they employed. Thus, the second pass through the transcription process added new layers of information and made them available for analysis.

Food for Thought

Take the transcript you developed above and do a transcription of it that takes more detail into account and uses some of the conventions explained on page 00. How does this new transcription provide additional insight into the data?

It can be useful to remember that up until the point that you put the transcript to work as part of the analysis, you can always rework it to capture new analytic foci. Your transcription protocol typically develops once your analytic direction has taken shape, and, like all drafts, the transcription isn't finished until you decide to stop working on it. At the most basic, you will probably always want to include details about the order in which characters spoke and the points when one character's turn ends and another one's begins. You may also want to keep in mind as you develop your transcription protocol that you want to maintain a balance between transcribing enough detail to make linguistic analysis feasible and making the transcription easy to read and, especially, search. It is one thing to work with a very detailed transcription of a few scenes; it is another issue entirely to use a large corpus (say, the entire run of a television show that aired for ten years) that you want to search in different ways. After you have transcribed the data in the level of detail relevant to your study, the next step is coding the data for the aspects that are of direct interest to the overall analysis.

Coding Your Data

Coding is the formal term for making notes about the phenomena you are interested in and for turning your transcriptions into data that can be analyzed. Coding is the process of organizing your transcripts so that you can look for recurrent patterns and recognize consistent patterns of actions and behaviors. For instance, you might code all the examples of a particular phenomenon in red or in some other way such as with a font change or textual label. Coding is most frequently discussed as part of the analysis in qualitative approaches; however, quantitative approaches based on relative frequencies will generally also require coding. Further, if you are using pre-existing data, such as is typical in the mass media, quantitative approaches that involve measurement (for instance, of vowel qualities, pause lengths, or other measurable characteristics) will involve coding your transcriptions so that the relevant phenomena can be found in order to be measured.

Just as the process of transcription typically involves some degree of analysis as you decide what exactly to transcribe, the process of coding your data typically involves degrees of analysis as well. Coding can involve any labeling scheme that makes it possible for you to see patterns and find occurrences of the "same" phenomena in a large set of data. Your codes may be text labels, numbers, letters, other graphic symbols, colors, or any device that makes it possible to systematically explore and explain your data. In my own work, I have frequently used color coding as a means of labeling particular phenomena. The scheme below is quite preliminary and combines different levels of observation, including aspects of conversational structure, interactional dynamics, styles, and affective orientations. It demonstrates that coding schemes can evolve over the course of an analysis and that schemes may focus on different aspects of analytic interest.

Example 3.1c   *Days of Our Lives*, Episode 7271, NBC, April 25, 1994
   Coding Scheme
   Casual/Informal
   Conversational facilitation
   <u>Long Pause</u>
   CONFUSION

1	Bo:	PLEASE, TELL ME, WHY DOES HOPE NOT **WANNA** COMMIT TO ME?=
2	Billie:	=Because she's still upset that you committed to me in Rome. that we conceived a child together.=
3	Bo:	=Yeah, she was upset about that [..] but WHY IS IT STILL AN ISSUE? I mean, we're divorced, we've moved past this, WHY CAN'T SHE?
4	Billie:	O.k. from a woman's point of view, when the man you love gives his heart to another woman [..] the hurt never goes away=
5	Bo:	=Right, and you have experienced that hurt. I'm sorry, I I shouldn't be **askin** you for advice on this.=
6	Billie:	=No no Bo, please, I I **wanna** be your friend [...] *go ahead, ask*.
7	Bo:	WHAT THE HECK IS GOIN ON WITH HOPE? I mean ever since that night when she had the accident, she's been distant and unlike herself=
8	Billie:	=*O.k. like how?* [..] *give me an example*=
9	Bo:	=Oh, I'll give you several, let's see. Today I saw her with DiMera. They were **acting** very friendly=
10	Billie:	=Hope and Stefano?, *are you sure?*
11	Bo:	I am very sure I mean she's been **having** memories of **bein** with him when she was Gina and I found this picture of the two of them together and they look like a couple. She was **sittin** on his lap. Isn't that a sickening thought?

For this transcript, I was particularly interested in features that indicated what I considered descriptively to be more casual speech. I was interested in this style of speech primarily because I hypothesized that the male characters were more likely to use casual speech than the female characters, something that was roughly borne out when I did a quantitative analysis of various forms. However, I was also interested in more qualitative components, particularly indications of characters' emotional states, such as being confused or being angry. Thus, I coded my transcriptions for those aspects. In some cases, the same element might be coded for more than one aspect, as occurs in the transcript above in lines 1 and 7 in which an element that is more casual occurs in a turn that indicates confusion on the part of the character.

Whatever coding system you develop, you will want be sure and maintain a coding protocol so that you know what your codes are labeling. Developing a coding protocol allows you to ask other people to code your data so that you can compare the degree to which different people label phenomena in the same way. This is known as *intercoder reliability*, and it is one mechanism through which the validity of a particular analysis can be judged.

Food for Thought

Take one of my transcriptions or one that you have produced yourself and code it for a linguistic feature you would be interested in exploring further.

Codes form the basis of your analytic categories and as such may continue to develop as your understanding of the data grows. Most researchers do several passes through the coding of their data as they gain more understanding of the data and thereby refine the kinds of questions they are asking. Through this process, the codes themselves typically shift, and sometimes a single code may be folded into another code or even eliminated entirely. In linguistic research, most of the codes will be related to some aspect of language form rather than specific aspects of the content. One area where aspects of content might be noted is when *metalinguistic comments* are being made. Metalinguistic comments are comments about language specifically and can be useful in the analysis of range of phenomena.

The next step in the analysis is bringing together your codes and transcripts in a form that makes them available for final analysis. If you are working with only one transcription, that process can generally just begin; however, if you are working with multiple transcriptions and a complex set of codes, you will generally want to build a corpus that you can search and otherwise manipulate.

Constructing a Corpus

At its most basic, constructing a corpus involves bringing together the relevant texts, such as transcripts or similar artifacts, and applying your coding, or annotation, scheme to them. The corpus represents a quantity of texts, usually larger than two or three, along with the codes that you have applied to them assembled together into some kind of searchable form. The corpus thus typically stands as a representation of a particular phenomenon or set of phenomena. The larger the corpus, the more representative and generalizable it is assumed to be; thus, an analysis of a single television series, such as *Friends*, would not be able to comment on television series in general or even situation comedies because it is a relatively small corpus. Nonetheless, a corpus of all the episodes of *Friends* has been analyzed for a variety of different components (Tagliamonte and Roberts 2005; Quaglio 2009; Heyd 2010). Similarly, Adams (2004) conducted an analysis of the entire run of *Buffy the Vampire Slayer* (1997–2003). In the case of my study of gender-linked language on *Days of Our Lives*, my corpus consisted of ten episodes that were all transcribed and coded for a set of relevant aspects of both language form and general pragmatics.

Once you have your corpus in place, you can use a wide array of computational software tools that have been designed to help search and manipulate corpora of linguistic data. Some are designed for elaborate coding schemes; some are designed to work with plain texts; and some are designed to work with specific corpora. There are too many to go into detail here, but some of the most basic include WordSmith, AntConc, and Simple Concordance Program. More complex tools designed especially for qualitative research include Elan (many platforms), Atlas.ti (PC), TAMSAnalyzer (Mac), and the Linguistic Inquiry and Word Count (Mac/PC/online).

Searching your corpus can reveal distributions, frequencies, and *concordances* (the environments in which particular phenomena occur). You can also search a corpus for *collocates*, which are elements that frequently occur together or very near one another, and keywords. Collocates and keywords can both illuminate characteristics of language use captured in the corpus. Finally, searching the corpus allows you to sort the data according to various codes and to remove extraneous information that may not be relevant to the analysis (see Baker 2010 for a more thorough discussion of using corpus-based approaches for sociolinguistic analysis).

Once you have decided on a perspective from which to view language in the fictional media as research data, have formulated questions concerning those data, have transcribed and coded the data in sufficient detail to address your questions, and have made it possible to search and manipulate the data, you have reached the point of doing your final analysis. Of course, in practice, you will have decided on your approach prior to the steps that we've just discussed since the approach you take has direct bearing on how you formulate your questions as well as how you transcribe and code the data. You then return to that approach when it's time to finish your analysis.

In what follows, I outline some of the major theoretical and methodological approaches people have taken for conducting and framing analyses of fictional media language. As you'll see, the approaches are quite varied and bring with them different ontological and epistemological assumptions. As is true of many social science endeavors, the study of language in the media can proceed quantitatively, qualitatively, or through a combination of qualitative and quantitative methods.

Quantitative Methods

As you saw at the start of the chapter, there are two major methods for exploring language in the mass media, quantitative and qualitative methods. Within each of these, there are further possibilities for orienting to the data depending on the types of questions and analytic interests the researcher has. Virtually all studies of language variation of any kind, and certainly of language variation in the mass media, use one or both of these methods.

First, you can elect to count or otherwise measure linguistic elements in some manner and then model the distribution or frequency of those elements quantitatively – for instance, with statistical models. This method is known as a quantitative method because it seeks to make generalizations based on the frequency with which some phenomenon occurs and frequently also on the probability that that phenomenon can be predicted or accounted for based on other information. Quantitative methods are generally based on the idea that you can generate a specific hypothesis and then test that hypothesis through measurement and quantification. A simple quantitative method occurs in Lukas Bleichenbacher's (2012) examination of multilingualism in Hollywood films.

Bleichenbacher looked at how often movies that were set in places where English was not spoken actually used English instead of the language in question. Bleichenbacher counted turns by speakers of English and by speakers of a different language across his corpus and found that even though these films were set in places where multilingualism was likely, more than 80 percent of the turns in his corpus were in English (Bleichenbacher 2012, 160). Beyond the raw frequency counts, Bleichenbacher did not perform any additional quantitative manipulation. Thus, he didn't attempt to correlate the use of English with any other feature, nor did he try to show that English use covaries with some other property. Still, based on his counts, he argues that not only does English predominate, but English-speaking characters also speak significantly more than characters with other first languages, something he attributes to the likelihood that non-English speaking characters will be in minor roles generally.

If you are interested in correlating variables in order to assess the likelihood that one variable will change under some kind of influence of another, there is a variety of ways in which to do this using statistical models. Statistical models consist of mathematical formulas that relate the data being influenced (the dependent variable) to the data that are hypothesized to be doing the influencing (the independent variables). An important consideration for deciding on which statistical test(s) to use concerns whether the variables are discrete (consisting of a clear choice between one or another variant) or continuous (consisting of a set of values between two points). While a discussion of different statistical tests is beyond the scope of this chapter, there are many resources available to help you make decisions about the statistical models best suited to your data. Simple searches of the Internet can help you find many of them. Useful texts for making statistical choices for work on language variation include: Johnson (2011), Gries (2013), and Rasinger (2013).

In Table 3.2, drawn from my *DOOL* study, I was interested in knowing whether the gender of the characters had an effect on whether they used [IN] or [ING], one of the variables we discussed in the last chapter.

For this analysis, I hypothesized that the female characters would be more likely than the male characters to use -ing. Using a statistical test

Table 3.2 Gender-based distribution of -in allomorph in progressive verbs*

	Female speaker	*Male speaker*	*Total*
-in	20 (6 %)	95 (28 %)	115 (17 %)
-ing	319 (94 %)	243 (72 %)	562 (83 %)
Total	339 (50 %)	338 (50 %)	677 (100 %)

*There is a significant difference in male and female productions (p<.0001).
Source: Queen 2012, 164. © Equinox Publishing Ltd 2012.

designed for discrete variables (the Chi-square test), I found that, while both male and female characters used more -ing than -in, the female characters used proportionally more -ing than the male characters, and this difference was significant. Significance within a statistical model means that the likelihood is very low that the relationship found between the variables was due to chance. In the case of the relationship between the characters' gender and -ing, the likelihood that the pattern found was due to chance was 1 in 10,000. In most social science research, a hypothesis can be considered supported with a finding when there is less than a 5 percent likelihood (this is often expressed as $p < .05$) that chance accounts for the patterns found.

Sali Tagliamonte and Chris Roberts (2005) used another kind of statistical test, a multivariate logistic regression, in their study of intensifier use on the television show *Friends*. That type of statistical test is meant to test co-variation between dependent and independent variables and how much influence, if any, different independent variables have on the dependent variable. Intensifiers are words like 'very,' 'really,' and 'so' that intensify the adjectives they modify, as in 'really cool.' Tagliamonte and Roberts were interested especially in the how 'so' related to several independent variables.

Tagliamonte and Roberts hypothesized that 'so,' the newest intensifier form, would be more likely to occur when used by female characters, when used to modify relatively frequent adjectives, and when used for adjectives that were more emotional in quality. They further hypothesized that intensifier use would be affected by the season of the show in which it occurred. Almost all of their hypotheses were supported, with the only exception being the use of 'so' to distinguish the quality of adjectives in Seasons 1 and 2. Table 3.3 illustrates this and also shows the degree of influence of the various independent factors, noted by the factor weight (FW) in the table. For the statistical program they use, VARBRUL, factor weights higher than .5 are conventionally considered to favor the occurrence of the dependent variable, while those below .5 are considered to disfavor it.[1]

If we look at the sex variable, we see that the female characters always used more 'so' than the male characters; however, there was a particularly strong difference in Seasons 1 and 2, something Tagliamonte and Roberts had predicted based on general paths of language change in non-media communities. Similarly, we see that highly frequent adjectives were more likely than less frequent adjectives to be modified by 'so' in Seasons 4 and 5, but lower-frequency adjectives were more likely to be modified by 'so' in Seasons 6 and 7 (these are shown by cell shading in Table 3.3).

Table 3.3 Multivariate analysis of intensifier 'so' by season

	Seasons 1 & 2		Seasons 4 & 5		Seasons 6 & 7		N
Corrected mean	.07		.11		.08		
Number	1,888		2,195		2,270		8,611
	FW	%	FW	%	FW	%	
ADJECTIVE FREQUENCY							
>600 ('good,' 'great,' 'sorry')	.48	8	.54	13	.42	6	1,964
>100 ('bad,' 'big,' 'cool,' 'crazy,' 'cute,' 'fat,' 'funny,' 'happy,' 'nice,' 'stupid,' 'weird')	.50	8	.53	12	.43	6	1,798
>30 ('amazing,' 'beautiful,' 'horrible,' 'old,' 'sweet,' etc.)	.63	14	.61	16	.64	13	1,535
>10 ('huge,' 'glad,' 'sick,' etc)	.46	8	.38	7	.47	7	2,679
<10 ('geeky,' 'murky,' 'rough,' 'unfair,' etc)	.47	7	.47	10	.66	14	635
Range	16		23		24		
SEX							
Female	.65	13	.58	7	.57	10	4,376
Male	.34	4	.42	4	.43	6	4,235
Range	21		16		14		
ADJECTIVE QUALITY							
Emotional	[.49]	10	.69	25	.69	21	518
Neutral	[.50]	9	.49	11	.49	7	4,301
Range			20		20		

Tagliamonte and Roberts argue that this indicates overall diffusion of 'so' across the lexicon, something also predicted in language changes occurring in non-media communities. Thus, based on the data represented here, Tagliamonte and Roberts argue that data found in the fictional media do often approximate patterns of variation found outside the media.

Food for Thought

Find a copy of the Bleichenbacher, Heyd, Tagliamonte and Roberts, or Quaglio study listed in the bibliography for this chapter. For each of the charts and tables in the article, explain in your own words what the quantitative data represent and what they illustrate.

For our purposes in this chapter, Table 3.3, along with Table 3.2, illustrate some of the ways that researchers are able to quantify data taken from the mass media and then model aspects of the distributional characteristics of those data. Being able to assess, and in theory predict, the likelihood of a given dependent variable occurring is a powerful tool for assessing how language variation contributes to the overall media product. It's also useful for assessing the degree to which language variation found in a source like the fictional media compares to variation drawn from other sources. Quantitative modeling further allows for experimental approaches to language variation in the media. An *experimental approach* controls variability in a deliberate way that is generally not possible with naturalistic data such as those found in the media (and in the majority of studies examining linguistic variation from a social perspective). Nonetheless, an experimental approach could be used to answer a variety of questions linked especially to the connection between the variation found in a media product and an audience's reception of that variation.

As powerful as quantitative models can be, it's important to keep in mind some of their limitations. For instance, since the majority of these models are based on probability, they can't explain or predict definitively the outcome of any specific case. Rather, they can at best suggest the relative likelihood of an outcome. Similarly, they are not well designed to provide information about the meanings embedded in the variation that occurs or about how variation may be structured within a given stretch of speech such as an individual scene or as produced by an individual character. For questions related to those issues, most researchers turn to the second major method of analysis used for language variation, which is the qualitative method.

Qualitative Methods

Qualitative research centers chiefly on doing highly contextualized inter-pretations of particular bits of data. If you have ever done literary analyses or critical readings of literary texts, you probably used largely qualitative research methods. There, you interpret, often within the context of a particular theoretical framework, some stretch of data (typically referred to as "a text" in fields where this type of work is most common). Qualitative analysis, like quantitative analysis, depends on defining and constraining a corpus of data for the purposes of addressing a particular question or interest. Qualitative research is largely the method of choice for disciplines that are more or less humanistically oriented, and fundamentally draws its power from probing for meaning within the data. Unlike in many of the other humanities, most linguistic analyses are at least as interested in, and frequently are more interested in, the general form of the linguistic output as the specific content. Within linguistics, there are quite a number of qualitative approaches.

There are three major qualitative research traditions within studies of language in the mass media (and within studies of language variation more generally), all of which are linked to continuous, naturalistic language output. First, there is *discourse analysis* (DA), which can refer either to an analysis of stretches of language larger than a single sentence or to the analysis of language as part of broader systems of cultural knowledge and practice. The latter approach is common in literary analysis, cultural studies, and similar humanities-oriented approaches. For the most part, linguists take the former approach to thinking about discourse, focusing on how elements in a stretch of speech or conversation are structurally or conceptually linked together (such as with words like 'well' or 'you know'). Discourse analysis from this perspective may also capture aspects of con-versational management and general narrative structure, connecting these to other aspects of the context of the language event, including the gen-eral setting, the participants, and the topics involved.

In my analysis of the scene transcribed above in Examples 3.1a, 3.1b, and 3.1c, I take a largely discourse analytic approach to showing different aspects of the scene to argue that Bo and Billie present a clearly binary portrayal of gender while also undermining gender-based stereotypes, particularly of rigid masculinity. I argue this point using details of their speech more broadly:

> The overall interaction is marked by Billie's facilitation of Bo's contributions
> and each of her turns provides a means through which Bo can continue
> with his own conversational interests. This pattern is particularly apparent

following her urging Bo in turn 6 to ask her for advice. As Bo launches into his evidence for Hope not being herself, his apology in turn 5 for placing Billie in an awkward position is seemingly forgotten. Indeed, his prosody and excited demeanor in turns 9 and 11 ironically show that his worry over Billie's feelings concerning his rejection of her are subordinate to his own jealousy and disgust at Hope having had a relationship with Stefano. Thus, in general, this conversation follows what Fishman (1997) has deemed the pattern of women doing the conversational "shitwork" in which they make sure that conversation progresses. At the same time, there is also clear interactional solidarity in the form of conversational overlap and rapid turn-taking. This sort of pattern is generally reported for friendly conversation and has been particularly widely noted in all-female conversations (Coates 1993, 1996). The friendly nature of the conversation is further supported by both characters' use of a casual speech style. Bo in particular uses the alveolar variant of -ing in turns 5, 7 and 11. Both characters also use cliticized variants of 'want to' and 'going to.' (Queen 2012, 167)

Here, we can see both how the whole scene can be analyzed and how that analysis can be linked to broader aspects of the social context in which it occurs, in this case both the social context as it is found in the narrative world of the drama and the social context in which an audience views the drama.

Critical discourse analysis (CDA) captures the second major form of qualitative analysis found in studies of language variation in the mass media. CDA seeks to understand how power circulates in and through different kinds of interactive and institutional contexts, including especially in the media. In some ways, critical discourse analysis combines the two notions of discourse noted above through its focus on power dynamics. CDA seeks analyses of language that reveal how language creates, sustains, and replicates fundamental inequalities in society. Many analyses of language in the mass media, particularly within media genres such as news, center on how language frames particular kinds of events. In his book *Media Discourse*, Norman Fairclough (1995) takes a CDA approach to explore data from the news, political debates, documentary sources, and various reality and lifestyle programs – all sources that are significantly less scripted than what we find in the narrative mass media. In his analysis of the medical program *Medicine Now*, for instance, Fairclough illustrates that the show's host and a doctor being interviewed systematically use linguistic strategies such as repetition, slow speaking rate, pausing, and lexical choices to construct positions of authority and professionalism, each of which contributes to the overall power of the doctor over the audience (1995, 133–135). Generally, CDA seeks to expose how powerful people maintain their power through various official and non-official channels (ten Have 1999, 10).

CDA tends to focus especially on issues of word meaning, word choice, metaphorical meaning, and strategies for managing and controlling word meaning. CDA lends itself well as an analytic framework for the following scene from the television show *Seinfeld* (1989–1998), which focuses specifically on matters related to word choices. In this case, those choices reflect relatively recent social norms around "political correctness." Throughout the scene, Seinfeld works to avoid using certain words, especially those that derive a negative connotation through their connection to ethnicity. In other words, Seinfeld seeks to avoid being politically "incorrect" in order to maintain a positive rapport with the woman he is dating. In each case (see lines 4, 10, and 28), he starts to say the word, stops himself, and then describes the activity that would have been denoted by the word.

Example 3.2 *Seinfeld*, "Cigar Store Indian," Season 5, Episode 10, Larry David and Jerry Seinfeld (creators), NBC, December 9, 1993

```
1  Girlfriend:  Okay, so where are we gonna eat?
2  Seinfeld:    Ah, I thought we'd eat at the Gentle
                Harvest.
3  Girlfriend:  Ooh, I love that place! But it's
                usually so crowded, can we get a
                table?
4  Seinfeld:    Oh, don't worry I made reser%
5  Girlfriend:  You made what?
```

6	Seinfeld:	I, uh, I uh arranged for the appropriate accommodations.
7	Girlfriend:	Oh.
8	Seinfeld:	And then, Knicks tickets! Floor seats!
9	Girlfriend:	How did you get these?
10	Seinfeld:	Got 'em on the street from a sc%
11	Girlfriend:	From who?
12	Seinfeld:	A, uh, one of those guys.
13	Girlfriend:	What guys?
14	Seinfeld:	You know, the guys, they sell the tickets to the sold-out events.
15	Girlfriend:	Ah.
16	Seinfeld:	Wait a second, you've got the Mark McEwin TV guide!
17	Girlfriend:	That's Al Roker.
18	Seinfeld:	Oh, well, they're both chubby weathermen. I get Don Deloise and Paul Proudhomme up too. Could I have this?
19	Girlfriend:	Sure, take it.
20	[Scene shift to Seinfeld's apartment]	
21	Girlfriend:	I like your place. It's very unassuming.
22	Seinfeld:	Oh why would I assume, I never assume. Leads to assumptions.
23	Girlfriend:	Oh by the way, that TV guide I gave you, I need it back.
24	Seinfeld:	Why?
25	Girlfriend:	Well, I'm doing a report on minorities in the media, and I wanted to use that interview with Al Roker.
26	Seinfeld:	It's too late, I gave it to Elaine, she's already on her way to give it to George's father.
27	Girlfriend:	Jerry, I really need it back. It is mine.
28	Seinfeld:	Oh, but you can't give something and then take it back, I mean what are ya, a [..]

29	Girlfriend:	What?
30	Seinfeld:	A uh, a person that [uh-
31	Girlfriend:	[A person that what?
32	Seinfeld:	Well, a person that gives something and then they're dissatisfied and they wish they had [uh
33	Girlfriend:	[And?
34	Seinfeld:	-never given it to the person that they originally gave it to.
35	Girlfriend:	You mean like an indian giver!
36	Seinfeld:	[raising hands and stepping back] I'm sorry, I'm not familiar with that term.

"Political correctness" is a complex topic that goes beyond our discussion here about methods of analysis (see however Cameron 1995, ch. 4, for a brilliant discussion of political correctness). Of interest from the perspective of CDA are both the choices that Seinfeld makes to avoid using certain terms as well as the somewhat extreme interpretation of those terms as being homophones with terms related to Native Americans. The discussion of the first two, 'reservation' (lines 4 and 6) and 'scalper' (lines 10, 12, and 14) set up the general perception that speaking without offending people is quite difficult and that speaking in general can be full of landmines when others are (overly) sensitive about language. Although these two terms aren't usually part of general conversations concerning "political correctness," the third term, 'Indian giver' (lines 28, 30, 32, 34, and 35), of course, is. In having set up the first two cases as linked clearly to unusual concern about causing offense, the third iteration of this same dynamic does the same for the term that has been part of actual discussion.

In turn, and of particular interest for analyses based in CDA, this scene links to broader sociopolitical conversations, beliefs, and norms about the place of language in the service of social power and social and political dominance. The scene also illustrates how *conversational repair* can work. One of the hallmarks of conversations about political correctness lies in the assumption that uttering certain words results in a conversational problem that requires repair, something apparent throughout this scene, but especially in lines 28–36. The means through which conversational repair occurs captures one of the major areas of interest for the third major qualitative approach to language variation, conversational analysis.

Conversational analysis (CA) differs from DA and CDA in that it takes a fairly strict etic approach to the analysis of linguistic variation. Etic means focusing only on what is overtly available in the data themselves, rather than extrapolating to broader social norms or stereotypes. For instance, in the scene between Billie and Bo, a CA approach would argue that gender is relevant specifically because it is mentioned in line 4. CA approaches data from the perspective that understanding conversational participants' use of resources is important. CA generally eschews including information external to the interaction as part of the analysis and thus differs further from other qualitative approaches in being more strictly focused on the details of interaction.[2] It may include aspects of gesture and body language, however, particularly as they co-occur with aspects of language.

CA addresses questions related to how we know when it's our turn to talk and how we signal to others that our turn is coming to an end. This might include, for instance, cases in which speakers jointly produce a turn. CA thus primarily examines the structuring of interaction and tends to focus on feedback in conversations, conversational overlap, conversational repair, and turn-taking.

Example 3.3   *Big Brother*, Season 3, Channel 4 (cited in Thornborrow and Morris 2004, 258)

```
1  Nick:   Darren has definitely voted boys out every
           time
2  Craig:  yeah
3  Nick:   Every time=
4  Craig:            =I think 'cos he feels we're the
           biggest to him
5  Nick:   [exactly
6  Craig:  ['cos he's a wimp
7  Nick:   I'm glad you spotted that
```

In this example, taken from the third season of the UK version of the reality show *Big Brother* (2002) in a study oriented primarily around gossip, Joanna Thornborrow and Deborah Morris (2004) discuss how Nick and Craig are conversationally aligned with one another in their negative assessment of Darren (2004, 258). Both Nick (line 5) and Craig (line 2) offer positive feedback to the other's assertions, indicating general agreement. Further, their turns occur in rapid succession, with no gaps or pauses, including in one case directly overlapping utterances. The overlapped turns 5 and 6 underscore the affiliation between the two within this scene.

Because many of the issues of central concern to CA, especially conversational overlap and conversational repair, are significantly less prevalent in scripted, fictional media than in other media forms and in non-media-based interaction, the use of CA is somewhat circumscribed for studies of language variation in the fictional mass media. Still, we see several examples of conversational repair in the *Seinfeld* example discussed above. For instance, in each of the repairs that he does related to word choice, the term 'uh' or 'um' precedes the reformulated part (lines 6, 12, and 30). In general, the preference in conversational repair is for the speaker to do a self-repair by him- or herself. In the scene, however, the girlfriend prompts the self-repair by asking 'wh-' questions (lines 5, 11, 13, 31). The prompting of self-repair is preferred to someone other than the original speaker doing the repair. In the two cases where the girlfriend does the repair, Seinfeld responds with additional information or clarification of what he meant, which doesn't happen in the cases of self-repair. In line 17, when the girlfriend corrects the mistake of who is on the cover of the *TV Guide*, Seinfeld explains (line 18) how he could have made the error. Then, in line 35, when the girlfriend calls Seinfeld on the use of a particular term, Seinfeld actually denies that that was the term he intended by claiming that he doesn't know the term.

Food for Thought

Take a transcription that you've already produced or produce a new one from a movie or television show. Make sure it's at least twenty-five lines long and do an analysis of how the conversation proceeds along the lines described in the chapter for CA. Could you also do a CDA analysis on the same transcript? What do the different methodological approaches point out?

The *Seinfeld* example nicely illustrates the potential for both CA and CDA, showing how the two approaches capture different components of language variation and how important careful framing of the driving question is for selecting an appropriate method of analysis. Using both approaches to examine the same data in different ways provides a final consideration for approaching the analysis of language variation in the narrative media. Given that it can be difficult to attend to all the relevant elements of language variation with a single method, *triangulating* your data using several methods can be a powerful alternative approach.

Triangulating Your Evidence with Different Analytic Approaches

Triangulating your evidence refers to using two or more methods to validate your analysis while also allowing you to overcome potential shortfalls in any single method. In this case the "triangle" emerges from using multiple sources of evaluation and is metaphorically connected to ways of measuring distance to arrive at a coordinated location. In social science research, triangulating your evidence allows you to ask different kinds of questions of the same data, and, in the best cases, those different questions (and their corresponding analyses) will point to similar general conclusions. In the work on the soap operas that we've discussed at different points in this chapter, I took a triangulated approach, using both quantification (including simple relative frequencies as well as different probabilistic models) and qualitative analysis (primarily a discourse analytic method) in order to support a general claim that daytime dramas simultaneously reinforced stereotypes about the binarity of gender (the idea that people come in male and female types and that those types are clearly and categorically distinct from one another) and alternative models for masculinity. In a study I did on dubbing American films into German (Queen 2004), I did something similar. In that study, I developed a corpus of films that had been coded for particular characteristics. Within that corpus, I selected some films for analysis and transcribed scenes that were relevant to my particular interests. For example, I wanted to count the number of times a particular character used a particular linguistic feature in the original and then how many times the same character used a corresponding feature in the dubbed version. Since the two versions showed similar general patterns but overall very different frequencies of the characteristics of interest, I also conducted a qualitative analysis of the dubbed version to show the relative importance of the characteristics when they occurred. Thus, even though the dubbed versions were not as frequent, they carried more narrative weight within the context of the dubbed film. Using multiple methods for exploring and analyzing language variation in the narrative provides a methodological balance to some of the challenges that this type of data can present. Further, triangulation of your evidence can allow you to explore multiple dimensions of the same media product using approaches designed to answer different types of questions.

Notes

1 VARBRUL is a statistical application that was developed by sociolinguists to perform logistic regression at a time when doing so on natural language data was difficult with existing software applications. In more recent work with variable language data, most researchers have been using more conventional statistical models, including especially mixed models, to quantitatively capture patterns in the data. The term *factor weight* is a specific artifact of VARBRUL and is not generally used or otherwise found in statistical descriptions. *Predictor variables* and *likelihood estimations* are terms associated with more conventional models designed to capture these same phenomena.

2 CA is increasingly used to understand conversations that are electronically mediated and thus, at least nominally, written. We'll discuss the distinction between writing and speaking more thoroughly in the next chapter.

References

Adams, M. 2004. *Slayer Slang: A Buffy the Vampire Slayer Lexicon*. New York: Oxford University Press.

Baker, Paul. 2010. *Sociolinguistics and Corpus Linguistics*. Edinburgh: Edinburgh University Press.

Bauman, Richard. 2011. The Remediation of Storytelling: Narrative Performance on Early Commercial Sound Recordings. In *Telling Stories: Language, Narrative and Social Life*, ed. D. Schiffrin, a. de Fina, and A. Nylund, 23–42. Washington, D.C.: Georgetown University Press.

Bednarek, M. 2011. Expressivity and Televisual Characterization. *Language and Literature* 20(1): 3–21.

Bell, A. 2011. Falling in Love Again and Again: Marlene Dietrich and the Iconization of Non-native English. *Journal of Sociolinguistics* 15(5): 627–656.

Bleichenbacher, Lukas. 2012. Linguicism in Hollywood Movies? Representations of, and Audience Reactions to, Multilingualism in Mainstream Movie Dialogues. *Multilingua* 32(2/3).

Bucholtz, M. and Q. Lopez. 2011. Performing Blackness, Forming Whiteness: Linguistic Minstrelsy in Hollywood Film. *Journal of Sociolinguistics* 15(5): 680–706.

Bucholtz, Mary. 2000. The Politics of Transcription. *Journal of Pragmatics* 32: 1439–1465.

Cameron, Deborah. 1995. *Verbal Hygiene*. London: Routledge.

Coates, Jennifer. 1993. *Women, Men and Language*. London: Longman.

Coates, Jennifer. 1996. *Women Talk: Conversation between Friends*. Cambridge, MA: Blackwell.

Fairclough, Norman. 1995. *Media Discourse*. London: Hodder Education.

Fishman, Pamela M. 1997. Interaction: The Work Women Do. In *Sociolinguistics: A Reader*, ed. N. Coupland and A. Jaworski, 416–429. New York: St. Martin's Press.

Gries, Stefan Th. 2013. *Statistics for Linguistics with R: A Practical Introduction.* Berlin: Walter de Gruyter.

Heyd, Theresa. 2010. How You Guys Doin'? Staged Orality and Emerging Plural Address in the Television Series *Friends. American Speech* 85(1): 33–66.

Johnson, Keith. 2011. *Quantitative Methods in Linguistics.* New York: John Wiley & Sons.

Mandala, Susan. 2008. Representing the Future: Chinese and Codeswitching in *Firefly.* In *Investigating Firefly and Serenity: Science Fiction on the Frontier,* ed. R. Wilcox and T. Cochran, 31–40. New York: I.B. Tauris.

Quaglio, P. 2009. *Television Dialogue: The Sitcom Friends vs. Natural Conversation.* Philadelphia: John Benjamins.

Queen, Robin. 2004. "Du hast jar keene Ahnung": African American English Dubbed into German. *Journal of Sociolinguistics* 8(4): 515–537.

Queen, R. 2012. The Days of our Lives: Language, Gender and Affluence on a Daytime Television Drama. *Gender and Language* 6(1): 151–178.

Rasinger, Sebastian M. 2013. *Quantitative Research in Linguistics: An Introduction.* New York: Bloomsbury.

Richardson, Kay. 2010. *Television Dramatic Dialogue: A Sociolinguistic Study.* New York: Oxford University Press.

Tagliamonte, S., and C. Roberts. 2005. So Weird; So Cool; So Innovative: The Use of Intensifiers in the Television Series Friends. *American Speech* 80(3): 280300.

ten Have, Paul. 1999. *Doing Conversational Analysis.* London: Sage.

Thornborrow, Joanna, and Deborah Morris. 2004. Gossip as Strategy: The Management of Talk about Others on Reality TV Show Big Brother. *Journal of Sociolinguistics* 8(2): 246–271.

Chapter 4

Dimensions of Variation

Introduction

Language can vary in a surprising array of ways. Although we sometimes think of language as fixed (and our grammar books and dictionaries suggest to us that this is so), language actually shifts around all the time, both in terms of the form it takes and the meanings it represents. For instance, imagine that you need to ask someone for help. There are many different variations on how you can ask for help, and the one you select will depend on the specifics of the situation, the nature of what you're asking for help with, whom you are asking, and a variety of other issues as well. These different dimensions of variability form part of your knowledge of any language you know. In this chapter, we'll delve into these different dimensions as a means of providing more analytic context for language variation in the audiovisual narrative media. In doing so, we'll see that language as crafted for the narrative mass media exhibits virtually all of the same dimensions of linguistic variation that occur in our everyday non-scripted, non-mediated lives.

For instance, let's look at a small snippet of text from Season 1, Episode 1, of the television show *Sherlock* (2010–). The setting is a press briefing following a series of what appear to be suicides. As the inspector explains the situation, a modern Sherlock Holmes texts first Inspector LeStrade and then all the reporters in the room.

Vox Popular: The Surprising Life of Language in the Media, First Edition. Robin Queen.
© 2015 John Wiley & Sons, Inc. Published 2015 by John Wiley & Sons, Inc.

Example 4.1   *Sherlock*, "A Study in Pink," Season 1, Episode 1, Steven Moffat and Mark Gatiss (creators), BBC, October 24, 2010

```
1  Deputy:        The incidents are now being treated as
                  linked, the investigation is ongoing
                  but Detective Inspector LeStrade will
                  take questions now
2  [Lots of talking]
3  Reporter 1:    Detective Inspector how can suicides
                  be linked?
4  LeStrade:      Well, they all took the same
                  poison, um, they were all found
                  in places they had no reason to be.
                  None of them had shown any prior
                  [indications
5  Reporter 1:    [But we can't have serial suicides
6  LeStrade:      Well, apparently you can.
7  Reporter 2:    These three people, there's nothing
                  that links them?
8  LeStrade:      There's no link found yet, but we're
                  lookin' for it, there has to be one.
9  [Text alerts go off. Text reads 'wrong']
```

Sherlock is a British crime drama that airs on BBC One, the flagship channel of the major public broadcaster in the United Kingdom. Thus, the characters speak British English, with some dialect variability. For instance, some of the reporters use the BBC pronunciation (the label used for British Standard English), while LeStrade's accent points to the eastern outskirts of London. In other words, some of the characters in this scene use what we might call a supraregional variety (the BBC pronunciation), while others use more locally specific varieties. One place where the localness of LeStrade's accent is apparent in the transcript is in line 8 where he says 'lookin' rather than 'looking.' While this feature in and of itself isn't specific to the eastern outskirts of London, it does generally *cluster* with features that are, just as it clusters with features that are specific to varieties in the United States and other places as well. If you recall the discussion of packages of linguistic features from Chapter 2, the term cluster is frequently used to capture the fact that linguistic features often occur together, meaning that our sense of a "language" or a "dialect" (the linguistic package) generally comes from our recognition that sets of linguistic features co-occur, or cluster.

The situation in the example is relatively formal, and LeStrade's role as the inspector explaining the case to reporters gives him license to speak more than the reporters; however, the reporters have license to challenge him. The context is relatively private, something made clear with the surprising text that everyone receives from someone ostensibly not in the room. As the scene will later reveal, Sherlock Holmes has unexpected access to this conversation and begins to participate in it via text message. The introduction of his texts poses a challenge for the show's creators because they have to introduce written forms of language into what is otherwise primarily spoken interaction, something they do in fairly creative fashion by adding text directly to the visual channel (see Figure 4.1).

This single scene illustrates a variety of dimensions relevant for language variation, including elements of linguistic form (accents, writing versus speaking, and so on) as well as elements of the general situation involved (formality, privacy, spontaneity, and such). When thinking about language variation, these dimensions can each provide various constraints and pressures that help explain why the variability shows up as it does.

In Chapter 2, we discussed several different considerations of form and function that are important for thinking through language and language variation. In this chapter, we look more closely at some of those considerations. As we'll see, some dimensions of variation are more linked to aspects of the linguistic form – for instance, whether something is more

Figure 4.1 Text messages being sent to journalists from Sherlock Holmes at a press conference he is not present for. *Sherlock*, "A Study in Pink," Season 1, Episode 1, Steven Moffat and Mark Gatiss (creators), BBC, October 24, 2010.

or less standard. Other dimensions of variation are more linked to some aspect of the context in which language occurs. Contextual features can include how spontaneous the interaction is, how much the interaction is subject to explicit or implicit norms, and how private the people involved assume the interaction to be.

Interestingly, the edges of various dimensions tend to line up with one another in terms of the occurrence of particular linguistic variants. If we take a single feature that we've discussed previously, nasal fronting in progressive verbs, we find that the fronted variant -in is relatively more frequent in spoken language, being used in more local, more unplanned, more informal, and more private situations, while -ing will be relatively more frequent in written language being used in more global, more planned, more formal, and more public contexts. While we can expect that both *can* occur in any situation of speaking, the relative probability of one or the other occurring will depend on the calibration of the various dimensions of the situation.

We can consider these various dimensions more as relative scales than as categorical distinctions, something that complicates our ability to create neat analyses based on clear taxonomies but that gives us a different kind of analytic flexibility. A *scalar* dimension means that the space between two points may include an uninterrupted series of steps, while a *categorical* dimension means that there is a clear boundary between one point and another. The points on scalar dimensions are much more granular and gradient, while categorical dimensions definitively distinguish one case from another. You can think of categorical distinctions as being black and white, while scalar distinctions include many shades of gray.

Considering dimensions of variation in scalar fashion allows us significantly more nuance and greater ability to model more directly the material experienced by the audience for any given media product. For instance, let's consider the television show *Modern Family*, where there is both dramatic action as well as talk directly to the camera (as in a documentary or reality program). This gives the illusion of rapid shifts in context and audience. The language similarly shifts, particularly the characters' styles. Likewise, if you think of yourself moving around the Internet, while also texting with your BFF, you know that you will vary your language as you do so, making different choices with respect to a wide range of issues including spelling, punctuation, choice of words, and so on. All of these choices are meaningful in that they construct the general social plane of interaction and interpretation.

Thinking about dimensions of variability in scalar, rather than categorical, terms has two major analytic benefits. First, scales allow the specification of edges, which provide the general parameters for the concept under consideration. At the same time, a scale captures the gradience that most accurately characterizes how people calibrate the social dimensions of interaction involving language and also how they may use language to situate an interaction within a conceptualized social space. We can exemplify these two benefits of scales by comparing hypothetical situations, such as an intimate dinner at home between two people and a surprise birthday party with 100 guests for one of those same people. What differences can you imagine in how language might be used in these two situations? Now, imagine that the person whose birthday it was is an important public figure whose speeches are regularly broadcast to millions via television. In comparison to that, the birthday party for 100 people would seem relatively private. The relative publicness of a given speech event is one of the dimensions relevant for thinking about language variation both generally and specifically within the case of the mass media. That dimension interacts with a host of other dimensions as well, as illustrated in Figure 4.2.

What we see in this figure are two broad dimensions along which we can think about linguistic variation. First, we can look to dimensions related to linguistic form, which will include dimensions such as how tied to language the form is; its general *modality* – for instance, whether it is spoken, written, or signed; how it clusters with other forms to create the sense of a linguistic package; and so on. Second, we can look at dimensions related broadly to the context in which language is used, which will include the formality of the situation, the public or private context, the relative planning

Non-linguistic/linguistic

Spoken/written

Non-standard/standard

Informal/formal

Unplanned/planned

Local/global

Private/public

Figure 4.2   Dimensions of variability.

involved prior to the speaking event, and other similar dimensions. The gradient area in the middle of the chart captures areas that are constituted by both form and context and thus constitute a fuzzier boundary.

Food for Thought

Take the previous paragraph and read it to yourself (or to a friend) in a way that you think of as very formal and then read it in a way that you think of as very informal. What differences do you notice? What could you do to the paragraph to make it more formal than it is now? What about less formal?

As we move through illustrations of these different dimensions, it's useful to keep in mind that within the context of the mass media, these scales are at work on two conceptual planes, one that is internal to the media product itself – the narrative world – and another that functions between the media product and its various audiences. For the purposes of this chapter, we are going to center our attention on the former; however, the latter should not be lost from view as we move through the discussion.

Non-Linguistic/Linguistic

The first dimension of variation we'll consider is seemingly the most obvious. This dimension involves distinguishing the linguistic from the non-linguistic. We communicate meaning in a variety of different ways, some of them tied to language specifically and some of them tied to more general processes. Facial expressions and physical gestures generally convey meaning outside of the system of language, though interestingly they can often support aspects of the language meaning. For instance, we may syncopate gestures with rhythmic aspects of speech. Additionally, some aspects of our vocal tone may be more linked to conveying emotion or affect than to specifically linguistic meaning. Thinking in terms of continua provides a means for not getting too caught up in trying to decide if some given feature is or isn't linguistic. We can think more in terms of relatively more or less linguistic. On this kind of scale, something like the character's costume will be on the far end of the non-linguistic, while the use of a passive sentence would be on the opposite end. In this book, we privilege the linguistic, but that doesn't mean that the linguistic is more or less important, and in fact most studies of the media have focused primarily on the non-linguistic side of things.

Researchers work to capture the relationship between the linguistic and the non-linguistic through a type of analysis called *multimodal* analysis (Kress 2010). Multimodal analyses examine the broad range of ways that meaning can be conveyed through different modalities, where modalities are understood as different channels of sensation (vision, aurality, touch, and so on). A hallmark of a multimodal analysis is being able to examine how different meanings that arise through different sensory experiences combine and interact to produce the broad or general meaning of the whole.

In Figure 4.3, a map of a high school found in the film *Mean Girls* (2004) nicely illustrates the layering and building of meaning through multiple resources that a multimodal analysis can facilitate. It also highlights the continuum between the linguistic and non-linguistic dimensions.

There is both linguistic and non-linguistic information embedded in this map of the social dynamics of the high school. This map is shown on screen and there is a voiceover explaining the different components of the map. Various elements of the map jump out as creating the meaning of the map, which functions overall to illustrate one student's conception of the social dynamics at the school. Each of the drawn elements includes a clear linguistic component as well. The football field and cafeteria are both labeled with words; the trees on the edge of the football field are described with linguistic elements ("Make-out scene – warning! There is sexual activity in these woods"). In turn those linguistic elements include aspects that are somewhat less linguistic in nature, such as the fonts and other

Figure 4.3 Map of North Shore High School. *Mean Girls*, Mark Waters (dir.), 2004, Paramount Pictures.

Figure 4.4   Detail of North Shore High School map. *Mean Girls*, Mark Waters (dir.), 2004, Paramount Pictures.

graphic elements like special underlining and location markers on the map, which we can see if we zoom in a little bit (Figure 4.4).

Here, there are squiggly lines under several of the words indicating perhaps word emphasis. The exclamation point after "warning" could be considered linguistic as it indicates a relationship between the term "warning" and the nature of the warning being issued. But it can also be interpreted as non-linguistic, indicating a general stance on the part of the map creator toward activities like making out in the woods next to one's high school. The differential use of capitalization and the font and script differences seem much more linked to the aesthetic qualities of the map and thus are more non-linguistic in nature.

Food for Thought

Examine the opening credits of some of your favorite films or TV series. How are linguistic and non-linguistic elements combined to create an overall effect in a film or television show?

As the *Mean Girls* map makes clear, language variation is virtually always embedded in other kinds of meaningful activity, providing additional nuance and creativity to the task of creating the media product. Although a multimodal analysis provides a more or less holistic approach to the understanding of media, for the remainder of this book, we focus almost exclusively on the more linguistic side of things. One of the aspects of interest with the map, for instance, is the voiceover narration that accompanies the visual image of the map.

Spoken/Written

The difference between written and spoken language provides one of the most transparent dimensions of variation in language. The *Mean Girls* map above includes aspects of this dimension because the voiceover combines with and describes the visual image of the map. The map itself doesn't contain any surprising features in the written representation, with the only slightly colloquial element being the lexical item "make out," though overall the tone of the map has a consistency with the voiceover, thereby lending a kind of consistency to the character, Janis, as a particular type of high school student. The image of the map on the screen and the voiceover in the audio channel capture the interrelationships between written and spoken forms of language by providing complementary information to the audience simultaneously.

People sometimes think of the written language as the more basic form of language and the spoken language as derivative of it. On this model, differences between the written and spoken forms of language may be evaluated as evidence of language problems, primarily in the spoken form. An example of this dynamic might be the difference between 'Wanna go?' and 'Do you want to go?' The first version, much more typical of spoken language than written language, may be evaluated as sloppy or lazy or just somehow not quite "right." On the other hand, you can no doubt think of cases where saying the second form might be evaluated as overly stiff or robotic.

Contrary to the way most highly literate people conceptualize language, most linguists think of the spoken language as the more basic form of language. As we discussed in Chapter 2, children acquire spoken language as they grow independently of whether they are formally taught. Written language, on the other hand, has to be formally taught, and you can be a perfectly good speaker without being able to write at all. It is difficult to imagine someone who writes but doesn't have (and never did have) any other means of linguistic expression.[1] There isn't really a clear-cut means for evaluating whether the spoken or written forms of language may be somehow "better"; however, we do know, based on the developmental evidence, that writing is more derivative of speaking than the reverse. Thus, it probably makes the most sense to think about them as related but separate channels of linguistic expression.

If we think of written and spoken language in this way, we can start to see how different constraints and pressures affect the nature of these two different forms, something that may be of special interest for those crafting audiovisual media products. One of the most basic distinctions between writing and speaking concerns modality. Speaking (or signing) is language that is processed through the ear/eye, whereas writing is processed only through the eye. Speaking is generally tied to an acoustic or gestural output, whereas writing is text-based output. Speaking has many more tools for conveying nuances of meaning, such as vocal tone, voice quality, speech rate and rhythm, and other similar effects. Writing, on the other hand, is more formal and often more permanent.

There's probably good reason to believe that these two modalities are cognitively processed in some ways that are quite different from one another as well as in some ways that are very similar, and in that sense it's not easy to make a categorical distinction between them. Table 4.1 highlights some of the differences between spoken and written language.

Table 4.1   Characteristics that differentiate spoken and written language

Spoken language...	*Written language...*
Universally found in human communities	Found in many but not all human communities
Acquired by children without formal instruction	Must be formally taught or studied
Highly variable across time and space	Highly standardized and slow to change across time and space
Used primarily in real-time, face-to-face interaction	Accessed primarily at a different time and in a different place than when it is produced
Has more limited distribution potential	Has wider distribution potential
Hard to preserve indefinitely	Designed to be preservable across time and space
More likely to be spontaneous	Less likely to be spontaneous
Significant information about message tone is encoded in the voice quality and body/facial configuration	Uses a variety of symbols (punctuation) and characters (emoticons, emoji, etc.) to try and convey message tone

Many of these distinctions become harder to make in the context of some forms of electronic communication, for instance, texting and other forms of messaging. In those forms, the need to consider variation on a relative scale becomes especially apparent.

Food for Thought

Look through the comment thread on an article from one of your favorite websites. What features do you notice that seem more spoken-like?

The context of the fictional audiovisual media (as well as many other media forms) similarly blurs the lines between speaking and writing, since so much of the writing is linked to a form that will ultimately be spoken. To see an illustration of this effect, we can compare the final scene as written in the script for the film *The Help* (2011) with the spoken words that occur in the final scene of the finished movie. *The Help*, based on a book of the same title, is set in 1962 in Jackson, Mississippi, and explores the relationships between African American domestic laborers and the European American families who employ them, primarily from the viewpoint of the European Americans. *The Help* is a useful film to examine precisely because it involves quite a range of interesting linguistic variation. In fact, the range of variation and the complex reception that the film received will motivate our returning to the film in several later chapters to discuss different layers and aspects of the place of language variation.

The Help is also useful because of the complex ways that language variation is represented across the different forms the narrative takes. The book and the screenplay, for instance, were written by people who do not appear to have much understanding of the grammatical characteristics of AAVE. In the case of the book, the language of the AAVE-speaking characters is rendered in ways that are fully ungrammatical in the linguistic sense for the variety being represented, particularly with regard to the verbal system of that variety. This is less the case in the screenplay; however, notably, the actors who animate the AAVE-speaking characters appear much more aware of the grammar of AAVE. They do not produce ungrammatical forms even as they do render much of their characters' speech in AAVE, even in cases where it is not written in the screenplay as such. The final scene involves only a voiceover from the main character, Aibeleen, who has just been fired from her job as a maid and nanny. Thus, its meanings come almost entirely from language.

Example 4.2a   Final scene of *The Help* (Tate Taylor [dir.], 2011, Dreamworks), script

```
Aibeleen:   Mae Mobely was my last baby. In just ten
            minutes, the only life I knew was done.
            God says we need to love our enemies. It
            hard to do. But it can start by telling
            the truth. No one had ever asked me what
            it felt like to be me. Once I told the
            truth about that I felt free. And I got to
            thinking about all the people I know and
            the things I seen and done….My boy,
            Treelore, always said we gonna have a
            writer in the family one day. I guess
            it's gonna be me.
```

Example 4.2b   Final scene of *The Help* (Tate Taylor [dir.], 2011, Dreamworks), finished film

```
Aibeleen:   Mae Mobley was my las' baby. In just
            ten minutes the only life I knew was
            done. [Mae Mobely screaming at the
            window] God says we need to love our
            enemies. It ha:' ta do. But it can sta:t
            by tellin the truth. No one had eve aks
            me what it felt like to be me. Once I told
            the truth about that, I felt free. And I
            got ta thankin about all the people
            I know and the things I seen and done.
            My boy Treelo' always sai? We gon: have
            a writer in the family one day. I guess
            i's gon: be me
```

It's important to note that only some of the most obvious pronunciation effects are included in the second transcript so that it remains reasonably easy to read. Even with just some of those effects noted, however, clear differences exist between the script, which is language written to be spoken, and the final outcome. For instance, in the words 'last,' 'hard,' and 'felt,' the final consonant is omitted in the spoken version due to the consonant clusters (more than one consonant in a row) at the end of the word. This is characteristic of the variety of English the character Aibeleen would have used (and is characteristic of most varieties of English: see Guy 1980). There is also variability in this feature in the spoken version. The word 'told' retains the final consonant. Throughout, the spoken version is non-rhotic (as we discussed in Chapter 2), though the written version has all the <r>s represented. There are several other differences notable between the spoken and written versions, including the character's pronunciation 'aks' rather than 'ask' and the omission of overt past-tense marking on that verb. This pronunciation is one of the most salient markers of AAVE, the variety of English that is used by the character. Interestingly, some other aspects of the grammatical variation characteristic of AAVE occur in both versions. The copula verb 'to be,' is absent in the sentence 'It hard to do'/'It ha:' to do' and the auxiliary verb 'have' is absent in the sentence '...the things I seen and done'.

Keeping the distinction between writing and speaking in mind while also remembering that most of the fictional audiovisual media start as language written with the intent to be spoken can help make sense of some of the aspects of variation that occur. This particular consideration further points to the issue of the relationship between standard and non-standard forms of language, since a script may be written using forms that are standard or non-standard and actors may voice the script similarly.

Non-Standard/Standard

One of the consequences of the common belief that the written form of the language is the more fundamental form involves what linguists typically refer to as *standardization*. A standard generally involves cases in which variability is being suppressed for some reason, most typically to provide a kind of uniformity. Once they gain a writing system, languages commonly undergo broader processes of standardization in which variability in spelling and punctuation in particular is minimized and in many cases erased entirely. Significant economic and social pressures often hasten the process of language standardization. Of some interest for our purposes here is the fact that once a language has been standardized, users of that language often come to think of the standard forms as inherently better than forms that are not standard. Once in place, beliefs about the superiority of the standard become widely circulated. Even though it's not always clear how we know what is "standard," those forms that are conventionally considered not to be standard can be used for particular kinds of effects, such as aspects of both plot development and characterization. Some of this use was apparent in those non-standard grammatical elements that appeared in both the scripted and the final spoken versions of the final scene of *The Help*. Much of the discussion in Chapter 2 centrally involved the distinction between forms American English speakers consider to be standard and those they don't.

Rosina Lippi-Green (2011) uses the term *Standard Language Ideology* (SLI) to highlight the importance of our beliefs about standard languages for the production and reception of language generally. Indeed most of the dimensions I am discussing in this chapter are tied in complex ways to the ideological distinction between "standard" and "non-standard." Such a presentation rests especially on how ideas about languages, including especially "standard" languages, circulate. While we'll discuss language ideologies in some depth in Chapter 5, it's useful here to think about how our generalized beliefs about what is or isn't standard affect language in contexts such as the fictional mass media. Lippi-Green defines the SLI as follows:

> A bias toward an abstracted, idealized, homogenous spoken language which is imposed and maintained by dominant bloc institutions and which names as its model the written language but which is drawn primarily from the spoken language of the upper middle class. (2011, 67)

The SLI is important for the media specifically because various media outlets are precisely the "dominant bloc institutions" referenced above. In other words, the media, including especially the fictional audiovisual media, are assumed by scholars to play an important role in creating and maintaining differential social evaluations of linguistic forms understood to be "standard" and those understood not to be. Lippi-Green goes on to describe standard and non-standard forms as they occur in children's animated films, demonstrating that the hero characters in such films virtually always speak a variety of English that corresponds roughly to a spoken American English standard. Characters who speak other varieties are much more likely to be villains or very minor characters. Lippi-Green argues that this particular pattern serves to socialize children into the SLI (2011, 71).

Food for Thought

Watch a couple of animated films or television shows. Do you notice anything about how different kinds of characters talk? Do you find the pattern of using the SLI for the heroes that Lippi-Green describes?

While this pattern is intriguing, it can also be useful to think more broadly in terms of relative standardness rather than as categorically standard and non-standard, and this is true for individual linguistic features as well as for larger units of language. As we saw above with Aibeleen in *The Help*, individual characters may well vary their pronunciation to achieve a variety of effects, something difficult to capture when characters are categorically labeled as "standard" or "non-standard" language users. An example of the usefulness of thinking relatively can be seen in the children's film, *Peter Pan* (1953).

Example 4.3   *Peter Pan*, Clyde Geronimi, and Wilfred Jackson (dir.), 1953, Walt Disney Productions

1	John:	I'm frightfully sorry old chaps, it's all my fault. <BBC accent>
2	Cubby:	Oh, that's alright Wild Cat!<American accents>
3	Lost boys:	We don't mind! That's okay!
4	Chief:	How.
5	Lost Boys:	Hi Chief!
6	Chief:	For many moons, Red Man fight pale-faced Lost Boys.
7	Lost Boys:	Ug ug!
8	Chief:	Sometime you win, sometime we win.
9	Cubby:	Okay, Chief, uh, you win dis time. Now turn [toin] us loose!
10	John:	Turn us loose? You mean this is only a game?
11	Slightly:	Sure, when we win we turn dem loose.
12	Raccoon 1:	When dey win, [dey turn us loose.
13	Raccoon 2:	[dey turn us loose!
14	Chief:	This time, no turn-em loose.
15	Slightly:	Haha, he's a great spoofer!
16	Chief:	Me no spoof-em. Where you hide Princess Tiger Lily?
17	Cubby:	Uh, Tiger Lily?
18	Slightly:	We ain't got your old Princess!
19	John:	I've certainly never seen her.
20	Twins:	Me neither! Honestly!
21	Chief:	Heap big lie. If Tiger Lily not back by sunset, burn-em at stake!

Figure 4.5 The Lost Boys, John Darling and Michael Darling, after being 'caught' by "Indians." *Peter Pan*, Clyde Geronimi and Wilfred Jackson (dir.), 1953, Walt Disney Productions.

Barbra Meek (2006) has done an extensive analysis of the linguistic representations in films that include Native Americans such as this one, focusing in particular on the ways that Native Americans are represented using what she calls "Hollywood Injun English." In Example 4.3, many of the features commonly found among fictional Native American characters are apparent, including the '-em' suffix (lines 14, 16, and 21), the absence of auxiliary verbs (lines 6, 16, and 21) and the use of 'How' as a greeting (line 4). Clearly, the Chief has significantly different linguistic production than the boys and in many ways shows aspects of being a non-native speaker of English (a characteristic also noted as frequent by Meek).

In addition to the relatively non-standard language output by the Chief, though, the boys also show variability, most notably between John and the Lost Boys. John speaks with the accent of the English upper class, though it differs from what we would generally find among actual speakers in the non-mediated world. The Lost Boys, on the other hand, speak with unequivocally American accents, and yet those accents are generally not the standard accent. For instance, in line 9, Cubby uses the vowel sound found in the word 'boy' in the word 'turn,' a variation found most typically in northeastern varieties of American English. Similarly, in lines 11 and 12 the use of a "d" sound instead of the more standard "th" in the words 'they' and 'them' occurs from two separate characters. Relative to the Chief, the boys are certainly more standard (or at least very differently non-standard), while relative to John, they are less standard. The effect, though, is that John appears much more formal than the Lost Boys (an effect enhanced by the fact that he is wearing a top hat). Similarly, even though the Chief is less standard in his linguistic production than any of the boys, he also seems much more formal than any of them, including John.

Informal/Formal

In the last few sections, we've primarily focused on what we might call dimensions of variation related to language form. Is the language in spoken or written form? Does it follow the expectations of the standard generally or not? How is language form embedded with other formal elements, such as the visual representations, other aspects of the soundtrack, and so on? Now, we'll look at dimensions of variation related in some broad sense to the context or situation in which language is being used. Example 4.3 from *Peter Pan* highlights contextual formality at the same time as it highlights the scale of standard and non-standard language form. For instance, in line 14, the Chief makes it clear that the situation is more formal than the Lost Boys are used to in their interactions with him, something captured in line 15 when Slightly calls him 'a spoofer.' In response in line 16, the Chief reiterates that this time is different from previous times when the activity was a game. This example nicely illustrates the formal/informal dimension of language variation as distinct from other dimensions such as relative standardness. Even though the Chief is being very formal, he continues to speak using relatively non-standard linguistic forms. Additionally, we see juxtaposition between John and all the other characters. John uses extremely standard speech, including a recognizable BBC accent. While the situation is generally a formal one, John as a character is relatively more formal than the Lost Boys.

The formality scale can be thought of in terms of the intimacy of the relationships involved. Generally, the better we know someone, the more informal we will be. Similarly, the more serious, important, or ritualized the situation is, the more formal we are likely to be. We interact differently with people we know well when we are in a formal situation, such as a business meeting, than in an informal situation, such as a game of racquetball. In the case of the *Peter Pan* example, the less intimate relationship between John and the other characters may help explain some of his speech while the relatively more intimate relationship between the Lost Boys and the Chief leaves the Chief having to do more work to shift the formality of the situation, since their interactions are often less formal.

Food for Thought

Construct both a formal and an informal e-mail message inviting someone you know to a birthday party. What are the features involved? How do the two messages compare to each other?

Language itself can play an important role in helping to define the relative formality of a situation. Formal linguistic styles typically include more standard grammar and lexical choice, including the general lack of what might be called "slang." Formal styles may also include more Latinate than Germanic lexical items (for instance, 'perspire' instead of 'sweat' or 'inquire' instead of 'ask') and will generally include more elements linked to formal writing, such as more complex syntactic structures and a lack of contracted forms.

Naming conventions provide fairly easy access to thinking about formality scales because it is often a shift in naming conventions that can signal (and hence create) changes to either the situation, the relationship between the participants, or both. We expect people who don't know us well and people whom we consider somehow subordinate to use some sort of title when they use our names. In the United States, for instance, children often use "Mr." and "Mrs." to refer to adults, even when the adults are close family friends. This usage is typically asymmetric in that adults virtually always refer to children using their first names. It is highly unusual for adults in the United States to have asymmetric naming practices, something that indicates a general ideology of equality. At the same time, it is not unheard of for such asymmetric naming practices to occur in highly formal business environments in which the people higher in the hierarchy are referred to with a title by those lower in the hierarchy but not vice versa.

An early scene from the film *Dodgeball* (2004) shows this kind of dynamic clearly. This scene represents the first encounter between Kate Veatch and Peter Lafour. Lafour is in danger of losing his business and Veatch has been secretly hired by one of his competitors to go investigate his books. Later in the film, as is expected in this type of comedy genre, the two become romantically involved. At this stage, however, the relative social distance between them as well as the formality of their encounter is being negotiated as Lafour tries to make the situation less formal and Veatch works to make it more formal.

Example 4.4   *Dodgeball*, Rawson Marshall Thurber (dir.), 2004, 20th Century Fox

```
1  Kate:    Fifty thousand dollars
2  Peter:   Personal check gonna be o.k.? Might have
            to wait to the end of the month? to go
            ahead and cash 'er because I do have
            to switch some funds unfortunately the
            charity I like ta work with is gonna take
            a hit
3  Kate:    Mr. Lafour I can assure you [puts clipboard
            in front of him] this is a very serious
            situation
4  Peter:   Yeah, no, I, gah, this is extremely serious
            Mrs. Uh Veach
5  Kate:    It's Ms. I'm gonna need to review all of
            your financial statements and assess any
            tax liabilities there may be
6  Peter:   Oh, absolutely. I dunno how you say Ms
            for Mr cause it's just mister but if
            there was Ms Mister, I'm a, I'm the, I'm
            a Ms as well
7  [She stares at him for 1 second]
8  Kate:    You do keep financial records don't you,
            invoices, revenue reports, taxable income
9  Peter:   You kidding me? I got a whole closet full
            yeah, call ['em keepers
10 Kate:                 [here?
```

Lafour and Veatch are generally at cross purposes in terms of the relative formality of the situation, something Veatch notes explicitly in line 3. Lines 4–6 are particularly insightful with respect to this question. In line 4, Lafour refers to Veatch as 'Mrs.' Veatch then corrects him, noting that she prefers 'Ms.' It is difficult to know whether Veatch is correcting Lafour's assumption about her marital status (e.g., "Mrs." is "incorrect") or is making a different kind of claim concerning professional credentials (e.g., "Mrs." is not as professional as "Ms."). Lafour largely interprets her correction in the latter sense in his comical discussion of how he would be the male equivalent of "Ms." if such a term existed.

While there are several likely explanations for his utterance, one of them is undoubtedly that he wants to indicate his understanding of how serious the situation is, even though he has to this point not indicated that understanding in how he has interacted with her. This scene provides a nice example of how people, or in this case characters, use language to simultaneously reflect and create interpersonal relationships as they are tied to specific interactions, a dynamic captured through scales of relative formality (and informality).

Unplanned/Planned

In addition to illustrating the dynamic between the written and the spoken and standard and non-standard language, the scenes discussed thus far illustrate an additional dimension linked to language variation. They also illustrate a relationship to overall planning. The planning dimension centers more on how much preparation is involved prior to the production of the language in question. It's probably most useful to think of planning as tied to particular demands of contexts. You are more likely to plan what you will say if you want to impress someone or be accepted as a member of some group. Lower-ranking people are more likely to plan their contributions than higher-ranking people (think of job interviews). Some situations require more planning of what you will say than others.

If you consider various components of your own language use, you know that when you are talking to your friends in a casual atmosphere, you don't do a lot of planning of what you are going to say. In contrast, if you must give a speech in front of a room full of people, you are likely to plan out more specifically what you are going to say. You may also practice what you have planned, adding yet another layer of planning to the overall production. When language use is more planned, it may also seem at once more formal and, typically, more standard – dimensions of variation we've just discussed. It may also have more of a written quality, though of course, language that has been written to be said aloud will differ in somewhat predictable ways from language that has been written to be read silently.

Food for Thought

Can you think of examples of seemingly unplanned language use that might have in fact been highly planned? (Social media is a good place for this kind of exploration; documentary-style productions in which a character speaks to the camera directly are another.)

Planning for language differs fairly significantly in the media as compared to everyday language use. We can't get away from the issue of scripting when considering language use in the media. Indeed, language variation often functions to make a media product appear less planned. In other words, scripts may be written specifically to make a scene seem more like everyday interaction, thereby creating the illusion of less formal planning. If you examine the third sentence from the script version of the final scene of *The Help* above, you'll see the line, 'It hard to do.' In this line, the copula verb (the verb 'to be') is absent. This is, of course, not the way that the line would typically be written, and only speakers of particular varieties of English will generally say it that way. As it happens, the character speaking that line is supposed to be a speaker of a relevant variety of English; thus, planning that element of her output helps make her, and the scene, both recognizable and believable for the audience.

On the other hand, sometimes unplanned things occur even in highly planned events, like scripted, fictional media. The technique known as *ad-libbing* provides a good example of this kind of slippage between planned and unplanned within the context of the scripted media. In fact, some of the most famous movie lines, such as "Here's lookin' at you, kid" from *Casablanca* (1942) and "I'll have what she's having" from *When Harry Met Sally* (1989) were ad-libbed (Martin 2011, 353). We can look at the dynamics of one such line, the famous "I'm walkin' here" line uttered by Dustin Hoffman's character, Ratso Rizzo, in the film *Midnight Cowboy* (1969).[2] As explained in a 2008 *Los Angeles Times* story about Dustin Hoffman (Abramowitz 2008):

> Like the famous scene in 1969's "Midnight Cowboy," when Hoffman as the creepy, crippled con man Ratso Rizzo walks down the street with his friend, the strapping Texas buck played by Jon Voight. The filmmakers had no permits to take over an entire New York City block, so director John Schlesinger had rigged up a hidden camera in a van and radio-miked the actors. It was finally going well after about 15 takes when a cab almost hit them as they crossed the street. "It went through a red light," and Hoffman, as Rizzo, screamed out with fearful fury: "I'm walking here!"
>
> "Now that is kind of a signature moment in that movie," he [Hoffman] says. "That was me reacting very angrily, partly out of fear because we almost got hit but also because he was ruining the take . . . I really wanted to say, 'We're shooting here! . . . And you are ruining it!' Luckily, he was able to react honestly and still keep in character. "And when that happens . . . it's the gift of movies."[3]

In this case, the iconic scene from the film involves both a planned component (much of the script remains intact), and, assuming that Hoffman's account is accurate, an unplanned component as the taxi comes close to hitting the actors and Hoffman (reacting as both Hoffman and Rizzo) responds.

Example 4.5   *Midnight Cowboy*, John Schlesinger (dir.), 1969, MGM

Joe Buck and Ratso Rizzo are walking down the street talking about the paid escort business that Joe wishes to enter.

1 Rizzo: Look, with these gals that wanna buy it, most of 'em are old and dignified. Social register types, you know what I mean? They can't be trottin' down to Times Square to pick out the merchandise. They gotta have some kind of a middleman. And that's where O'Daniel comes in, you know what I mean?

2 [Joe and Rizzo step off curb, Rizzo links arms with Joe]

3 [Cab screeches and honks, Rizzo turns to look as cab moves into screen]

4 Rizzo: <register shift, deeper pitch, more vernacular>Hey [slams hood open palm, cab honking] What the. I'm walkin' here. [bangs hood again while cab honks] I'm walkin' here.

5 Cabbie: Get outta the way

```
6  Rizzo:    Up yours you son of a bitch. You don't talk
             to me that way. Get outta here.
7  [Cab continues to honk, Rizzo does a crude gesture.
   Joe and Rizzo continue walking].
8  Rizzo:    <register shift, higher pitch, more
             nasal>Don't worry about that. Actually
             that ain't a bad way to pick up insurance,
             you know
```

What is particularly notable in the scene is the radical shift in speech style between the conversation prior to and following the interaction with the cab and during the interaction itself. During the conversation, as in the film as a whole, Rizzo's character speaks in a fairly high-pitched, nasal, somewhat feminine manner. However, his pitch drops noticeably, his speech rate slows, and he generally uses a more authoritative-sounding tone in the interaction with the cab driver, a tone that is supported by his hitting the hood of the cab and using a cursing gesture as the cab drives off. In the context of the film, this scene adds depth and nuance to Rizzo's character as the audience comes to understand that he is not as weak and conniving as he appears. The fact that this component was apparently unplanned added, as Hoffman himself suggests in the interview, an element of serendipity to the process of creating this film. It also highlights why this dimension of language variation can be useful to keep in mind when considering the various pressures that influence language variation generally and language variation in the mass media more specifically.

Local/Global

The next dimension that we'll consider is linked to context of use and has to do with the relatively local or global context of language use. The narrative media of course are quintessentially global; however, most stories are set in a place and time, and often that place and time are critical components of the story itself. In those cases, we can argue that there is a local component – in this case, local to a particular media product. In other cases, though, local can have a meaning tied more to a specific place, such as a geographic region or space. Barbara Johnstone (2004), for instance, has written extensively about how various media outlets, including especially the Internet, help create and reproduce a sense that there is a "Pittsburgh dialect" called *Pittsburghese*.

The more a message or a context extrapolates away from the particulars of a situation or a place, the more the context may be understood as global. Comparing Pittsburghese to English can help illustrate this difference. English is often called a "global" language, which can mean several different things, though in most cases it has to do with the number of people who know English as either a first or a subsequent language. At the same time, of course, there are many local varieties of English, such as Pittsburghese.

Food for Thought

What argues for thinking about American English as a local variety and what argues for thinking about it as a global variety? Do you consider it more local or more global? Why?

The directors Joel and Ethan Cohen are generally well known for producing films that are set in local places and that come along with local accents. The most famous of these is perhaps *Fargo* (1996), but other films, such as *No Country for Old Men* (2007), *Miller's Crossing* (1990), and *Raising Arizona* (1987), also make significant use of local accents. As one reviewer writes:

> Each of the movies you've seen by them employs hilariously intricate dialect. They're almost love letters to the words of the people: respectfully precise, provincially astute, and knowingly clever. There's a fine line between funny and making fun, and the Cohen brothers toe it expertly. (Matheson 2007)

The Cohen brothers don't just use local accents to be true to a specific place. They also use them to juxtapose characters from different places against one another and against more generalized accents. In *Fargo*, for instance, the midwestern accent of Marge and her husband is juxtaposed with the New York accents of the kidnapers, Carl and Gaear. Similarly in *Miller's Crossing*, Irish and Italian varieties of New York English help sustain the central tension between competing crime syndicates.

The Cohen brothers' films provide an excellent source for thinking specifically about how language variation can be artfully incorporated into representations of locality. At the other end of the spectrum, we can also look at the ways in which the global context of English can play a role. For instance, Lukas Bleichenbacher (2008, 2012) has demonstrated that mainstream American film products represent characters/situations using English even though a language other than English would be expected (because they are set outside of an English-speaking place, for instance). He notes that when non-English languages appear in films (with or without subtitles), they typically function to set up local situations of "narrow communication" (2008, 141). Thus, minor characters are much more likely than major characters to use a non-English language. Further, characters with negative motives are also more likely to speak a non-English language than are characters with positive motives (2012, 159).

Bleichenbacher refers to these kinds of practices as *linguicism* and discusses the particular role they play in reflecting and sustaining the belief in the global reach of English. He provides an analysis of the scene in Example 4.6 as one illustration of linguicism.

Example 4.6   *Just Married*, Shawn Levy (dir.), 2003, 20th Century Fox (cited in Bleichenbacher 2012, 169)

```
1   Henri:  My grandparents installed the wiring in
            the hotel before World War First. It
            worked fine until you young kids had to
            bring out your toys and ignore the sign.
2   [A small monolingual sign on the wall is shown
    in close-up DEFENSE D'UTILISER DES APPAREILS
    ELECTRIQUES (Do not use electric equipment)]
3   Tom:    The % that is the the% that's in French
            for Christ's sakes.
4   Henri:  That's because we're in France.
5   Sarah:  Is there anything we could do?
6   Henri:  Pay the damages.
7   Tom:    <chuckles>Hold on there Jacques.
8   Henri:  <slowly and clearly>Je m'appelle Henri
            Margeaux.
9   Tom:    Whatever. Look, this hotel gets guests
            from all over the world. It's your
            responsibility to put some American on your
            signs.
10  Sarah:  He means English.
11  Tom:    Sarah, <whispers>I'm trying to negotiate.
```

As Bleichenbacher writes,

On a macro level, the scene reflects and comically exploits the long-standing conflict (reheated at the moment of production due to disagreements over Iraq) between the USA as a de facto global power, and France as a country with dwindling global influence. Then, the scene is interesting from a socio-linguistic view in that the dialogue explicitly refers to the status of English and French as world languages in a concrete context, the linguistic landscape in a tourist environment. On the one hand, the fact that an important security message is presented in monolingual French can be interpreted as a comment on the rather strict and purist language policies against the use of other languages (particularly English) in public space (and elsewhere) that the French state is known for. On the other hand, the French mono-lingual ideology, vigorously defended by Henri, the eminently inhospita-ble hotel owner, is contrasted with its American counterpart, when Tom calls his language "American" and implies that the use of the national language on the sign is absurd, even though his wife actually knows French. (2012, 170)

In addition to Bleichenbacher's observations about the scene, we can consider this scene as an excellent illustration of the local/global dimension of language variation. Henri's shift to French in line 8 in particular pro-vides a kind of pivot point around the local/global as he simultaneously uses the shift to critique Tom's behavior and to challenge the global dom-inance of English. For his part, Tom does something similar, though in reverse, in his reference to English as "American." Here, Tom critiques the local provincialism he perceives in Henri while asserting that a local variety of English is synonymous with English itself.

Private/Public

The final dimension of variation we'll cover deals broadly with the general breadth of the audience for a given message. Messages that are intended for only a few people, maybe even only one person, are more private than are messages intended for many people. The commercial media, which are the primary focus of this book, are clearly on the public end of the private–public continuum. At the same time, the representations within media products are often of interactions that are more on the private end of the continuum. For instance, one of the hallmarks of mockumentary-style audiovisual media is speaking directly to the camera as if in private conversation with the audi-ence. The language used by the various characters on *Modern Family* (2009–), for instance, varies considerably, not just in terms of content but also in terms of how they are speaking, when they are speaking to the camera as compared to when they are interacting with one another.

There is no linguistic element that is specific to this dimension, just as is true of the other dimensions. You can have very formal private conversations, such as a job interview, and very public informal interactions, such as during a music concert. Nonetheless, some linguistic elements become more or less common as you move along the private–public continuum. The use of taboo language, for instance, is more common in more private contexts than in more public ones. Similarly, language that is written to be spoken is more likely to occur in more public contexts. You'll generally pay more attention to what you're doing the broader your audience is. With very private language you typically worry less about interpretation from others. But the more you expect an audience of some kind, the more attention you are likely to pay to your speech.

Food for Thought

What differences do you notice when you are speaking relatively privately versus relatively publicly? In what contexts might you use very informal language in a public setting? What about very formal language in a private setting?

In Example 4.7, there are two simultaneous conversations going on that have different degrees of privacy linked to them. The film *No Strings Attached* (2011) is a romantic comedy involving two people who start a sexual relationship with the assumption that there will be no emotional involvement. Example 4.7 starts after their first hookup but before they have decided to have a strictly sexual relationship (which eventually fails, as the genre predicts that it must):

Example 4.7   *No Strings Attached*, Ivan Reitman (dir.), 2011, Paramount Pictures

```
1  [Walking down the sidewalk to a bar]
2  Eli:      You know, you shouldn't a gotten her a
             balloon actually. Who do you think you
             are, the old guy from Up?=
3  Adam:     =You told me to get her a balloon.
4  Eli:      Well, I didn't think you'd actually do
             it. It's a terrible idea
5  [Sitting down at table in bar]
6  Adam:     Listen, hey nobody knows about this so
             don't say anything to anyone. O.k?
```

```
 7  Eli:       Alright, I won't
 8  [Text ding]
 9  Adam:      It's from Emma=
10  Eli:                  =What's it say?
11  Adam:      Where are you?
12  Eli:       Ahhh. Whaddare you writing?
13  Adam:      Hi how are you doing [while typing] and
                then a winky face
14  Eli:       No, Adam, it's after 10pm. Come on.
                The where are you text is like sayin'
                hey, I wanna have sex with you. I just
                need to know how drunk ya are
15  Wallace:   Hey. Did you fuck Emma and then bring 'er
                a balloon?
16  Adam:      What? Did you [tell
17  Eli:                     [no. Yes.
18  Adam:      you can't tell any one.
19  Eli:       She just texted 'im where are you
20  Wallace:   Oh, she wants the dick.
21  Eli:       Now Adam you gotta come back strong here.
                You know, go from a position of power.
                Somethin' like where am I? Why don't you
                check your [underpants?
22  Wallace:              [Yeah=
23  Eli:                    =Yeah=
24  Wallace:                    =Don't write that
25  Adam:      I would never write that.
26  Wallace:   See, I like to be kinda scary. Like
                Boo! Here comes my dick.
```

```
27  Joy:      Did you have sex with some girl and give
              her a balloon.
28  Adam:     Can we not tell everyone<growly voice>
29  Eli:      Apologize
30  Wallace:  So what'd you write back?
31  Adam:       Hi
32  [..]
32  Eli:      Yeah, that [works
34  Wallace:             [Yeah that's not bad. That's
              fine
35  [Text ding. Screenshot of text "Your place in 30?"]
```

This conversation shows one of the modern conventions of negotiating personal relationships electronically while in the company of friends, who the text interlocutor may or may not know are present (see Gershon 2010). In the text conversation (lines 11, 13, 31, and 35), Adam and Emma engage with one another in a somewhat perfunctory way, this being the first conversation they've had after their first, unexpected, sexual encounter. In this sense, the conversation is relatively private. At the same time, it lacks a certain kind of social intimacy. Even though they have had sex, it's clear they don't know each other very well and the lack of much conversation between them highlights that fact. Most of the conversation between Adam and his friends involves how to interpret Emma's text from line 11 and how to best respond. Adam's male friends in particular provide sexualized potential responses intended, presumably, to highlight Adam's sexual prowess (lines 21 and 26). Their lexical choices include conventional taboo terms and colloquial terms for body parts, something much more common in relatively private than relatively public conversations.

Both conversations are relatively private conversations and the face-to-face conversation is also focused on general issues of privacy since part of what they are discussing is Eli having told other friends about Adam's actions even though he agreed not to. The two conversations are private in different ways, and one more so than the other. The general situation constrains the type of language that the characters are likely to use. As a mass-produced, widely released film, we see language that is likely more polished and definitely more rehearsed than what we would likely find in a non-media conversation; however, the internal situation being represented is much more private, and the language choices simultaneously reflect that and also remind the audience of its private nature. Adam's rejection of his friends' text suggestions and his relatively minimal output with Emma create for the audience a private interaction between people who don't know one another very well, while the playful ribbing and teasing among the different friends construct another kind of private encounter, but this time among people who know each other reasonable well already. The fact that there are no serious consequences for Eli having told so many people about something he was told in confidence and asked not to repeat further constructs aspects of the relationship among the friends for the audience.

Putting It All Together

While the *No Strings Attached* example above nicely demonstrates the private–public dimension of language variation, it also serves as an excellent illustration of all the dimensions at work simultaneously. For instance, in line 13, Adam makes reference to the "winky face," a *non-linguistic* element of electronically mediated communication that typically indicates prosodic or tonal qualities of the utterance. The interaction involves both *spoken* and *written* language, including spoken representations of potentially written forms (lines 21 and 26). While the interaction is roughly recognizable as involving the *standard* form of American English, there are also elements that we wouldn't expect in some other kinds of contexts, including taboo words, particular kinds of contractions, -in, and a few other somewhat less than standard forms. The general setting of the film (and this conversation) is not particularly specific to a location, and thus the language used has a more *global* character than we would expect in a film in which the place was a central component of the narrative. The conversation between the set of friends is less *formal* than the conversation occurring between Adam and Emma even while that conversation is more *private* than the one happening among the friends. Finally, the entire conversation among the friends is about *planning* what Adam should say to Emma and formulating turns that would facilitate both his masculinity and his further sexual involvement with Emma.

What becomes immediately clear when doing an analysis of the language variation in a fictional media scene like this is that each dimension provides a slightly different heuristic for thinking about language variation. The choice to focus on one or another dimension will be largely dependent on what the researcher is working to address in the context of a particular analysis. The different dimensions are at work more or less simultaneously in any interaction; however, one or another may be particularly attenuated in a specific case, including in a fictional scene. Further, while it may not be possible to pinpoint exactly where on a given dimension the language variation in an interaction should fall, some generalizations are possible based on the edges of each continuum. If we convert Figure 4.2 into a set of scales, it looks as follows:

Casual	Dressed up
Spoken	Written
Unplanned	Planned
Non-standard	Standard
Informal	Formal
Private	Public
Local	Global

I've removed the linguistic/non-linguistic dimension from this outline in order to focus on linguistic elements alone. What you can see is that the edges of the various dimensions tend to cluster together. I've called these two clusters "dressed up" and "casual" to illustrate their connections to relative stylistic orientations (something we'll explore in much more depth in Chapter 8). The overlap between the different dimensions allows for certain kinds of predictions; thus, we can expect a language event that falls at the far right edge of all the continua, such as perhaps this very book, to have a predictable set of characteristics, ones we might well describe as your "Sunday best." For the left edge, we might think of a face-to-face interaction between close friends over dinner. In that case, the language used will be much more casual, more like "weekend lounge-wear." The fashion metaphors are, of course, not perfect; however, they hint at some of the complexity involved in exploring the different factors that might be relevant for language variation.

These clusters also allow us to formulate predictions that involve differences along the individual scales as well. To continue the fashion metaphor, this type of variation would capture cases in which someone might be wearing a dress shirt, athletic socks, and underwear, as occurs in a classic scene from *Risky Business* (1983), in which the main character dances and sings while home alone (Figure 4.6).

In other words, just because there is a tendency for the edges of the scales to cluster together doesn't mean that the scales are dependent on each other or that they will always align with one another. The specific benefit of thinking about these dimensions as scalar rather than categorical is that it allows each to be considered in relation to the others and allows us to capture cases in which a character or scene may mix and match elements of the scales to create complex situational dynamics that may be

Figure 4.6   Joel Goodsen dances in a dress shirt, underwear, and tube socks. *Risky Business*, Paul Brickman (dir.), 1983, Geffen Company.

formal and non-standard or standard and unplanned at the same time. The scalar relations in this model provide for an infinite number of possible combinations that language variation can take.

For instance, if you take a situation like an early romantic encounter, let's say a first date out to dinner, you can use the relative scales to predict what kind of language you'd expect the two (or more, depending on the nature of the date) people involved to use.

Casual		Dressed up
Spoken	♦	Written
Unplanned	♦	Planned
Non-standard	♦	Standard
Informal	♦	Formal
Private	♦	Public
Local	♦	Global

In this instance, we'd expect something close to what we in fact find in the early interactions between Adam and Emma in *No Strings Attached*, including in the interaction discussed above. The narrative media turn out to be a reasonably good source for representing these various dimensions in part because of the heavy planning that is involved in creating the representation.

Food for Thought

Consider a few other situations that vary along these different dimensions and make some predictions about what you believe you might find in terms of the language use. Can you find examples in the media (or elsewhere) that might allow you to test your predictions?

Thinking about the different dimensions and the interactions between them leads us to one of the fundamental issues tied to language variation more generally, namely, the relationship of language variation to meaning. Developing an understanding of the important role that language variation plays for constituting meaning provides a central motivation for considering these various dimensions that are tied to variation more generally. It's within the context of constructing meaning that the creative power of these dimensions rests.

Notes

1 People who are deaf may well write in a standardized language, such as English; however, they also generally have access to a signed language, which is their native language and often the language they learned prior to learning the written conventions of a language like English.
2 *Midnight Cowboy* won an Academy Award in 1969 and was the only X-rated film to ever win an Academy Award. The rating was later changed to R when X ratings became primarily associated with films that were especially sexually explicit.
3 There is some question whether Hoffman's account is accurate in terms of the scripting of this scene. In the extras that accompany the DVD release of *Midnight Cowboy*, Jerome Hellman, the producer, disputes Hoffman's account (*Encyclopedia of American Cinema*, smartphone edition). The significant shift in tone, otherwise not found in this character in the film, offers some support for Hoffman's account.

References

Abramowitz, Rachel. 2008. *Soaking up Success.* Retrieved July 10, 2013 from http://articles.latimes.com/2008/dec/24/entertainment/et-hoffman24.
Bleichenbacher, Lukas. 2008. *Multilingualism in the Movies: Hollywood Characters and Their Language Choices.* Tübingen: Francke.

Bleichenbacher, Lukas. 2012. Linguicism in Hollywood Movies? Representations of, and Audience Reactions to Multilingualism in Mainstream Movie Dialogues. *Multilingua* 32(2/3).

Gershon, Ilana. 2010. Breaking Up Is Hard to Do: Media Switching and Media Ideologies. *Journal of Linguistic Anthropology* 20(2): 389–405.

Guy, Gregory R. 1980. Variation in the Group and the Individual: The Case of Final Stop Deletion. In *Locating Language in Time and Space*, ed. W. Labov, 1–36. New York: Academic Press.

Johnstone, Barbara. 2004. "Pittsburghese" Online: Vernacular Norming in Conversation. *American Speech* 79(2): 115–145.

Kress, Gunther. 2010. *Multimodality: A Social Semiotic Approach to Contemporary Communication*. New York: Routledge.

Lippi-Green, Rosina. 2011. *English with an Accent*. New York: Routledge.

Martin, Ray. 2011. *Ray Martin's Favourites*. New York: Victory Books.

Matheson, Jessie. 2007. Dialect with Joel Chandler Harris and the Coen Brothers. Retrieved August 20, 2013, from http://www.wrensnest.org/dialect-with-joel-chandler-harris-and-the-coen-brothers/.

Meek, Barbra A. 2006. And the Injun Goes "How!": Representations of American Indian English in White Public Space. *Language in Society* 35: 93–128.

Chapter 5

Making Language Variation Meaningful

Introduction

In the previous chapters, we looked at examples of how language can vary and the dimensions along which it varies as a means of establishing that variation is both an expected part of any language and fully systematic. We also linked variation broadly to social meaning and social types; however, the process through which language variation becomes socially meaningful has been left relatively vague. Understanding how variation becomes socially meaningful, though, is the critical glue connecting language variation to the work that it actually does in the context of narrative mass media, something we'll explore in depth in Chapters 6 through 8. It's one thing to notice that we can find many examples of language variation in the mass media or even to notice exactly where the media use the variation, but it's something else entirely to think about what language variation means and, even more specifically, how it comes to have those meanings. In this chapter, we'll examine how the raw material of variation becomes socially meaningful in ways that go beyond the basic content and dictionary meanings of the words.

As an example, compare these two transcripts from the movie *Happy Feet* (George Miller [dir.], 2006, Warner Bros.).

Vox Popular: The Surprising Life of Language in the Media, First Edition. Robin Queen.
© 2015 John Wiley & Sons, Inc. Published 2015 by John Wiley & Sons, Inc.

Example 5.1a

1	Boss Skua:	Quiet. Little buddy, there is something out there. Creatures. Not like us. Big. Fiercer. Smarter, too. Ask me how I know.
2	Mumble:	How?
3	Boss Skua:	Because I've been captured by them, that's how.

Example 5.1b

1	Boss Skua:	Quiet. Little buddy, there is somethin' out dere. Creatures. Not like us. Big. Fierca. Smarta, too. Aks me how I know.
2	Mumble:	How?
3	Boss Skua:	Cause I been captured by 'em, that's how.

What differences do you notice in the lines by Boss Skua across the two transcripts? The dictionary meanings of the words are of course the same between the two transcripts, but the one with the non-standard features provides more data about Boss Skua in particular. And the overall feel of the character – what we might call the *social meaning* – changes. In fact, it becomes pretty similar to the social meaning set up by the first line of synchronized dialogue that occurred in the first commercially released film to combine sound and image, *The Jazz Singer* (1927), when Al Jolson says, "Wait a minute, wait a minute, you ain't heard nothin' yet." Of course, it's different, too, in ways linked to the specific context of each film and the different characters involved.

When people encounter variation in the real world, they do a version of the same thing that they do when they confront it in the mediated world. They give it a kind of meaning that goes beyond the specific content of the words. In this chapter, we'll explore more or less how that happens and some of the ways that we can model and understand it happening.

Meaning

In the broadest terms, meaning is a relationship between a way of referring to something and the thing itself. So, for instance, if you see an animal that purrs, you make a connection between that and the conventional English label for it, "cat." In this case, the particular string of sounds /k/, /ae/, and /t/ come together to be the way we refer to that animal in English. The only way that you can know about this relationship is if you learn it. You can't deduce it from anything about the sounds or about the concept/thing that they are connected to. For this kind of meaning relationship, you can only know it by virtue of convention.

Convention captures the idea of a shared process or concept, pattern of use, or custom. If you do something by convention, it means that there is a kind of unspoken agreement of sorts among the people in a group about how something will be done, what it means, or what kind of behavior is expected. Importantly, conventional behaviors cannot be deduced by characteristics of the behaviors themselves. It's conventional in the United States, for instance, to drive on the right side of the road, whereas it's conventional in the United Kingdom to drive on the left. There's no way to know which side of the road to drive on in terms of the laws of physics or biology or other things we know how to do just because we are human beings (like, say, walking). The only source of knowledge about which side of the road to drive on is seeing people do it over and over, and also seeing what happens when someone who is expected to do it doesn't (in the case of driving, of course, that can have dire consequences). The majority of linguistic (and other) meaning is conventional in the same way. Words mean what they do because people in some sense come to agree more or less on their meaning. In fact, we even come to agree on meanings that are novel or uncommon (for instance, using the term "cat" to refer to a person as in "That cat is a fine musician").

One of the earliest modern thinkers about language, Ferdinand de Saussure, called this particular kind of meaningful relationship *the linguistic sign* (Saussure 1959). The sign is the connection between something that denotes something else (what Saussure called the *signifier*) and the something else (what Saussure called the *signified*). As children learn a language, part of what they learn is what those relationships are. One of the important aspects of many linguistic signs, particularly in their most basic instantiations, is that the relationship between the signifier and the signified is arbitrary and conventional. In other words, you can't predict what set of sounds (or, in the case of signed languages, gestures) will be used to capture a specific object or concept out in the world. This is true for terms that denote actual objects or actions as well as for terms that are what we might call operators, the various parts of language that themselves signify spatial, temporal, or logical relations (e.g., 'up,' 'the,' 'then,' 'not,' and so on). The particular set of sounds used for these is just as arbitrary and conventional (and thus has to be learned) as the set of sounds used for material objects in the world, like 'cats,' 'pencils,' and 'rivers.' In being arbitrary and conventional, the only way to learn the connection between the set of sounds and what they denote is essentially to memorize it.

As we memorize more and more of these signs, of course, they start to get organized in certain ways. We link them together by the part of speech they are ("nouns," "prepositions," "verbs") or by the set of things they may be related to either conceptually (other signifieds, so that 'cat' may be linked to 'tiger,' 'kitten,' 'purr,' 'lolcat') or acoustically (other signifiers so that 'cat' might be related to 'cap,' 'cab,' 'can,' 'cad,' and the like as signifiers that are monosyllabic and start with /k/ and /ae/). We might also link them together based on our ideas about what kinds of people generally say them (most English speakers will say 'cat' for the animal, but only a subset are likely to say 'cat' to refer to a person as in, "That cat is a fine musician"). Or we might link them to the kinds of situations in which they are typically said. (It might be surprising to talk about a "cat" in the context of a job interview, unless, of course, the job was pet-oriented or the interviewer had pictures of his cat on the desk.) Leaving aside the cognitive and interactional models that need to be in place for linguistic meaning to happen at all, at its most basic, meaning emerges as representations (e.g., words) are connected to items being represented (these can be objects, actions, thoughts, and so on). This relationship is also known as *reference*. Referential meaning is similar to what many people call the dictionary meaning.

There are other relations of meaning, though, beyond the strictly representational. In the theory of meaning developed by Charles Sanders Peirce (1958), there are three basic types of meaningful (or sign) relations: symbols, icons, and indexes. A *symbol* is what most linguistic signs are. These are relationships of meaning that are arbitrary and conventional. To learn them, you just have to memorize them (though the more of them you know, the more tricks you'll have for memorizing them since you can rely on the ways in which you've organized previously learned signs). An *icon*, by contrast is not (as) arbitrary or (as) conventional. Instead, an icon more directly represents (signifies) the thing it denotes. In this sense, you can often figure out what it means based on properties of the signifier. So, for instance, the image in Figure 5.1 of the game *Plants vs. Zombies* iconically represents the game itself by using the characters from the game.

In fact, this representation is iconic in another way, too, since the characters are also iconic of particular items in the (imagined) world of the game. They are meant to iconically represent zombies and sunflowers and other recognizable items. If you know the item, you can tell what the icon means. Thus, the image represents the game *Plants vs. Zombies* as well as plants and zombies.

Figure 5.1   *Plants vs. Zombies* start menu. PopCap Games (2009).

Some regular linguistic signs are iconic. The best-known class of iconic linguistic signs is onomatopoeia, words like "boom" or "eek." At some level, you can figure out what they mean just by hearing them. Of course, this isn't entirely true as there is some degree of conventionality to these as well, but in general the meaning of onomatopoeia is that the word (sign) sounds like what it references. Another class of linguistic signs that works this way is the names for animal sounds. These kinds of words are meant to directly represent the sound the animal makes and in that sense they are iconic. But, of course, they aren't entirely iconic since different languages use slightly different labels for the same animal sound. A rooster says 'cock-a-doodle-do' in English but 'kikiriki' in German.

Symbolic and iconic meanings are two basic kinds of meaning relationship. One of them is mostly arbitrary and conventional and the other isn't. The final type of meaningful relationship within Peirce's system is what is called an index. An *index* is a sign in which the meaning changes depending on the context of use. Like a symbol, an index is a relation of meaning that may be conventional. Unlike a symbol, the relationship is not entirely arbitrary but rather linked to the context in which the index occurs. For instance, a classic index is captured in the relationship between smoke and fire, since the appearance of smoke generally points to (or indexes) a fire. A classic example of a linguistic index is a pronoun. Any use of the pronoun 'I,' for instance, "means" the person speaking. If Robin says "I," it "means" Robin, but if Susan says "I," it means Susan. Overall, of course, it broadly means "the person speaking." When we start to talk about *indexical meaning*, the relationships can get infinitely more complicated than that broad definition. We'll explore that complexity below. For now, the important point is that the index gets its meaning from the context in which it is used and, critically, has different meanings in different contexts.

Indexical Meaning

As it turns out, indexical meaning occurs with more than just lexical items (words). Any part of the grammar, including whole languages, can carry indexical meaning, which means that the occurrence of that part can point to issues in the context. Further, indexes work at different levels of meaning. Some indexes, for instance, are direct in that something external to the linguistic content is embedded directly in the referential meaning. Kinship terms often work this way, as do gendered terms of reference (the pronouns 'he' and 'she' referentially encode the sex/gender of the pronominal antecedent). This more direct indexical encoding into the referential (or symbolic) components of a linguistic sign is not as common as a second type of indexical meaning, what we might think of as *indirect indexicality*.

   Most of the ways of using language that get linked to particular kinds of people are linked to them non-referentially in terms of conventional expectations of patterns of use. This kind of indexical meaning might broadly be captured as "different ways of saying the same thing." So, for example, you might think that the two transcriptions of *Happy Feet* above are basically saying the same thing, and, from a strictly referential standpoint, that might be right. And yet we know that we get a different kind of information about Boss Skua in the second transcription relative to the first. The information there might include something about street smarts versus book smarts, masculinity and toughness, regional dialect, or socioeconomic class.

Food for Thought

Children's animated films are an excellent source of indexical information. Can you think of other examples of the kind of indexicality we see in the *Happy Feet* transcript? Think about what linguistic elements seem to go with what kinds of characters and what kinds of situations.

The second transcript, which provides a more narrow transcription of the dialogue (remember the discussion of transcription in Chapter 3), represents more directly how the characters actually produced the speech and provides a different kind of information as it creates links to social categories and other kinds of information about the characters' (here primarily Boss Skua's) traits and motivations.[1] That categorization is also, in a sense, conventional as there's no way to deduce directly what the social meaning is. Further, different viewers may have a very different sense of the characters based on the information embedded in the example. By looking at the longer scene from which the sample above is drawn, we get an even richer sense of how language connects to differences among the various characters.

Happy Feet is about a young emperor penguin from a community of emperor penguins who all sing, and who use their "heartsong" as the critical mechanism of finding their lifelong mate. The protagonist of the film, Mumble, is a terrible singer but an excellent dancer. Because he is different, he is ostracized from the community and decides to leave. In Example 5.2, he has been found wandering alone by a group of skuas looking for a meal.

Example 5.2   *Happy Feet*, George Miller (dir.), 2006, Warner Bros.

```
1   Boss Skua: Whatchu doing there, flippa boid?
2   Mumble:    Nothing. What are you doing?
3   Boss Skua: Nuttin. Just dropped in for a
               little lunch
4   [Two more skuas land.]
5   Mumble:    There's food? Here?
6   [Another skua lands. Skuas all laugh.]
7   Mumble:    Oh, no, no, wait, not me!, I'm a
               pen!guin.
8   Boss Skua: Exactly. The flippa boids, that's you,
               eat the fish=
9   Skua 2:    =Yeah=
10  Boss Skua: =Flyin' boids, that's me, eat the
               flipper boid and the fish. Lately there
               ain't a lotta fish, so uh
11  [Skuas start talking, making mocking,
    intimidating noises]
12  Mumble:    Wait, watch this!
13  [Mumble dances. Birds laugh]
14  Boss Skua: Yeah that's wei:d<<weird>>
15  [Boss Skua steps on Mumble, pinning him to
    the ground. Zoom in on the band on his foot.]
```

16	Mumble:	Hey, what's that on your leg?
17	Boss Skua:	What, this little thing?
18	Skua 4:	Oh, no, don't start 'im on [that.
19	Boss Skua:	[Shut up. The little flippa boid asked me a perceptive question. A question like that desoives<<deserves>>an answer.
20	Skua 3:	Here we go.
21	Boss Skua:	I got two words for ya. Alien! Abduction!
22	Skuas:	Aw, ya had to ask
23	Boss Skua:	Quiet [bird noises] Little buddy, there is somethin' out dere. Creatures. Not like us. Big. Fierca. Smarta too. Aks me how I know.
24	Mumble:	How?
25	Boss Skua:	Cause I been captured by 'em, tha's how
26	Mumble:	Unbelievable
27	Boss Skua:	Whaddu mean unbelievable, it's true. I'm sitting on a rock mindin' my own business when suddenly they're on me. These beings, like big ugly penguins, fat flabby faces with frontways eyes no fedders<<feathers>>no beaks and these these appendages.

```
              They probe me, they tie me up, they
              strap me down, they take this pointy
              thing and they stick it into me. And
              then blackout.
28  Mumble:   Gosh.
29  Boss Skua: I woke up and there's this this thing
              on me. Every flyin' bird is dissin'
              me. Hey what's happenin' yellow leg!
              It was humiliatin'.
```

Several interesting linguistic elements are apparent in this example even beyond those we saw in the shorter version. Mumble and Boss Skua are distinguished from one another almost immediately (lines 2–3) in the use of the <ing> variable, with Mumble using '-ing' and Boss Skua using '-in,' something that he does consistently throughout the scene. While Mumble's linguistic output conforms more or less to what we'd expect for the unmarked case (here, more or less the spoken standard), Boss Skua has a whole host of features that set his character apart. In almost all of the cases, the /r/ is non-rhotic (e.g., 'bird,' line 1; 'flipper,' line 8; 'smarter,' line 23; and so on). The vowel sounds are all characteristic of the vowels found in northeastern urban areas of the United States like New York City (the 'oy' vowel in 'bird,' for instance). The initial strings of wh- questions like "what do you" or "what are you" are said as if they were a single world ('whatchu,' 'whaddyu') and in general the overall rhythm of the speech is characteristic of a speaker from the northeastern urban areas of the United States, with many of the vowels reduced to the schwa vowel (the vowel in the second syllable of 'sofa') and some unstressed syllables omitted (e.g., line 25). Further, Skua Boss uses 'ain't' (line 10) and the present instead of the past tense in his abduction story (line 27) with a shift between past and present in the conclusion to the narrative (line 29). So, the entire bundle that we see emerging in this scene points to a character with traits that are culturally recognizable.

There are multiple kinds of meanings going on in this example, including those relative to demographics like region and gender but also to more intangible traits like masculinity, toughness, and control. Further, it's not a single linguistic feature doing this work but a bundle of features working together to create an indexical package that makes it clear to the audience who Boss Skua is. The movie producers could of course have done it differently and given Boss Skua a British accent (in fact, they do use British accents among some of the elder penguins who want to ban Mumble from the community). But British varieties don't bring along the same links to a particular kind of street smarts, low level of formal education, and toughness, at least not for an American audience.

The differences in how different audiences will recognize indexical meaning in mass media are of further interest. Certainly, different linguistic characteristics will have somewhat different indexes for different viewers. For instance, a child viewing this film in London might not have any knowledge of the regional associations that a child in New York might have. Similarly, the child in London might notice only the differences in how Boss Skua and Mumble talk without making any specific connections to the urban northeastern United States. Additionally, in line 23, Boss Skua says 'aks,' a pronunciation of 'ask' not typically associated with the regional varieties of the urban northeast (even though it may be found there). It is most commonly heard among speakers of AAVE, though others may use it as well.

In this case, some of the background for the film might be interesting to consider. The film is largely an Australian production, created by George Miller, an Australian director, screenwriter, and producer. The actor who voices Boss Skua, Anthony LaPaglia, is also Australian, as are several of the other voice actors. While it is impossible to know for sure, it's conceivable that the more common indexical associations to African Americans that Americans make with 'aks' could well be absent for speakers of other varieties of English. Thus, for them, perhaps the 'aks' variant does serve as an index to the urban, northeastern United States.[2]

Example 5.2 shows that indexical meanings can be quite complex and are much more dependent on both their context of occurrence and the context that both the speakers and the listeners bring to the interpretation of the index. Barbara Johnstone and Scott Kiesling (2008) have made this point about *indexicality* more generally in their discussion of the meanings that people in Pittsburgh attach to some of the canonical features of the dialect used in Pittsburgh. For many, those features are indexes of a local identity; for others, the features are indexes of individuals whom they know and like. They write:

> Our results highlight the degree to which the indexical meanings of speech features can vary within a community. Such variation arises because indexical meaning is created and reinforced in local practices in which different people participate in different ways, if at all. While it is often possible to find recurring semiotic relationships between linguistic variants and social meanings, the way in which a particular person will interpret a particular form is not determined by such larger-scale patterns. This is because different

people experience the sociolinguistic world differently. Some people's experience of local forms and their indexical meanings is relatively regimented by widely circulating metapragmatic practices that link forms and social meanings in the same way, repeatedly, for many people. (2008, 30)

While Johnstone and Kiesling's account is surely accurate, the issue of indexicality within the mass media requires a bit more nuance to explain. While the local practices in which indexical meaning arises are clearly still in play, as the example of 'aks' demonstrates, one of the specific goals of narrative mass media is to create characters who are recognizable. In some sense, the narrative mass media seek both to differentiate characters from one another in a believable way and to minimize the degree of variability in the interpretation of those characters, particularly with regard to character traits that will later be important to understanding character motivation as well as other aspects of the plot development.

It's specifically this strategy of using recognizable variability that makes the narrative mass media such a useful source of information about indexical meaning generally. For instance, even though there is no clear, direct indexical tie to the urban northeastern United States in the example from *Happy Feet*, such as an overt reference to a particular place like New York City, there is a longstanding indexical relationship in movies and television shows between the bundle of features used by Boss Skua and the urban northeast, going back in fact to the first line of synchronized dialogue in *The Jazz Singer* (set, not coincidentally, in New York City). Even viewers not familiar with the specific regional index or the index to masculinity and toughness noted above will notice that there are broad differences between Mumble and the skuas. They are also likely to notice that the skuas sound a lot like other characters they've seen in films, particularly films set in places like New York City.

Food for Thought

Watch one of your favorite animated films and note which non-human characters speak in ways that you recognize as indexing particular places or particular types of people.

The emergent nature of the indexical meanings in narrative captures one of the other important facets of indexical meaning, namely, that indexicality builds in a dialectic fashion, with one indexical relationship feeding into a second relationship that gets its meaning in part from the nature of the first, and then that second relationship feeding into a third. Michael Silverstein (1996) has called this dialectic relationship *order of indexicality*. For an American viewer, for instance, that package of features might first index the urban northeastern United States. A second index might capture the fact that many of the real people in the urban northeast who use these features share some traits: they are most typically working-class, male, and very much associated with a local identity. A third, interrelated, index could be to specific kinds of characters who use this package in narrative films, especially characters involved in organized crime. For a viewer outside the United States, the ordering and nature of the indexes could differ somewhat, for instance, a first index might be to the United States generally rather than to a specific region. A second could be linked more directly to educational status rather than class status, and so forth. While this degree of potential variation makes the nature of the meaning of the linguistic variation in the film dependent on the viewer, it also points out how the cyclical and interconnected nature of indexical meaning must be anchored in the interpretive mechanisms the audience brings to the film. One important kind of mechanism for the interpretation of linguistic variation concerns the mental models we all use to categorize and otherwise make sense of experience. Those mental models can broadly be captured as ideologies.

Ideology

Part of what we know when we know a language is how to think about or talk about that language. We know what kinds of expectations we have for how different kinds of people will use language and what different ways of using language might tell us about a given situation or context. We also have lots of ideas about how language works. This constellation of knowledge constitutes our ideologies about language. An *ideology* is a given belief or a system of beliefs, explanation, or rationalization about how something works. Critically, this system of explanations or understandings may or may not be directly connected to how the phenomenon actually works. For instance, the discussions in Chapters 2 and 3 illustrate that how people think language works doesn't always correspond to how it actually works.

If we think of ideologies as belief systems linked to ideas about how groups do or don't behave and relate to one another, we can also start to think of ideologies in terms of presenting us with *cognitive schemas*. Cognitive schemas are ideas that we use to imagine and constitute our social world. The social scientist Benedict Anderson thought about nationalism as a cognitive schema (1991). He noted that there isn't any "real" way to define who is French or American or Kenyan. Those definitions emerge through the ideas and beliefs people have about who is or isn't French, American, or Kenyan. Those ideas then create or define what a nation is. In this sense, Anderson argued, nations are imagined, a concept that can extend to most communities. The main idea behind *imagined communities* is that our ideas about communities, more so than specifically our face-to-face engagements within them, make those communities "real." Further, such imagining is inherently ideological in that it constructs the community based more on a system of beliefs, understandings, explanations, and rationalizations than on direct knowledge and interaction with other people who are part of the same community. Anderson's ideas can be extended much more broadly to all kinds of social groupings and to the various cognitive schema that provide our sense of the social types, groups, and persona it is possible to inhabit at a given time and in a given place, something Chapter 8 explores in more detail.

This can be a kind of unsettling way to think about things because it makes it seem like life is not based in some kind of specific reality. I like to think that what an ideological approach does is help us to organize our direct sensory experiences (what we see, feel, hear, smell, and touch). It seems inherently important to acknowledge that how we think about and conceive of those experiences is no more or less "real" than the sensory experiences themselves. Our ideologies have effects on how we understand the world and are probably central for being able to understand the world at all. They manifest in the most basic ways by helping us decide who is similar to us (and thus a member of some group of which we consider ourselves a member) and who is different from us.

Food for Thought

Think of two or three groups that you consider yourself a member of. What makes you a member of those groups? How does your understanding (your ideology) of yourself and of the groups relate to your sense of belonging? Now think of two or three groups you know about but don't consider yourself a member of. Again, how does your understanding (your ideology) of yourself and of the groups relate to your sense of not belonging?

Ideologies are beliefs that explain how/why a group of people behave or are believed to behave. Kathryn Woolard and Bambi Schieffelin (1994) have explored this facet of ideology in some detail and lay out four basic ways in which ideologies are connected to social and cultural life. First, ideologies provide a "shared" set of ideas that serves to independently rationalize or explain various social and cultural phenomena. This sort of orientation to ideology is particularly visible in the fictional audiovisual media. In Example 5.2 for instance, Boss Skua's explanation of his leg band being the result of alien abduction rather than for tracking purposes captures this kind of rationalization. It illustrates, via the familiar genre of alien abduction stories, the drive to give seemingly uninterpretable events and experiences a rational explanation.

The second way that ideology connects to social life according to Woolard and Schieffelin is through the experiences and interests of specific social positions or groups. Ideology helps us construct groups and then base membership (or lack thereof) in the group on a set of ideas about what the group members share. In Example 5.2, Boss Skua articulates exactly this kind of ideology in lines 8 and 10 when he describes the "flipper birds" and the "flying birds" and the properties that each share as an explanation for why he and the other birds are going to eat Mumble.

Woolard and Schieffelin's third and fourth connections of ideology to social life are tied directly to power, a notion that I'll discuss in detail below. One way that ideology connects to power is tied to the construction of social groupings discussed above. Once social categories are available to be applied to a group of people, the groups are often arranged in some kind of social hierarchy based on beliefs about the naturalness of the arrangement. This hierarchy usually results in those people belonging to groups at the top exerting power over those lower in the hierarchy. This conception of ideology is also at work in Boss Skua's discussion of flipper birds and flying birds when he explains that flying birds typically eat flipper birds when there aren't enough fish.

The final connection between ideology and social life that Woolard and Schieffelin discuss involves obscuring the bases on which some groups' interests are defended or promoted at the expense of the interests of other groups. This connection is revealed in the *Happy Feet* example in the differences between how Mumble, the film's hero, and the skuas talk. Mumble uses Standard English while the skuas don't. The connection of Standard English to heroes creates a connection between the standard and desirable qualities that hides how using the standard promotes the interests of middle- and upper-class people and the highly educated over those who are not.

Schieffelin and Woolard are primarily interested in articulating a connection between ideologies generally and ideologies about language more specifically. My general interest both in this chapter and in the book as a whole shares their orientation. Ideologies, including ideologies about language, provide the conceptual frameworks for making use and sense of language variation generally and within the context of the audiovisual narrative mass media more specifically. Ideologies create the paths from which the indexical relations and indexical meanings discussed above emerge.

Ideology about Language

Now that we have two critical concepts, ideology and indexicality, in place, we can move to link these to language in a general sense but also more specifically to language in the mass media. The analysis of *ideologies about language* began, in many ways, with Michael Silverstein's (1979) articulation of language ideologies as beliefs and ideas about language that justify, explain, or rationalize language structure and use. Ideologies have effects in terms of organizing linguistic variation conceptually, particularly in the service of distinguishing individuals and groups of individuals from one another (Irvine and Gal 2000) and in the service of interpreting similarity between individuals and groups of individuals (Bucholtz and Hall 2004; Queen 2004). While it's important not to reduce all forms of conceptual categorization as tied to language to ideology, it's clear that beliefs about language can be powerful. In the discussion about languages and dialects in Chapter 2, for instance, beliefs about shared cultural histories proved to be one of the critical elements for calling some codes 'languages' and others 'dialects.' These ideologies together form an important part of what we might call an ecology or culture of language.

Beliefs about standard languages may be especially salient in the overall set of language ideologies within a given language ecology. You'll recall the discussion of the standard language ideology from Chapter 4. As we saw there, beliefs about language do not typically capture the actual range of variation that we find even in the standard language or in its written forms. Still, speakers of languages that have a standard often share beliefs about the inherent accuracy, clarity, and logic of the standard. Rosina Lippi-Green (2011) has done a fascinating analysis of a large corpus of animated films, primarily from the Disney production company, showing that the protagonists of a story invariably speak Standard American English, while antagonists and especially side characters are more likely to speak some other variant. In this way, the standard becomes indexical of certain kinds of people, basically those who have the characteristics of Disney heroes, and a wide range of other language varieties become indexical of other characteristics. For instance, Lippi-Green (2011, 120–121) points to scrappy sidekicks such as the guardian dragon Mushu, voiced by Eddie Murphy in *Mulan* (1998), as well as other characters with generally scrappy behavior such as a trio of crows in *Dumbo* (1941) or King Louie, voiced by Louis Pima, in *The Jungle Book* (1967).[3] As Chris Rock articulated it fairly clearly at the 2012 Oscar ceremony (in reference to his own role as Marty the Zebra in *Madagascar*, 2005), "I love animation. I love animation because in the world of animation, you can be anything you want to be. If you're a fat woman you can play a skinny princess. If you're a short wimpy guy, you can play a tall gladiator. If you're a white man you can play an Arabian prince. And if you're a black man, you can play a donkey, or a zebra. You can't play white, my God!"

We have many different ideologies about language beyond those noted above for a standard language, including the belief that language is primarily made up of words that refer to things, that people's intentions are the source of most linguistic meaning, and that varieties other than the standard are simply poor versions of the standard rather than systematic codes in their own right. These ideologies may be expressed directly or indirectly, in as well as outside the media. An example of a direct *metalinguistic*, or *metapragmatic*, commentary can be seen in Example 5.3 from the film *Akeelah and the Bee* (2006). In the film, a middle-school-aged girl seeks to win a national spelling bee and in the process works with a spelling coach, played by Laurence Fishburn.

Example 5.3   *Akeelah and the Bee*, Doug Atchison (dir.), 2006, Out of the Blue … Entertainment

```
[Akeelah walks to the back of a house and finds
Dr. Larabee gardening.]
```

```
1  Larabee:   You're late
2  Akeelah:   You didn't answer the door
3  Larabee:   That's because you're late. Come in.
              Come come come<very enunciated>[..]
              [Larabee walks to some flower beds and
              kneels down] So [..] you wanna learn
              how to spell
4  Akeelah:   I know how to spell
5  Larabee:   Spell staphylococci
6  Akeelah:   Um [..] s, t, a, f
```

```
 7  Larabee:  There is no f [..] it's derived from
                the Greek so there can't be an f.
                Staphylococci s. t. a. p. h .y. l. o.
                c. o. c. c. i. winning word National
                Spelling Bee 1987. The first thing most
                serious spellers do is learn all of the
                winning words and their origins
 8  Akeelah:  Well maybe I ain't that serious
 9  Larabee:  Maybe neither am I
10  [..]
11  Akeelah:  So why you home today? Ain't you got no
                job?
12  Larabee:  Do me a favor. Leave the ghetto talk
                outside all right
13  Akeelah:  Ghetto talk? I don't talk ghetto=
14  Larabee:  =Mm ain't you got no job<imitating
                Akeelah>You use that language to fit in with
                your friends. Here you will speak properly
                or you won't speak at all. Understood?
15  Akeelah:  Yeah [..] whateva' [puts hand on hip]
16  Larabee:  You can leave now
17  [Larabee gets up and starts walking away.]
18  Akeelah:  Excuse me?
19  Larabee:  I said you can leave
20  Akeelah:  How come?
21  Larabee:  Because I don't have time to waste on
                insolent little girls
22  Akeelah:  Insolent? I ain't ins% I mean I'm not
                insolent. It's just the first thing you
                do is start gawking on criticizin'
```

```
the way I speak. I thought this was
just about spelling words. [..]
[Larabee doesn't look up] Well then
fine [..] [Akeelah turns to leave,
stops, and turns back around] You know
what? When I put my mind to it I can
memorize anything and I don't need help
from a dictatorial[.] truculent [.]
supercilious gardener. [..] I'm sorry
to be so insolent
```

The scene pivots most specifically in line 12 in which Larabee tells Akeelah that she is speaking 'ghetto talk.' In line 13, she rejects his admonition, saying that she doesn't speak ghetto. He then mimics her utterance from line 11, 'ain't you got no job?' to illustrate his point. Akeelah produces several grammatical elements associated with different nonstandard varieties of English, including AAVE. In addition to 'ain't,' these include the omission of /r/ in 'whatever' (line 15), negative concord in line 11 ('ain't you got no job'), and the omission of the auxiliary verb to be, also in line 11 ('So, why you home today?'). The general rhythm of her speech is characteristic of AAVE, particularly in urban areas. This set of features offers a clear index to working-class, lazy speech, an indexical relation articulated by Larabee both in his labeling of Akeelah's speech as 'ghetto talk' and also in his juxtaposition of her speech with 'speaking properly' (line 14). His analysis that her speech is linked to wanting to fit in with her friends, rather than, for instance, being the variety of English used in her community, captures many of the components of contemporary ideologies about language in the United States. One particularly common ideology is that varieties of English like AAVE are fundamentally poor versions of the standard and that speakers of AAVE know the standard and can choose to use it if they wish to. This belief is reinforced when Larabee tells her that she can leave after she utters 'whateva'' in line 15. Akeelah's turn in line 22 further supports this belief about the relationship between the two when she starts to use 'ain't' and then changes to 'I'm not.' She goes on to gain the upper hand in the interaction by illustrating a hyper-standard, hyper-formal lexicon, thus in a sense using language to turn the tables on Larabee. Akeelah achieves her goal by accepting, or appropriating, the very metalinguistic commentary that Larabee used to critique her. Both of their ways of using language further reinforce the indexical relationship between AAVE and characteristics such as lack of education, an orientation to the street, and a host of other features captured by the term 'ghetto talk.' Their language use also reinforces the relationship between Standard English and properness, politeness, education, and a more global rather than local identity.

In the following example, from the television series *Weeds* (2005–2012), we see a similar metalinguistic comment concerning the same basic indexical relationship to AAVE, although in this case the connection is to a broader social context. The series *Weeds* is about a suburban mother who turns to selling marijuana after she is widowed. One of her early suppliers is Heylia, who appears in Example 5.4. Joseph is one of Heylia's suitors and a member of the Nation of Islam. He hoped that she would also join the Nation of Islam, but she has declined.

Example 5.4   *Weeds*, 'Bash,' Season 2, Episode 9, Jenji Kohan (creator), Showtime, October 9, 2006

```
1    Joseph:  It's a shame.
2    Heylia:  Yes it is.
3    Joseph:  You sure look good in white=
4    Heylia:  =Well, all them rules, ain't no way I
              could keep it up for long=
5    Joseph:  =Don't say ain't. Ain't's a slave word.
6    Heylia:  Well, I ain't no slave. So I can
              says what I wants.
```

Like Larabee in Example 5.3, Joseph links a specific linguistic item, the word 'ain't,' to characteristics associated with lack of education. Whereas Larabee references this as 'ghetto talk,' Joseph links it to slavery (line 5), and indirectly to a longer-standing discourse about the connection of slavery to the prohibition of education and to subordination more generally. For Larabee, the use of this index is a choice Akeelah makes. For Joseph, the index is more essentialized and connected to longer-standing social and historical trends that necessitate its avoidance by African Americans in particular. Like Akeelah, Heylia contests this representation (in line 6). However, unlike Akeelah, she rejects the ideological component concerning 'ain't.' Not only does she repeat the word, she uses further elements associated with AAVE, including negative concord and the regularization of the present tense verbal paradigm with the extension of the third person singular present tense morpheme -s to the first person singular. In this case, though, her use is intentionally ironic and in a sense hyper non-standard, illustrating that she can make decisions about the meanings behind her words herself.

These two examples illustrate the complex relationships between ideology, indexicality, and metalinguistic commentary as each illustrates one speaker policing the language of another, with the language variety being policed being one of the most widely discussed, and stigmatized, varieties of American English. While an in-depth discussion of all the aspects of the grammar of AAVE is beyond the scope of this chapter, what is important here is that the variety is associated not only with African Americans as the first level of indexicality (and independently of the facts that many African Americans do not speak this variety and that not only African Americans speak this variety), but also with a whole host of characteristics tied to education, class, and possibly gender at higher levels. A further layer of indexical relation emerges via its connection to the standard language ideology.

Once we start to see examples of characters not only being constructed via linguistic variation but also being specifically evaluated based on those characteristics, we move to another level of understanding the relationships between ideology and indexicality, and that level involves the nature of power, such as the power involved in attempting to change someone's language. In *Akeelah and the Bee*, Larabee is able to successfully exert that power, but in *Weeds*, Joseph's similar attempt is rejected. In what remains of this chapter, I want to further explore the relationship of ideology and indexicality to power as discussed by Woolard and Schieffelin, using an example from the 2011 film *The Help*.

Ideology, Indexicality, and Power

In addition to providing information about character traits, what we might call their identities, language variation is also a source of plot development and action in its own right. I showed an early example of this sort of action in Chapter 1 in the discussion of *Love Actually* (2003). In that example, the juxtaposition of British and American pronunciations of particular words moved the action of the film forward. The indexical properties of British English in the context of the United States also provided Colin with the power to influence the women's romantic interest in him. As with indexicality, power is largely founded on specific ideologies about how it can circulate, who can wield it, who can resist it, and who must accept it.

Most simply, *power* refers to the ability to influence the actions of others. As Foucault (1991) and others within the scholarly tradition known as postmodernism have discussed, power is not really something that some people have and other people don't. Rather, power is a dialectic that exists between people. The ability to influence others occurs largely through the ongoing and complex means of accepting and resisting that very influence. In fact, power only exists because people come to accept, resist, or ignore it, and thus it is both always circulating and recognizable through the interaction between its exertion and the reaction to the exertion. Exerting power is primarily linked to the deployment of sets of available resources – resources that are distributed in a variety of different ways. This distribution is especially apparent in the film, *The Help* (2011).

The Help, based on the eponymous book by Kathleen Stockett, is set in Jackson, Mississippi, in 1962 and is chiefly a domestic drama in which the main characters are all women. The narrative seeks to reveal the specific experience of African Americans working as domestic labor as understood through the eyes of an Anglo American woman who grew up in Jackson, was raised by a domestic worker, and has returned to Jackson following her graduation from college. The film received wide critical acclaim and was nominated for numerous awards, including several Oscars.

Many critics of the film pointed out that the experiences being narrated were more linked to the interests of the narrator as a young white woman, albeit a generally liberal one, living in that time and place than to the interests and experiences of the domestic workers ostensibly at the heart of the story. Further, many critics pointed to the ideologies held by many viewers of the film that the abject racism depicted was no longer relevant and, more centrally, that the problem of racism was, and remains, a problem linked to individuals rather than broad systems of social power (see also Jane Hill's 2008 discussion of this dynamic as relevant for language). For instance, in a review of the film in *Time* magazine, Touré (2012) notes,

> I'm not sure why so many people flocked to spend hours in this world of American apartheid. Do whites like visiting a world where blacks are docile and controlled and the racial hierarchy is clear? Or do they like seeing a white girl saving blacks? Could the success of *The Help* be divorced from national subconscious anxiety about a future that includes minority status for whites and the loss of total power, as symbolized by the first black President? Or is it easy to watch because of an incorrect sense of having reached a world beyond racism?

Similarly, the Association of Black Women Historians (2012) published an open letter in which they state:

> Portraying the most dangerous racists in 1960s Mississippi as a group of attractive, well dressed, society women, while ignoring the reign of terror perpetuated by the Ku Klux Klan and the White Citizens Council, limits racial injustice to individual acts of meanness.

Thus, even as the film can be seen as exploring one dimension of power, namely, the power of racism, others dimensions circulate, too, as people receive the film (and the book on which it is based) and interpret and react to it. This back and forth illustrates exactly what it means to say that power isn't something that some people have and others don't but rather is a force that exists between people. In this particular case, some of the issues are about the power to represent and the power to contest those representations. It is this ideological work that the critics of *The Help* were particularly focused on, arguing largely that the film hid the real (and lasting) nature of the racism of the 1960s, and also that it used a story ostensibly about African Americans as a vehicle of the moral, social, and cultural elevation of several of the white characters and as the vehicle of a critical comeuppance for the white antagonist.

Food for Thought

Compare the first and last scenes of book and film versions of *The Help*. How does the author represent the different characters? Is that same representation present in the film? What do those representations reveal about power?

The final scene, shown in Example 5.5, illustrates not only connections between ideologies, indexicality, and power, but also the broader ways in which these concepts are integrally bound to the language used. In the case of this film, those broader connections are interwoven with (a) the book itself, partially written in ways that seek (often unrealistically and ungrammatically) to represent the putative spoken language of the characters; (b) the screenplay, which includes some vernacular representations, though largely not the same ones as those found in the book;

and, finally, (c) the actual verbal output of the actors in the film who represent the characters. The differences between a screenplay and the final output were discussed in some detail in the last chapter. For the discussion here, I am examining a transcription of the verbal output of the characters in the film.

Example 5.5 *The Help*, Tate Taylor (dir.), 2011, Dreamworks SKG

Characters:
A: Aibeleen Clark, African American, domestic labor for the Leefoldt family and a main character of the narrative
E: Elizabeth Leefoldt, Anglo-American, employer to Aibeleen, society climber, reluctant mother
H: Hilly Hollbrooke, Anglo-American, at the top of the power structure among the Anglo-American women in Jackson and strong supporter of pre-Civil Rights era race relations
M: Mae Mobley, Anglo-American, Elizabeth Leefoldt's daughter, age 3 or so, primarily reared by Aibeleen

Aibeleen walks in carrying groceries; Elizabeth, carrying a baby, and Hilly are in the living room.

Transcription note: ? at the end of the word indicates a glottal stop [the sound that occurs between the syllables of "uh oh"]. Other features are roughly transcribed.

1 E: [off-camera] Aibeleen, can you come in here please?
2 A: Goo? mornin'
3 H: Aibeleen, the silver I lent Elizabeth last week [head nods down]
4 A: [It not] polish goo? ? Humidity been fightin me on polishin day.
5 H: When you returned it, three pieces were missin from the felt wrapper. A fork and two<fronted [u] >spoons

6   A: Le, Lemme go check in the kitchen, maybe
        I lef some behin
7   H: You know as well as I do that silver's not
        in the kitchen
8   A: You check in Mae Mobley's bed? Since
        little May was born, she been puttin
        things in there[
9   H: [do you hear her Elisabeth? She's tryin to
        blame it on a toddler.
10 A: Ain't got no silver<shift to lower pitch>
11 E: She says she doedn't have 'em
12 H: Then it behooves me to inform you that you
        are fired, Aibeleen. And I'll be callin the
        police
12 [Mae Mobley runs in]
13 M: Aibie, my froat hu:ts
14 A: I'll go get some syrup Miss Leefoldt=
15 H: =Elizabeth can take care of her own
        [children
16 E: [I'll go get the cough syrup
17 A: [walks over to E] Come here lil man
18 [Hilly steps between Aibeleen and Elizabeth]
19 E: I, I'm o.k.
20 [Elizabeth turns and leaves. Aibeleen steps
    back]
21 A: I'n't steal no silver.
22 H: Maybe I can't send you to jail for what
        you wrote. But I can send you for bein
        a thief.=
23 A: =I know sump'n about you, don't you
        forget that!<style shift>And from
        what Yule May says, there's a lot of time to
        write letters in jail. Plenty of time
        to write the truth about you. And the
        paper's free.
24 H: Nobody would believe what you wrote!
25 A: I don't know! I been told I'm a pretty good
        writer, already sold a lot of books!
        [Hilly gets tears in her eyes. Elizabeth
        walks back in with syrup. Hilly turns toward
        Elizabeth]

```
26  H:  Call the police, Elizabeth.
        [Aibeleen steps quickly closer to Hilly.
        Hilly gasps]
27  A:  All you do is scare and lie to try to get what
        you want!=
28  E:  [off-camera] =Aibeleen, stop!
29  A:  You a godless woman! [..] Ain't you tired,
        Miss Hilly< [hillI] >? Ain't you tired?
30  [Hilly's face screws up with anger, defeat,
    and tears and she storms away]
31  E:  Aibeleen, you have to go now.
32  [Aibeleen turns to Mae Mobley]
33  M:  Don't go, Aibie. [Aibeleen leans down to be at
        Mae Mobley's height]
34  A:  Baby, you need to get back to bed.
35  M:  Please, don't leave.
36  A:  [kneels to Mae Mobley's level] I gots to,
        baby. I am so sorry< [sorrI] >!
37  M:  Are you going to take care of anotha little girl?
38  A:  No, that's not de reason. I don't wanna leave
        you. But it's time for me to retire. You my
        last little girl.
39  M:  No!
40  A:  Baby. Baby, I need you to member everything I
        told you, kay?
41  M:  kay.
```

42   A: You remember what I told you?
43   M: <sing song voice>You is kind. You is smart.
          You is important.
44   A: That's right, baby girl. [quiet]
45   [in tears she hugs and kisses Mae Mobley]
46   M: Don't go, Aibie!

47   A: I gots to, baby!
48   [to Elizabeth before she leaves]
49   A: You give my sweet girl a chance.
50   [Leaves the house to the voiceover below. Final
     shot of Aibeleen walking down the street with Mae
     Mobley pounding on the window inside the house and
     wailing]
51   A: May Mobley was my las' baby. In just ten
          minutes the only life I knew was done. [May
          Mobley screaming at the window] God says we
          need to love our<[a]>enemies. It har' ta do.
          But it can sta:t by tellin the truth. No one
          had eva aksed me what it fel' like to be me.
          Once I told the truth about that, I felt free.
          And I got ta thankin about all the people
          I know and the thangs I seen and done.
          My boy Treelore always sai? we gon: have
          a writer in the family one day.
          I guess it's gon: be me

This scene exemplifies some basic linguistic indexes that occur throughout the film. The dimensions of social variation that are present include age, race, and social class, with race and social class being more or less overlapping. All of the Anglo American characters are wealthy with privileged social positions and all of the African American characters are domestic workers, the large majority of them women who work in the homes of the Anglo American characters. There are Anglo American men in the film; however, their roles are relatively minor and their language does not differ in significant ways from that of the women. Finally, of course, all of the characters are speakers of some variety of southern American English. These basic dimensions, which involve linguistic bundles that the characters share as well as those that distinguish them, are present in Example 5.4 above.

First, all three of the adult women categorically use '-in' rather than '-ing' pronunciations of <ing>. Second, all three characters also use the monophthongal /aI/ ['maht' instead of 'might' in which the vowel is a diphthong] before voiceless consonants. While these are certainly expected features for characters located in the southern United States in the early 1960s, the effect for the audience in 2012 (and later) is to have a shared index to region.

The characters are distinguished based on a set of other phonological and grammatical features, with grammatical features being one of the primary ways that Aibeleen is distinctive from Elizabeth and Hilly. Those that Aibeleen uses include many that we have seen in one of the other examples discussed in the earlier parts of the chapter, including 'ain't' (line 10), negative concord (lines 10, 21), and regularized singular verb agreement (line 36). We also see the use of the 'aks' form, here in a more expected context relative to the real-world dialect AAVE. There are some additional grammatical elements that we haven't seen in earlier examples, including the omission of the copula (the verb 'to be,' line 38) and the omission of auxiliary verbs more generally. Aibeleen also shows some phonological distinctions. In particular she uses a non-rhotic pronunciation of postvocalic /r/, reduces consonant clusters to a single consonant wherever permissible in the grammar, pronounces final alveolar stops (t, d) as a glottal stop (lines 2 and 4), and uses a lax pronunciation of final /i/ (as in 'sorry' in line 36). All of the characteristics are part of the conventional grammar and, unlike in the book, the characters are animated using these features in more or less the ways we would expect a native speaker of AAVE to use them.

The two Anglo American characters also share some pronunciation characteristics that distinguish them from Aibeleen—notably, all of their postvocalic /r/ pronunciations are rhotic. As I discussed in Chapter 2, this use is particularly interesting because some of the older Anglo American characters in the film have non-rhotic pronunciations, and this distinction captures what was likely occurring in this area in the early 1960s, with the Anglo American southern dialects, particularly in the inland south, shifting from non-rhotic to rhotic variants. Finally, Hilly and Elizabeth also both produce the vowels /u/ [goose] and /o/ [moat] much more in the front of the mouth than we find in other varieties of American English. This feature, too, is characteristic of speakers of southern varieties of American English and was an innovation to those varieties among younger speakers in the 1950s and 1960s, having now spread through the population and beginning to spread outside of the traditional area for southern American English.

There are several different types of power in play in that scene, and each is associated with some kind of linguistic output. Each of the four characters variously seeks to exert power over the others. The most transparent moves linked to power occur between Aibeleen and Hilly. Hilly is seeking to have Aibeleen fired as retribution for a book that Aibeleen helped write (but whose author is listed as Anonymous) that exposed negative information about the white employers of domestic help. In terms of most of the social structures depicted in the film, Hilly has the upper hand, something that is fully supported by the beliefs (ideologies) that many people in Jackson, Mississippi, in the early 1960s held about African and Anglo Americans. Throughout the scene, we see that Aibeleen's reactions indicate initial acceptance of (lines 4, 6, and 8) and then resistance to (line 23) the power Hilly seeks to exert. Alternatively, we can also see in lines 24, 26, and 30 how Hilly reacts to the power that Aibeleen applies in return, initially resisting it and then accepting it. Ultimately, of course, the cost of Aibeleen's power move is to Aibeleen herself as she loses her job. But even that loss is not absolute as the audience is left to understand that Aibeleen will continue to write for a living and in that sense has ultimately empowered herself.

Scott Kiesling (1997) has pointed out that not all power is the same, and that the basis for the circulation of power can differ significantly, as can the resources linked to power. For instance, many people conceive of the ability to physically dominate someone as more coercive than the power to nurture someone; however, both can be implicated in the desire of one person to influence the behavior of another. Kiesling's model includes seven different sources of power, and each can be found at work in Example 5.5 from *The Help*.

Table 5.1 Kiesling's seven different types of power

Basis	Description
Physical	General physical ability and/or ability to physically coerce
Economic	Income, wealth, or other commodities
Knowledge	Information or understanding, especially that is not shared
Structural	Position within a structural unit such as a family, a company, or a social group
Nurturant	Ability to care for and/or help; also, the ability to request care and/or help
Demeanor	Personality, especially as related to ability to influence the positive feelings of someone else
Ideological	Ratification of some traits as powerful while defining what social positions/traits are possible within a given social constellation

Source: Kiesling 1997, 68.

These different notions of power highlight different kinds of relationships between interactants and different resources available for the exertion of and reaction to power. Example 5.5 offers an insightful means for thinking about how language serves as one of the resources available to exert and react to power. Power intertwines with ideas about how different kinds of people behave and what kinds of social relations hold between different groups of people. Because this is a case drawn from a media source, those ideologies are mutlilayered, tied to the world being depicted in the film, as well as tied to the context in which the film was produced, viewed in the moment of release, and viewed over time. These different beliefs about how people behave and how power circulates are always a matter of temporal and spatial context. Usefully for our purposes, Example 5.5 includes the circulation of all seven of the types of power found in Kiesling's model.

Food for Thought

What do you think of the idea that power is a property that circulates rather than being something people have or don't have? Observe a situation of interaction, either in the media or outside of it, and think about the different kinds of power being exerted by the people involved. Which of Kiesling's seven kinds of power seem the most common?

We can break the final scene into four broad narrative movements, with the final monologue providing the conclusion to the movie. While that portion of the scene is important for both plot and characterizations, and for concluding the story, I'm going to focus here on those parts of the scene that involve interactions between the characters, since those parts are where the linguistic indexes to power is most apparent. While physical power is clear at various points in the scene (for instance, in line 18 when Hilly prevents Aibeleen from taking the baby, or in line 36 when Aibeleen kneels down to be at Mae Mobley's height), there are no clear cases of physical resources linked to language in this scene (such resources might include, for instance, having a louder or significantly deeper voice).

In the first part of the narrative, lines 1–20, the basic plot conflict for the scene is established, namely, that Hilly, with Elizabeth's complaisance, plans to fire Aibeleen. There are complex power dynamics here between each pair of women – Hilly and Elizabeth, Hilly and Aibeleen, and Elizabeth and Aibeleen. Hilly and Elizabeth are ostensibly friends; however, Hilly is the more dominant person, both within their social circles and in terms of her personality. Hilly fired one of Aibeleen's best friends early in the film and is generally among the most racist of the white women in the film. Finally, Elizabeth is Aibeleen's employer, but Aibeleen raises (and loves) the Leefoldt children and is also the more mature of the two.

The two white women variously use resources connected to structural and economic power, while Aibeleen primarily has access only to demeanor power. These resources are particularly clear in line 12, when Hilly uses the very formal verb "behoove" and also commits the act of firing Aibeleen via the verb "inform," which is a verb that performs the action it names. In other words, by saying it, Hilly has done it (here she's done the act of informing and, by implication, the actual firing). (We'll talk in much more depth about these types of verbs in Chapter 7.) Her phrasing, "It behooves me to inform you that you are fired" is noteworthy because it is actually an indirect way of firing Aibeleen. A direct way to do it would have been to say "You are fired." The phrasing that Hilly uses not only creates/recalls social distance via its formality, it also recognizes that ultimately Hilly is not the one who has the power to directly fire Aibeleen. That power belongs to Elizabeth. Hilly's phrasing instead suggests that she is voicing what Elizabeth and she have already discussed.

This phrasing highlights both the structural and economic resources of power that Hilly and Elizabeth work with in the scene. Hilly uses her higher structural power within the community of white women to influence what Elizabeth does. Elizabeth actually attempts to resist this use of Hilly's structural power in line 11 when she affirms Aibeleen's claim that she doesn't have the silver. Her resistance, though, is ineffective as Hilly moves ahead in line 12 with firing Aibeleen. The economic power is Elizabeth's but the structural power is Hilly's. In the dynamic between Hilly and Elizabeth, structural power is clearly the more effective type of power.

For her part, Aibeleen does not have many resources that she can use to influence Hilly and Elizabeth. She is structurally and economically subordinate to them. However, she attempts to use her general demeanor in lines 6 and 8 to provide an alternative to the implication (line 5) that she has stolen the three pieces of silver. Line 8 is specifically of interest because she appeals to her shared identity with the other two as adults and marks this shift prosodically, shifting her pitch range down and lowering her amplitude. This move is fully resisted by Hilly in line 9. Here, she shifts from talking to Aibeleen with Elizabeth as the over-hearer to speaking directly to Elizabeth and as such appeals to Elizabeth as holding the ultimate power to fire Aibeleen as her employer. Aibeleen's demeanor-based resources have clearly been ineffective in influencing what is happening to her, so she shifts her style again to a resigned declarative (line 10); however, her use of 'ain't' highlights the ongoing structural differences between her and the other women not only in terms of the labor relationship but also in terms of relations of race and class.

The entrance of Mae Mobley (the young child being raised primarily by Aibeleen and generally disliked by Elizabeth, her mother) provides a plot device for Aibeleen to reappeal to her resources of structural power in being Elizabeth's, not Hilly's, employee. She also makes use of her nurturant resources as the primary caregiver to the child. When the child complains of a sore throat, Aibeleen directly addresses Elizabeth, noting that she'll go and get some medicine (line 14). Hilly again asserts her structural power over Elizabeth, though indirectly, by addressing Aibeleen. Here, Elizabeth accepts Hilly's move by saying that she'll go and get the medicine (line 16). When Aibeleen again tries to use her nurturance of the children to gain some control, Hilly physically intervenes so that Aibeleen can't take the baby, and Elizabeth again accepts Hilly's power over her in line 19, taking the baby with her to get the cough syrup.

Elizabeth's departure marks the second part of the scene, which encompasses lines 21–31. Here, the major power resources belong to Aibeleen as she uses her knowledge both of the fact that Hilly unknowingly ate a pie that contained the feces of her capriciously fired maid and that this story appeared in the anonymously published book that Aibeleen was behind writing. While Hilly suspects that Aibeleen was involved, as implicated in line 22, she doesn't know for sure. Aibeleen deploys her knowledge in both line 23 and line 25. What is especially interesting about this is that Aibeleen's speaking style shifts significantly as she delivers line 23. Not only does she latch on directly to Hilly's utterance in line 22, she states explicitly that her knowledge has direct power over Hilly, who is deeply embarrassed to have been made a fool. Whereas all prior examples of final consonant clusters have been reduced (e.g., line 6 with 'lef' and 'behin'), in line 25, the clusters of 'told' and 'sold' are fully articulated. Hilly's reaction to line 25 is to get tears in her eyes and when Elizabeth returns, she tells her to call the police.

In lines 27 and 29, Aibeleen again engages the power of demeanor to try and affect Hilly, but here it is not their shared identity as adults that she appeals to, as she did above, but rather basic morality. By naming Hilly as a fear-monger, liar, and "godless," Aibeleen gains the upper hand in the conversation. When she delivers the final two utterances of line 29, she shifts her tone, again, making use of resources associated with her demeanor in an effort to affect Hilly. This is effective in that Hilly remains speechless and tearful and ultimately leaves the room. Elizabeth, however, reasserts her economic position as Aibeleen's employer by telling her that she must leave. Her utterance is made in a more confident tone relative to her earlier comments. Speaking independently of Hilly, she marshals the necessary resources of her economic position to fire Aibeleen on her own.

Elizabeth's firing of Aibeleen leads to the final segment in the scene, which occurs between Mae Mobley and Aibeleen as Aibeleen says goodbye to the little girl. Here, although the little girl tries to use her ability to ask for nurturance to influence Aibeleen to stay, Aibeleen has accepted Elizabeth's authority to fire her. For her interactions with the little girl, though, Aibeleen relies on both her nurturant power (lines 34, 38, 40, 42, and 44) and her demeanor power (lines 36 and 44) as she tries to empower the little girl. The most interesting aspect of this scene from the perspective of language comes in line 43, in which the child reproduces Aibeleen's voice (and her grammar), illustrating that she has learned an important lesson from Aibeleen. Critically from the perspective of language variation, the child speaks as does her nanny rather than her mother.

While the entire scene, and really the entire film, is driven by an overarching set of resources linked to ideological power, those resources here are employed in especially nuanced and complex ways. At some level, the scene depends on the power of the standard language ideology to work; however, in this case, resistance to that ideology provides the overall effect. Further, the effect is as much for the characters in the film as it is for the audience watching. In voicing Aibeleen, Mae Mobley affirms not only the nurturant power Aibeleen is able to wield but also the demeanor power as apparent in her moral upper hand over the two white women (and by extension the power structures of the film's time and place). It is only through the resources of linguistic variation that this move is possible: the only way for it to be clear that Mae Mobley has learned the lessons taught by Aibeleen is to have a clear way of distinguishing Aibeleen's voice from that of other potential caregivers like her mother, Elizabeth. That mechanism occurs because of the grammatical variation between Standard English and AAVE. This power is further enhanced in Aibeleen's parting words to Elizabeth (line 49), which impugn her as a mother and solidify Aibeleen's moral authority. Of course, ultimately, Aibeleen has had to accept the economic power used by Elizabeth in confirming that she has been fired, but, as we learn in the final scene, Aibeleen intends to write further and thus to ultimately find a new source of economic support.

We have seen two major ways in which language variation is a central component to a narrative arc. On the one hand, language variation can actually be an important component of the overall plot development; on the other, it can be critical to the means of creating recognizable characters. Both of these effects will be explored further in the next two chapters. This chapter has shown the close relationship between beliefs about language (ideologies) and the ability of language to index character traits, character motives, and character interactions. The chapter has also illustrated how the linguistic variation we discussed in the previous chapters becomes meaningful beyond the referential content of words and grammar and thus emerges as a potent resource for narrative media productions.

Notes

1 As we discussed in Chapter 3, it's important to keep in mind that all transcription frames speakers in particular ways based on the decisions made about what exactly should be transcribed and how. Although there is no neutral transcription, being as clear about what you are transcribing, how, and why can help avoid unintended value judgments about the people being transcribed (see Ochs 1979 and Bucholtz 2000 for extended discussion of transcription).

2   It's noteworthy that one published script for *Happy Feet* represents most of the skuas' non-standard features, including 'aks' (Miller n.d.).
3   Louis Prima is presumably not a native speaker of AAVE; however, as Lippi-Green points out, the character King Louie is characterized in particular for scat singing, a style of singing with strong ties to both blues and jazz. As Lippi-Green comments, "it's not surprising that movie viewers generally believe that King Louie is voiced by an African American" (2011, 123).

References

Anderson, Benedict. 1991. *Imagined Communities*. New York: Verso.
Association of Black Women Historians. 2012. An Open Statement to the Fans of *The Help*. Retrieved June 6, 2013 from http://www.abwh.org/index.php?option=com_content&view=article&id=2%3Aopen-statement-the-help.
Bucholtz, Mary. 2000. The Politics of Transcription. *Journal of Pragmatics* 32: 1439–1465.
Bucholtz, Mary, and Kira Hall. 2004. Theorizing Identity in Language and Sexuality. *Language in Society* 34(4): 501–547.
Foucault, Michel. 1991. *Discipline and Punish*. London: Penguin.
Hill, Jane. 2008. *The Everyday Language of White Racism*. Malden, MA: Wiley-Blackwell.
Irvine, Judith, and Susan Gal. 2000. Language Ideology and Linguistic Differentiation. In *Regimes of Language*, ed. P. Kroskrity, 35–83. Santa Fe, N.M.: School of American Research Press.
Johnstone, Barbara, and Scott Fabius Kiesling. 2008. Whose Social Meaning? Indexicality, Identity, and Awareness of /aw/-monophthongization in Pittsburgh. *Journal of Sociolinguistics* 12(1): 5–33.
Kiesling, Scott Fabius. 1997. Power and the Language of Men. In *Language and Masculinity*, ed. S. Johnson and U.H. Meinhof, 65–85. Oxford: Blackwell.
Lippi-Green, Rosina. 2011. *English with an Accent*. New York: Routledge.
Miller, George. n.d. Happy Feet. Retrieved March 15, 2014, from http://www.imsdb.com/scripts/Happy-Feet.html.
Ochs, Elinor. 1979. Transcription as Theory. *Developmental Pragmatics:* 43–72.
Peirce, Charles Sanders. 1958. *Collected Papers of Charles Sanders Peirce*. Boston: Harvard University Press.
Queen, Robin. 2004. "Du hast jar keene Ahnung": African American English Dubbed into German. *Journal of Sociolinguistics* 8(4): 515–537.
Saussure, Ferdinand de. 1959. *Course in General Linguistics*. New York: McGraw-Hill.
Silverstein, Michael. 1979. Language Structure and Linguistic Ideology. In *The Elements: A Para-session on Linguistic Unites and Levels*, ed. P.R. Clyne, W.F. Hanks, and C.L. Hofbauer, 193–247. Chicago: Chicago Linguistic Society.

Silverstein, Michael. 1996. Indexical Order and the Dialectics of Sociolinguistic Life. Paper presented to the Salsa III, University of Texas at Austin.

Touré. 2012. Is *The Help* the Most Loathsome Movie in America? *Time.* Retrieved July 15, 2014, from http://ideas.time.com/2012/02/02/is-the-help-the-most-loathsome-movie-in-america/.

Woolard, Kathryn, and Bambi Schieffelin. 1994. Language Ideology. *Annual Review of Anthropology* 23: 55–82.

Chapter 6
Language Variation and Characterization

Introduction

Having thought about language variation in general, including how it becomes meaningful, we can start to look at how language variation does specific work for the narrative found in mass media. In the first part of this book we focused primarily on how narrative media provide a good venue for exploring language variation more broadly; then we looked at how language variation adds an element of social meaningfulness to interactions found in the media and at the basis upon which that meaning is made. Now we're going to turn to examine what language and language variation add to the media (rather than what media can reveal about language variation). Language achieves three main contributions to the media, and we will be addressing each of them in the remaining chapters. First, language variation adds substantially to the exposition, particularly of characters and their various identities, and that is the topic of this chapter. Second, language variation can push the story forward, which is the focus of Chapter 7, and finally, language variation connects the media product to its audience in various ways. That connection will be the topic of the final chapter of the book.

In Chapter 7 we explore how language variation helps move the narrative forward. While it is obvious that plot and characterization cannot be fully disentangled from one another, they are nonetheless slightly different lenses when focusing on language variation. For issues of characterization, we look at language variation based on how it is distributed

Vox Popular: The Surprising Life of Language in the Media, First Edition. Robin Queen.
© 2015 John Wiley & Sons, Inc. Published 2015 by John Wiley & Sons, Inc.

among characters and how those distributions add to the overall gestalt of a given character or set of characters (Androutsopoulos 2012). *Characterization* is linked to achieving individual distinctiveness, on the one hand, and to engaging general ideas of social similarity and social difference on the other. These two facets of characterization highlight why a given character might be simultaneously stereotypical and uniquely individual. Language becomes part of characterization through its connection to attributes that we might broadly consider the character's "identity." Often, it suffices to come close enough rather than to model exactly what people who inhabit these various identities may do in non-narrative life. When the narrative media hit that mark, great characters often emerge.

Some recent great characters from television include Omar Little, from the series *The Wire* (2002–2008); Carrie Mathison from *Homeland* (2011–), Walter White from *Breaking Bad* (2008–2013), and Liz Lemon from *30 Rock* (2006–). Similarly great recent film characters include the Bride from *Kill Bill* (2003, 2004), the Joker in *The Dark Knight* (2008, 2012), Tyler Durden from *Fight Club* (1999), and Ree from *Winter's Bone* (2010). What all of these characters, as well as many others, have in common is that they are memorable as individuals with knowable strengths and weaknesses, and they are recognizable as particular kinds of people in particular kinds of time and space. There are lots of different components for making characters memorable, but fundamentally it comes down to the question of convincing viewers that characters are who they are supposed to be within the context of the narrative itself.

Characterization is less about what the characters are doing specifically (though that of course is part of being believable as characters) and more about who the characters are. It may seem a little bit odd to talk about "what" or "who" characters are, given that they are in the most general sense figments of the imagination. In this case, it refers to various components of their identities, stances, and general personas and how those are created and maintained so as to be retrievable for the audience. These components may include the broad demographic characteristics the character inhabits, the personality quirks and traits s/he exhibits, and the connection of all of those to the situations in which s/he is narratively placed. Language variation, along with many other meaningful elements like costuming, gestures, and facial expressions, creates characters that are fundamentally believable.

In this chapter we look at the language of characterization, exploring how characters emerge as both recognizable versions of certain social kinds while, in the best of cases, also existing as distinctive individuals. Characterization is fundamentally about performance, a concept that we'll discuss in more detail in Chapter 7. The performance of a character (rather than, say, the idea of the character that a writer, director, or actor might have) engages the imagination of the audience and allows the audience to evaluate how believable the character is within the narrative context. The opportunity to explore the overt performances of fictional characters represents one of the real benefits of investigating characterization in the context of the narrative mass media because of the light it sheds on the more mundane, everyday performances all of us engage in as we go about our lives.

While it is certainly possible to render characters in ways that are extremely flat and stereotyped, including with respect to their language, narrative audiovisual media generally attempt to construct and present characters that are a nuanced blend of broad identity types and more individualized personality traits. These attempts are complicated by the fact that characters develop out of a writer's or director's imagination but are animated and performed by real people (actors) who have their own histories, identities, and personality traits. The language of characterization is thus influenced not only by who the characters are supposed to be but also by who the actors performing them are.

Characterization and Language

We use the stories of characters to get a sense of broader moral, cultural, and social landscapes, but, unlike in novels, the characters that emerge in audiovisual media are typically also real people who differ in distinct ways from their characters. Yet actors are frequently tasked with rendering characters in fictional dramas more or less independently of who the actor is in non-media life. Actors who look different from the characters they portray can alter those looks in various ways. Actors who sound different from their characters can do the same thing. If characters are from the American south, they need to sound like it; if they are from Australia, they need to sound like that.

Food for Thought

As quickly as you can, write down three things about yourself that you think make you yourself. Now, write three things about a character you really like from the narrative media. What do you know about them? How do your two lists compare with one another?

Many aspects of character identity, such as socioeconomic background, ability status, general personality, sexual orientation, place of origin, and general life experience, are assumed to be creatable through the craft of acting. Meryl Streep, for instance, is well known for her ability to sound like a realistic version of the characters she portrays, particularly when they have recognizable accents, and she has portrayed characters as varied as a Polish immigrant to the United States in the 1950s, Margaret Thatcher, a nuclear plant worker in the American south, an Australian in the outback, and a Danish aristocrat living in eastern Africa. Other actors, for instance, Tom Cruise, are not well known for managing accents, and in cases like his, the director may forgo using language as part of the background characterization. This was the case in *Valkyrie*, in which Tom Cruise plays the German colonel Claus von Stauffenberg but does not adopt any particular accent in doing so. Even though he didn't sound like a German speaking English, he did alter his language in other ways to convey a sense of von Stauffenberg as a character.

Androutsopoulos (2012) notes three specific ways that language variation connects to characterization and specifically to distinguishing characters. First, individual characters may use different codes. In Example 1.2 from the film *Love Actually* (2003), discussed in Chapter 1, Colin uses British English and the three women in the bar use American English. The codes themselves distinguish the characters. Second, individual characters may use the same code differently, either in terms of the frequency with which features of the code are used or the bundle of features from the code that a character uses. For instance, in Chapter 2, [IN] and [ING] pronunciations by the characters Phil and Jay from the television show *Modern Family* (2009–) were compared, with Phil using [ING] more frequently and Jay using [IN] more frequently. Finally, codes may be associated with different groups of characters. This differs from individual characters using different codes because, in this case, codes function to group sets of characters socially. A good example of this function between language variation and characterization occurs in media products that use invented languages. Thus, the Dothraki in *Game of Thrones* (2011–) speak Dothraki, and the Westerosi speak English. We will examine the concept of whole codes in much more detail in Chapter 8. For now, we can take Androutsopoulos' model as a broad theory of how the dynamics of language variation become married to characters.

For the most part, this aspect of characterization is established early in narrative media, either in the first episode of a new television series or in the first ten or fifteen minutes of a film. It also happens whenever a new character is introduced or when an established character's circumstances are significantly altered. An example of this early characterization can be seen in Example 6.1, which captures the first few minutes of the pilot episode of the crime drama series, *The Closer* (2005–2012), which stars Kyra Sedgwick as Brenda Johnson, the Deputy Chief of the Major Crimes Division of the Los Angeles Police Department.

Example 6.1   *The Closer*, "Pilot," Season 1, Episode 1, James Duff (creator), TNT, June 13, 2005

```
Three men with a general, regionally non-specific but
noticeably urban accent are examining a crime scene
involving a dead and mutilated body. The camera is
focused on the corpse.
```

```
1    Brenda:   Looks like love. <fronted vowel
                on<<love>>>
2    [Camera pans up to Brenda Johnson]
3    Tanaka:   who might you be?
4    Gabriel:  Dr. Tanaka, Deputy Chief Brenda Johnson,
                head of our new priority murder squad from
                Atlanta.
5    Brenda:   Nice ta meet ya Doctor.
6    Gabriel:  And you remember detectives Flynn and
                Waters, don't cha mam?
7    Brenda:   Yes, I do, nice to see y'all again.
                Mind if I jus' jump right in here,
                Doctor. Scuse me. Any sign of sexual
                assault?
```

8   Tanaka: I dunno. I'm not gonna examine until
                tomorrow. I'm just here to declare
                the victim dead and write it up as a
                homicide. Something a coroner's
                attendant usually does but some
                asshole in Parker's center insisted
                on a doctor.
9   Brenda: MM-hmm, that asshole would be me.
10   Tanaka: Oh, scuse me.
11   [The men look at each other]
12   Brenda: Look< fronted vowel>, Doctor, just inside
                the ear canal and on the edge of the
                lobe, that's not blood, it's dried vomit.
                Killer threw up, over here. See. The
                rug's discolo:ed.
13   [Brenda crawls over and sniffs at the rug]
14   Brenda: [coughs] Someone used detergent here
                to clean up the vomit. Might wanna move
                this light and put a marker over here.
                This crime doesn't look premeditated
                to me. Sorry to interrupt your evenin'
                doctor, but I'm gonna have to ask you
                to expedite this autopsy, and when the
                body's ready I'll go with you to the
                morgue. Thank you very much. <vowel
                in< <you> >very fronted>
15   [Brenda walks away]

The transcript starts 2:33 from the start of the show, and in less than two minutes Brenda Johnson's characterization is well established, largely through what she says. In addition to her general personality as smart, demanding, and highly competent, she is also unquestionably southern, which includes a specific form of performed politeness, evident in particular at the end of line 14. Her southernness is also clear in the set of linguistic features she uses. In the example, which represents the audience's first exposure to the character, Brenda uses very consistent /aI/ monophthongization, 'ya'll,' three instances of r-omissions (in lines 12 and 14), and several cases where the word final /r/ is nearly omitted. Additional features include lax final /i/ ('any,' line 7; 'sorry,' line 14), '-in' on 'evening' (line 14), fronted /u/ in virtually all cases, elongated vowels on most monosyllabic words, consonant cluster reduction, and raised /ae/ in 'asshole.' Although the audience is told that she is from Atlanta, it isn't until she speaks that the audience also understands that she is southern.

Food for Thought

Watch the first ten minutes of a movie or the first episode of a television show. How are the characters established in relation to one another? How is language part of character establishment?

Who the characters are in the narrative will also matter for how codes are connected to them and how they make use of the codes. In many animated films designed for children, the protagonist is more likely to use Standard American English while the antagonist is more likely to use an accented variety of some sort, as we discussed in Chapter 5 (see also Lippi-Green 2012). Alternatively, peripheral characters often serve the purpose, particularly early in the narrative, to provide an index to the local cultural context, in this way fulfilling the third function noted by Androutsopoulos (see also Bleichenbacher 2008, 2012). In *The Hunger Games* films, for instance, the main characters all speak Standard English, but some of the peripheral characters use grammatically and phonologically marked forms as a means of distinguishing different parts of the narrative universe, Panem. For instance, the peripheral characters in District 12 speak quite differently from those in the Capitol. These linguistic moves are typically linked to the same impulses around costuming, film locations and sets, and sound effects, which generally serve to create a knowable, "believable" context.

Realness and Authenticity

Despite considerable research into language in the mass media, a lot of the work that has concentrated on spoken language has centered on media venues that revolve around the broadcast of "real" events rather than on broadcasts of more obviously scripted events. Interesting presuppositions lurk in that decision, the clearest one being that such broadcasts approximate real-world language use in that they are more or less spontaneous and unscripted. In other words, non-fictional, less scripted media venues are presumed to involve language that is more real, more authentic. The dialects and accents portrayed are understood as the real speech patterns of the people on the screen. There are two related problems with this view. First, part of the illusion of the news and lifestyle media is this very realness since we have no way of knowing how real the language actually is. But the second problem with this view is its very perspective on realness. Is Meryl Streep's language less real when she is in character?

It may be true that a character exists only in the context of the media vehicle she appears in, but the embodiment of that character is real flesh; the sounds emerging from that character's mouth are real sounds; the grammar is (usually!) the real grammar of a human language. The patterns of variability may differ from those found in non-media communities, but that's only a problem if we assume that they should be the same. From my perspective, having watched and listened to a great many fictional media products, the more interesting questions concern linking the language patterns we find being used by characters to the broader language ecology we find in human communities generally. Monika Bednarek (2012, 200) writes, "audiences are interested in the 'lives' of televisual characters and engage with them emotionally and otherwise." In other words, fictional characters exist in that ecology just as you or I do. As James Atlas writes of watching the series, *Breaking Bad* (2008–2012),

> But if the story line propels me into my TV grotto, it's the realism that keeps me there. There's nothing artificial about "Breaking Bad" – the spell is never broken. The dialogue is pitch-perfect... . There comes a point when these are no longer actors to me: they are real people leading their lives. I spot a familiar face on the red carpet at the Academy Awards and exclaim, "That's Walt!" It turns out to be someone named Bryan Cranston. (Atlas 2013)

An important component of characterization, of placing a character into the language ecology of both the narrative and the ecology of the potential audience, involves being real enough to permit recognition (Marriott 1997, 183). This is the point at which it is likely useful to distinguish "real" and "authentic." What language variation in the narrative mass media shows us is that authenticity may be the more critical component of understanding how to place the media within the linguistic landscape. We know that the language Dothraki, as seen in the television series *Game of Thrones*, is not real in the sense that it is used natively in a human community. It is a language partially constructed for the fantasy series on which the television series is based and elaborated further by a linguist for the series. Even though it's not "real" in the sense that English is "real," it is authentic as a means of characterizing those characters who use it. For instance, Daenerys Targaryen learns the language when she is married to a Dothraki ruler as a means of securing his allegiance to her brother. Over the course of her character's development, however, the language becomes a means of indexing her growing persona as a ruler in her own right.

Food for Thought

The issue of accents and authenticity is often a source of intense fan discussion, as you can see in an online commentary on the accents on the television show *Game of Thrones* (Read 2013: you can access the discussion at http://goo.gl/OYi4Y). Do you agree with the author of the article that a discussion of accent authenticity is nitpicking?

Authenticity brings a variety of elements together to provide a degree of believability and a sort of truth about characters. Some of these elements include sincerity, trust, genuineness, and authority. Ultimately, authenticity captures a relationship between the ideas we hold about types of people or things (generalizations) and the ways individual people or things actually exist in the world (particularity). The more we perceive those to overlap, the more likely we are to perceive any given instantiation of them as authentic. Thus, we can think of authenticity as the cognitive and social work we do to connect generalization with particularity. Sometimes people refer to *authentication*, which moves more to questions of the processes by which authenticity is constructed rather than specifically a particular(ly) authentic outcome.

Authenticity may be why it doesn't matter entirely if the variation that shows up in the media is an accurate representation of the speech of actual members of whatever group is being represented. The media show us that our notions of what is and isn't real are tied to a set of ideologies – in other words, beliefs about how we know what is real, legitimate, and authentic. Authenticity is the link between ideological types and a specific character engaging in specific actions with other characters and contexts in an imagined narrative space.

Now we have two different concepts that link ideology to actual behavior out in the world: indexicality (which we discussed in detail in Chapter 5) and authenticity. We can think of these two concepts as capturing different aspects of the same basic process of connecting language variation to the wide range of possible social types and social actions that we encounter (and produce) and about which we hold ideas. Indexicality takes the raw language material and connects it to our rich set of beliefs about the world. Authenticity orders our indexical connections to help us make sense of individuals (characters or "real" people) as simultaneously singular and generalizable. Both indexicality and authenticity are thus tied to questions of identity and, by extension, to questions of characterization.

Identity and Identification

It's important to remember that the media are trying to evoke in the audience a sense of character identity. At its most basic, *identity* is about who or what something is perceived to be by either the self or others. What you are perceived to be (or not be) is linked to the available social categories that you have, the practices and attributes associated with those, and your ability to connect those in a way that others recognize. This link between person, behavior, and perception is true of most of the major social categories that people use to divvy up the cultural landscape.

Identity is about the representation of a self (one's own self or someone else's). On the one hand, that can mean something like a specific individual – Olivia instead of Owen. On the other hand, it can mean various characteristics that can be applied to different individuals who somehow share (or are believed to share) characteristics. For instance, many societies group people into gender categories, and the category you are grouped into becomes part of your identity (you are a "woman"). As with authenticity and authentication, there is a difference between identity and identification. *Identification* is more tied to the process of achieving, or of being recognized as possessing, a particular identity. The differences between the pairs *identity/identification* and *authenticity/authentication* point to how different processes of word formation allow us to clearly distinguish what we might call outcome from process. These distinctions allow us to shift our interpretive lens back and forth between a (possibly imagined) state of being at some specific point in time (identity) and the various processes we may engage in order to achieve that state of being (identification). Different analytic moments will necessitate different analytic lenses.

With those distinctions established, we can think of identity as a descrip-tion of the framings through which individuals and groups are socially categorized (by themselves or others) as particular selves, and we can think of identification as a description of how that social framing and social categorization occurs. With regard to narrative media, identity is the ideo-logical component of characterization, and identification is the outcome of the intersection of indexicality and performance that occurs in the course of enacting a character. In Example 6.1 from *The Closer*, Brenda Johnson is framed as from the south. Although Gabriel says that she has come from Atlanta, this in and of itself wouldn't necessarily construct the character as southern. After all lots of people who aren't southern might live in Atlanta. Her identity as southern comes more from framings that connect her language ideologically to southern American English and that juxtapose her language with that of the other people investigating the crime scene. Thus, her characterization includes an identity as southern American, and she is identified as such because of the linguistic indexes to the south that appear in her speech. You'll recall from Chapter 5 that indexicality is the mechanism of meaning that links ideology to performance (the actual instantiation of some kind of behavior). Brenda Johnson becomes southern as soon as the actor Kyra Sedgwick uses linguistic elements indexical of the south, and this performed identity is reinforced through its juxtaposition with the performances of the other characters on the show. This particular constellation points us beyond general questions of identity and identification and toward a slightly more complicated model for how identities are related to one another.

Relational Identity

As Mary Bucholtz and Kira Hall (2004) have talked about it, identity is always created relationally, though engagement with other people and material objects. This means that identities don't simply exist in people but emerge and are constantly developing as new interactions take place. For language, this means that we don't vary our language because of who we are; instead, varying our language is part of how we become who we are. The idea that the language we use makes us who we are helps explain why characters often have accents and dialects that differ from those of the actors portraying them and why people may complain about accents they don't perceive as authentic.

This can be a difficult idea to get our heads around because our own beliefs (ideologies, see Chapter 5) about identity lead us to understand behavior as largely driven by who we are. It seems obvious that Americans speak English because they are American or that men speak differently from women because they are men. However, where language is concerned, the relationship really seems to go in the other direction. One of the ways we become American is by speaking English (even though speaking English isn't a legal requirement for being an American citizen and certainly there are plenty of American citizens who don't speak English), and speaking English, specifically American English, will generally lead people to perceive you as American. In this sense, identity is always emergent rather than a fixed part of a person's being.

Relational identity works especially well for thinking about media because fictional characters are an example par excellence of emergent identities, as was apparent with Brenda Johnson in *The Closer*. In the media, clues to who a character is are necessarily highly *focused* (or concentrated). It's in the interest of the producers of the media product to make sure you have the information you need as a viewer to make the assessments they want you to make quickly. In other words, they are framing the story for you, and part of that is giving you the relevant clues to who the characters are supposed to be. It's this concentrated, or focused, framing (in real life, cues are often quite *diffuse*, and it may or may not be easy to do the work of categorization) that makes the media such a great source of information about cultural categories and the elements or features that are assumed to go along with them.

Brenda Johnson doesn't use every feature in the linguistic bundle that makes up southern American English but rather those features that are ideologically associated with the south, like the word 'y'all' or the '-in' pronunciation of <ing>. The more she interacts with the other people at the crime scene (and over the course of the seven-season series), the more her southernness emerges as a component of her identity in relation to the other characters and to the various situations in which she's placed. In a sense, Brenda Johnson becomes southern while the other characters do not, and this occurs by virtue of the differences between her language use and theirs.

As another example, take *Modern Family*, which we have examined in several previous chapters. The show revolves around three related families, the Dunphys: Phil, Claire, Haley, Alex, and Luke; the Tucker-Pritchetts: Mitchel, Cameron, and Lily; and the Pritchetts: Jay, Gloria, Manny, and Joe. Jay is the father of Claire, Mitchell, and Joe, who is an infant. He is the stepfather to Manny. All the families live in the suburbs of Los Angeles and are staunchly upper-middle-class. One adult in each household is a stay-at-home parent. The adult who works outside the home works in a white-collar environment. The majority of the characters are white; however, Gloria and Manny are Colombian and Lily is adopted from Vietnam. The majority of the characters are straight; however, Cameron and Mitchell are gay. Thus, we see some broad similarities that unite the characters as well as some juxtapositions among them.

All the characters but Gloria speak Standard American English. Gloria speaks Spanish-accented English, and her accent is the source of frequent commentary and misunderstandings and thus part of the humor of the show. The two boys on the show, Luke and Manny, differ from one another in their general orientation, with Manny being very dapper and hyperstandard and Luke being fairly goofy with a much more colloquial linguistic style. As we discussed in Chapter 2, the four adult male characters reflect somewhat different personalities and general orientations, in addition to being juxtaposed based on their sexual orientations. These differences map onto the relative frequencies with which they use the '-in' variant of < ing > .

What we see in *Modern Family*, as is the case with virtually any media product, is that there are many qualities that the characters share, including some of the ways they use language, but there are also ways in which they differ based on certain aspects of their identities, including their individual styles and personalities. Both the similarities and the differences among the characters are reinforced in each episode as they all interact with one another and with the audience (the show is a mockumentary, and the characters frequently address the camera directly).

Food for Thought

Pick a movie that you've watched recently and map out what characteristics different characters share and which ones are unique to individual characters. How might you represent the similarities and differences in the characters visually? Could you use a chart? A map? A diagram?

Hall and Bucholtz (2004) elaborate further on the relational dimensions of emergent identities and their framework provides a useful heuristic for thinking about fictional characters (and of course for thinking about regular people, too, which is who their model is intended to explain).[1] Three axes of their model are especially pertinent for thinking about characterization. First, there is a dimension based on similarity and difference. In this dimension, clues about how to group people based on how they are similar to one another come to the forefront. For instance, we look for things that all women, or all children, or all people who are wealthy, seem to have in common. At the same time, we pay attention to how groups of people are different. For instance, we look for what distinguishes women from men or children from adults or wealthy people from poor people. When we are paying more attention to distinctiveness, we tend to overlook the ways in which people who are in different groups may be similar and vice versa.

The second axis on which relational identity revolves is between being real and being fake. This axis is particularly important for characterization because of course at some level all fictional characters are "fake"; however, what Bucholtz and Hall have in mind here are cases in which people obscure some aspect of themselves, either intentionally or not. The film *Victor/Victoria* (1982) is a particularly good example of this. In this film, the main character, Victoria Grant (played by Julie Andrews), can't find work as a singer, so she decides to pretend to be the gay female impersonator, Victor Grazinski. Here, the "real" character is a woman and the "fake" character is a man. The artifice goes even further in that the "fake" man impersonates a woman. Of course, the impersonation is also fake. In the case of the impersonation, the artifice is fully known to the audience in the clubs at which Victor/Victoria performs; the fake is known to be fake (and the artifice is revealed in every performance in which Victor removes her head covering to reveal herself to be male). What is not known to the club audience is that Victor is being animated by Victoria, the "real" character. The film is a wonderful illustration of this particular axis, and the language use is similarly interesting. Without going into a lot of detail here, it is made more complicated by the positioning of Victor as a gay man, something done in part to account for his unusually (for a man) high pitch.

Bucholtz and Hall's final axis concerns legitimacy, or authority. In Bucholtz and Hall's formulation, this is where the workings of cultural and social power intersect with the emergence of identities, making some identities more legitimate than others. We can think here of the film we discussed in Chapter 2, *Chasing Amy* (1997). In that film, a young lesbian falls in love with a man, and the two of them must work out a variety of problems associated with that relationship. In Chapter 2, we examined her sharing with her friends that she is in love and using the gender-neutral singular "they" to obscure the gender of her attraction. In terms of the characterization/identity component of the character, Alyssa's identity as lesbian presents an issue of legitimacy for people evaluating the relationship between her and Holden. Being interpreted as a legitimate lesbian generally entails not being sexually/romantically involved with a man, and Alyssa's friends strongly sanction her for her involvement with Holden. More generally, though, Holden's friends and his business partner, Banky, have prejudice against lesbians, seeing that identity in a more essential, homophobic way. Here, two different sources of authorizing power are at work, one linked to the broad culture (of the time) in the case of Holden and his friends and one linked to a lesbian subculture in the case of Alyssa and hers. The broader culture saw lesbians as culturally and socially problematic; the subculture of lesbians depicted in the film saw a lesbian dating a man as problematic.

Bucholtz and Hall's model of relational identity takes us a long way toward understanding not only how identities are achieved in the "real" world, but also how they work in the worlds of narrative media. One component not explicitly built into this model, however, is the role of stereotypes and norms in the construction of emergent identities. With regard to characters as particular examples of emergent identities, it is clearly the case that some characterizations are more readily recognizable than others, a fact related to social norms and stereotypes.

Norms and Types

Holden and Alyssa, Victor/Victoria, Manny and Luke, and all the other characters we've discussed so far emerge because they, in a sense, bring ideologies about identity to life. As we saw above, identities are tied to interactions with other people, situations, and material objects. Over time, another dynamic occurs, namely, that expectations about identities appear in the form of norms. Like identities, norms emerge through the ongoing dynamics of interaction. In the narrative media, these interactions occur both among characters and between characters and the audience. Bednarek (2012), for instance, describes a case of a fictional character's death being discussed on the evening news, something she attributes to audience members' interest in the "lives" of characters and in engaging with those characters emotionally and otherwise.[2] After the "Red Wedding" episode in the third season of *Game of Thrones*, many fans had powerful emotional responses to the deaths of beloved characters (Smithsonian 2013).

A *norm* refers to the usual, typical, or average example of behavior. We can think of norms as the often unstated rules, or patterns, that regulate interaction and ways of being that are perceived by others as culturally or social appropriate. The adjective "normal" means conforming to a norm and suggests a particular state of being, while the adjective "normative" indicates the processes and institutional forces that seek to enforce a norm. Norms are the building blocks of generalization, and an implicit assumption involved in being "normal" is that it is desirable to be so. As one of the central institutions in most modern societies, the media are essentially normative, which means that the very process of representation available to mass audiences highlights some patterns and ways of being as typical. This normativity can lead to the perception among viewers that the media are also fundamentally stereotypical. Stereotypes and norms should be viewed as somewhat different analytic lenses with which to understand the relationship of individuals to social groups or social categories.

With respect to language, Labov (1972) has defined *linguistic stereotypes* as variation that is both noticed by speakers and about which speakers have specific judgments that may be widely discussed. He juxtaposes linguistic stereotypes against two other kinds of linguistic indexes: indicators and markers. *Linguistic indicators* are largely unnoticed correlations between language behavior and a particular social grouping of people. For instance, the construction 'needs' + past participle as in 'the car needs washed' is a linguistic indicator for parts of Ohio, Pennsylvania, and West Virginia. Most native speakers of English from those places use this construction, but there are few if any social judgments about it, even though speakers from other areas typically interpret it as not part of the grammar of English. *Linguistic markers*, by contrast, are correlations that people notice but don't generally have strong judgments about. Many of the vowel sounds associated with different regions of the United States are linguistic markers. Given the media's general normativity, it is precisely linguistic stereotypes that are most likely to be used by fictional characters. Language variation that the audience doesn't notice or have strong judgments about isn't particularly effective as an instrument of characterization.

As analytic lenses, however, norms and stereotypes can be slippery to work with because judging a representation to be normal (or normative) and/or stereotypical depends as much on the perspective of the audience as it does on the representation itself. Some viewers of *The Closer*, for instance, perceive Brenda Johnson's accent to be stereotypical; others perceive it to be non-normative (in the sense of not conforming to the norms of native speakers of southern American English). There is no clear-cut means for deciding if one, the other, or both perspectives are more accurate, which brings us back to the interactive and relational nature of characterization.

Food for Thought

Pick a favorite television series and focus on the characters as types of people. What types do you find represented? Do you think any of the characters are stereotypes? What makes them stereotypical? How does language variation figure into your assessment?

Viewers who are well acquainted with the types of people being represented may feel a degree of frustration when those characters don't seem to have the kind of complex and multilayered identities that we typically experience with non-fictional people. As we can see from this quote from a trade manual on using dialect in voice animation, what matters for media producers is that the characterization is both recognizable and retrievable to a broad audience.

> What is most important is that a dialect SEEMS authentic and that we can easily understand you. Does your character have a heavy accent or only a hint of an accent? In either case we must understand you clearly. No one is going to laugh at a gag or be touched by an emotional moment if they are concentrating on understanding the words instead. Remember that dialects used in animation may be less about authentic realistic speech and more about portraying a character in a way that is believable to the audience and funny. (Wright and Lallo 2009, 60)

Many citizens of Minnesota and generally the upper midwest in the United States, for instance, were dismayed at what they perceived to be the unrealistic representation of the dialect found in their part of the country in the film *Fargo* (1996).[3] However, people unfamiliar with the accent were often mesmerized and charmed by it. This pair of reactions taps into exactly the place of norms as components of identity and identification.

The role of familiarity in the evaluation of a character's language use points us to a few other concepts that can be placed in relationship to stereotypes, as they too involve the role of judgment in evaluating a given character. We can call this constellation of concepts *typification*, which includes archetypes, prototypes, and stereotypes. Broadly speaking, an *archetype* is the idealized example of a particular type against which all other examples are evaluated. A *prototype* denotes an initial sketch or early version of a type. Finally, a *stereotype* captures the relative social value, often negative, of a given type. Thus, we can think of an archetype as the more ideological concept, a prototype as the initial version of a particular instantiation of a type, and a stereotype as the evaluative overlay on the archetype. Stereotypes are perhaps the most consequential for characterization because they tend to oversimplify the type, rendering a character potentially flat and thus unbelievable as an actual person, as we see reflected in the quote below about *Fargo*.

> It's the cultural stereotypes in the film that are arguably more problematic. *Fargo* portrays Minnesotans as a group of people with an unwavering friendly reserve that remains unshaken even in the face of violence. As with many fictional works satirizing rural people, the film straddles the line between using loving humor and painting its characters as backwater oddballs. The accent has become emblematic of these stereotypes. (Trawick-Smith 2011)

The degree to which a given character is perceived as stereotypical will often depend on who is doing the evaluating and what their position is relative to the work or character being evaluated. For instance, compare the way that Frances McDormand, who plays Marge Gunderson in the movie *Fargo*, articulates the role of language for character background to the commentary about the film above:

> Marge was the most pronounced accent. Generations of her family came from there. So she wore it as a badge of authenticity. I was trying to make it authentic. I worked with a really wonderful dialect coach, Liz Himelstein, who is great because she just doesn't work with the technique of a dialect, she works with the character of a dialect. We really worked on how it could come out of me, through the script and then become Marge Gunderson. (Carey 2012)

Figure 6.1 Marge Gunderson from *Fargo*, Joel Cohen and Ethan Cohen (dir.), 1996, Working Title Films.

It is probably impossible to determine definitely when a character is problematically stereotypical since that determination occurs through ongoing critique and discussion among different audiences, including critics, fans, and researchers, as well as ongoing interactions among different media products. Our modern understanding of the characters in a film like *Gone with the Wind* (1939) has been strongly influenced by the range of films dealing with similar topics over the course of the many decades since the original release. Our understanding isn't necessarily more accurate or better than earlier understandings; however, it is based on a broader range of experience and information.

It is also probably not possible to completely avoid stereotypical representations given the variation noted above in people's familiarity with different social types and the characteristics and behaviors that we use to construct those types. What we can do, though, is understand that characters are always working with the same kinds of social norms that the rest of us do and that it is rare indeed for a character to have no connection whatsoever to a preexisting social type.

Social Personae

An alternative model to identity for thinking about characterization and types is a model based on social personae. Whereas identities may be conceived in terms of some particular state, *social personae* focus instead on the various roles, acts, and activities that it is possible for a person/ character to engage in. Thus, a role such as a diva, a mother, or a president can be inhabited by a range of types of people, just as different types of people may be involved in activities such as falling in love, robbing a bank, finding a treasure, or mitigating injustice.

One social persona that has been well represented in the US media since the 1980s, particularly in television, has been the nerd or geek persona. As Bucholtz (1999) describes this persona in her discussion of real-life nerds, the nerd persona stands in opposition to what we might call being "cool." This opposition may be marked through a host of different characteristics, including studiousness; technological, scientific, and/or science fiction and fantasy interests; hyperstandard language and delight in obscure aspects of language, including the lexicon; non-cool fashion sense; no interest in sports; not fitting conventional ideas of attractiveness; introversion; and generally non-cool means of social interaction (see also Bednarek 2012).

Lorna Jowett (2007, 33) describes the character Fred, from the television show *Angel* (1999–2004), for instance, as follows:

We know Fred is a science nerd because she talks like one ... although Fred often talks about "masculine" science ... her communication styles are feminine. She speaks with a sweet Southern drawl using a recursive (feminine) rather than linear (masculine) speech pattern – she says science words but doesn't actually talk like a scientist.

Here, the social persona of the nerd is intertwined with the identity category of gender, highlighting both that the normative nerd is male (we'll ignore the description of feminine styles as 'recursive' and masculine styles as 'linear' since this description makes little linguistic sense) and science-oriented.

Monika Bednarek (2012) has done a fascinating analysis of the character Sheldon in the television comedy, *The Big Bang Theory* (2007–), a show about two physicists and some of their friends. The show is fundamentally a representation of nerd or geek culture. Bednarek's analysis illustrates the connection between Sheldon's character traits and widely circulating stereotypes about nerds that exist outside the show (2012, 203). Bednarek focuses centrally on exploring the content of Sheldon's interactions, and shows specifically how a concordance analysis using a corpus of *Big Bang Theory* scripts (see Chapter 3 for more discussion of this type of methodology) provides the lexical basis for Sheldon's nerdiness. However, in Example 6.2 we can also see how the framework for thinking about identity and characterization that I've laid out in this chapter is at work in all areas of the grammatical systems used by the characters.

Example 6.2 *The Big Bang Theory*, "The Peanut Reaction," Season 1, Episode 16, Chuck Lorre and Bill Pardy (creators), CBS, May 12, 2008 (cited in Bednarek 2012, 13)

```
1  Penny:    Uh, Sheldon, I didn't see your present.
2  Sheldon:  That's because I didn't bring one.
3  Penny:    Well why not?
4  Howard:   Don't ask.
   Sheldon:  The entire institution of gift giving
             makes no sense.
5  Howard:   Too late.
6  Sheldon:  Let's say that I go out and I
             spend fifty dollars on you, it's a
             laborious activity, because I have
             to imagine what you need, whereas
             you know what you need. Now I can
             simplify things, just give you the
             fifty dollars directly and, you could
```

```
                    give me fifty dollars on my birthday,
                    and so on until one of us dies leaving
                    the other one old and fifty dollars
                    richer. And I ask you, is it worth it?
 7   Howard:        Told you not to ask.
 8   Penny:         Well, Sheldon, you're his friend.
                    Friends give each other presents.
 9   Sheldon:       I accept your premise, I reject your
                    conclusion.
10   Howard:        Try telling him it's a non-optional
                    social convention.
11   Penny:         What?
12   Howard:        Just do it.
13   Penny:         It's a non-optional social convention.
14   Sheldon:       Oh. Fair enough.
```

Bednarek presents this scene as an example of Sheldon's essential nerdiness and general lack of social skills. The majority of the characters on the show share the basic social persona of being nerds. The major exception is the character Penny, who is fundamentally juxtaposed against the others as a non-nerd, though someone with a lot of sympathy for nerds (in later seasons of the show, Penny and Sheldon's roommate Leonard are romantically involved). Although Penny is supposed to be from Nebraska, having moved to California to pursue acting, she speaks a more or less unmarked form of American English. Thus, Penny provides the relational component to the cast that helps foreground the nerd identities shared by the others. Second, even among the major characters who are nerds, there are distinctions. For instance, some viewers interpret Sheldon as having qualities associated with Asperger's syndrome (Bednarek 2012, 210). Unlike the other major characters, Howard doesn't have a PhD, something that is a regular source of narrative tension and humor. The two main female characters besides Penny are not physicists but biologists. While they are all native English speakers and in fact speak in very standard, often formal ways, each comes from a different location, something apparent in many of their accents. The character Raj has the most notable accent in that he speaks Indian English rather than American English. Sheldon's vowels place him from southeastern Texas, and Leonard's place him squarely in northern New Jersey. While Howard himself doesn't speak with a marked accent, his mother, with whom he lived for some time, has the canonical accents of someone Jewish from New York, an accent that Howard freely and frequently imitates.

As Bednarek (2012, 201–202) writes, "the focus is not on how 'real' or 'authentic' the analysed scripted dialogue is, but rather on how characters are established as stylised representations of particular social identities and on how narrative personae are constructed with recourse to stereotypes shared by audiences." By examining the character of Sheldon, we start to see how all the pieces of the characterization puzzle fit together and especially how language variation provides an integral means through which to achieve characterization, whether it is conceived in terms of identity, typification, or social persona, the three main concepts that have been linked to characterization in this chapter. Further, as a character, Sheldon from *The Big Bang Theory* works authentically as a nerd because he looks and behaves like the image that many of us have of nerds. And, of course, he sounds like a nerd.

At the same time, he differs from other nerds on the show through his own mix of particular characteristics that make him Sheldon and not Leonard or Raj or Howard, who also look, behave, and sound like nerds. This particularity adds to the sense of his authenticity because it keeps the character from flattening into an obvious stereotype. He seems believable as an actual person, not only as a figment of someone's imagination. He is both a type and an individual. As the next section illustrates, language plays an important role for creating characters (and people more generally) that are a believable blend of individual traits with more general social types/identities.

Food for Thought

Think about some of your favorite characters from television or film. What makes them individuals rather than just types or stereotypes? What components of language do you think add to your sense that they are individuals?

Indexical Authenticity

Both social traits and personality traits can be tied to indexicality, but the indexicalities are a little bit different from one another. Here, I will call them "type" indexicality and "trait" indexicality. In general, it's types that we typically think of as linked to something like language. *Type indexicality* is the meaningful connection of language to the broad set of social kinds that characters often inhabit. We can think of these both as their social demographics, like race, gender, age, sexual orientation, and class, as well as specific kinds of personae, like nerds, jocks, and girly girls. *Trait indexicality*, on the other hand, is the connection of language to variability within categories of social demographics and personae, such as being quiet, cheerful, melancholy, or energetic.

The film *Boyz n the Hood* (1991), directed by John Singleton, provides a clear example of how type and trait linguistic indexicality are at work. This film is set in south Los Angeles in the early 1990s at a time when there was much cultural concern over gang violence and the trafficking of illegal substances in urban areas. The film focuses on the friendship between three main characters, Tre, Doughboy, and Ricky, who live in a neighborhood that deals with both of these issues, but the film also contends with more mundane issues of teenagers' relationships to their parents, growing into adulthood, and general friendship. All three characters, as well as the majority of other characters in the film, use the dialect AAVE.

Although the characters all use the same variety of English, and although shifts to Standard American English among the three are quite restricted, they don't all use AAVE in exactly the same way, as demonstrated in Table 6.1, which highlights Tre and Doughboy. It turns out that many of the differences in how they use AAVE are related to aspects of each character's characterization and specific positioning in the film.

Figure 6.2   Tre and Doughboy from *Boyz n the Hood*, John Singleton (dir.), 1991, Columbia Pictures.

Table 6.1   Frequency of multiple negation and the null copula in *Boyz n the Hood*

	All characters	Tre	Doughboy
Multiple negation	78% (146/187)	65% (17/26)	82% (18/22)
Null copula	71% (385/402)	62% (51/82)	74% (35/47)

Source: Queen 2004, 527.

In Table 6.1, which is based on data from the last 60 minutes of the film, the frequency of multiple negation and the null copula are given for all characters and then for the characters Tre and Doughboy. Multiple negations are cases where more than one negative morpheme occurs in the utterance, such as "You don't know nothing," and the null copula is when a form of the verb 'to be' would occur in many varieties, including standard varieties of English but may be omitted in others, such as in AAVE, with an example being "We straight." In *Boyz n the Hood* overall, the frequencies of the AAVE variant of each strategy are relatively high, exceeding 70 percent for both features. Tre and Doughboy differ from one another with respect to their overall orientation to local street culture, with Doughboy being tightly connected and Tre being somewhat more peripheral. Correspondingly, Doughboy shows a higher frequency in both multiple negation and the null copula than does Tre.

The characters share most of the "type" characteristics we've discussed as markers of identity: their age, gender, race, neighborhood. Both are being raised more or less by single parents. There are some differences between them in terms of socioeconomic status; however, what distinguishes them is primarily their "trait" characteristics, something reflected in fundamentally different orientations to similar circumstances. This distinction between them is revealed through a range of cues, one of them being clearly in terms of language.

When characters exhibit different orientations toward the situations in which they are interacting, we can think of that in terms of their general *stance*. Stances represent an orientation toward activities and utterances, and are often signaled linguistically, for instance, with particular stylistic choices. The difference between "drug dealing is wrong" and "I think that drug dealing is wrong" can be understood as a reflection of stance. In the first instance, the stance of the speaker is of a generalized position presupposed to be shared. In the second instance, though, that position is relativized somewhat, which captures a slightly different stance toward the proposition about drug dealing. Broadly speaking, Tre and Doughboy have different stances with respect to involvement in street culture, and they also show different frequencies of use of various linguistics features.

Food for Thought

Choose a movie in which a couple of characters share type indexicality but differ on trait indexicality and/or stance. Then, choose a linguistic element (<ing> is often a very good feature to listen for) and find a transcript of the film. Can you do an analysis like the one I did for Tre and Doughboy? What makes such an analysis challenging? What makes it fun? If you actually do the analysis, can differences in stance explain any differences you find in the use of the linguistic elements you focused on?

What about cases in which the characters share both their general demographic characteristics and a stance toward the narrative situation in which they are placed but differ on something somewhat less tangible, like their basic personality? Here, we can turn again to the film *The Help* (2011) and the two main domestic workers, Aibeleen and Minny, in the film. In Chapter 5, we examined Aibeleen in an interaction with three of the white characters. There, it was clear that the demographic differences between the characters were connected to general type indexicality in the characters' language use. Aibeleen also exhibited clearly different stances toward each of the three characters: Elizabeth, her employer; Hilly, Elizabeth's domineering friend; and Mae Mobley, the child Aibeleen has raised. These different stances were linked to language as Aibeleen altered her language as she interacted with each of them.

In the case of Aibeleen's best friend, Minny, the situation is somewhat different. Here, the women share their basic demographic characteristics and many aspects of their stances toward the situations in which they find themselves.[4] Where they differ from one another is in having fundamentally different personalities. Aibeleen (played by Viola Davis) is quiet and dignified, and Minny (played by Octavia Spencer) is loud and sassy. Aibeleen tends to control her emotions, while Minny tends to express hers. One of the recurrent topics of conversation when Minny is involved is how her "mouth gets her into trouble." When she sends her oldest daughter to begin work as a domestic laborer, she expressly tells her to be careful not to "sass-mouth."

These differences in personality can be linked to language in the same ways that differences in stance and in broad demographic types can be. For instance, though neither character uses 'God' in any sense other than referring to a deity (while other characters frequently use 'Oh my God'), Aibeleen does not use any curse words, while Minny uses both 'damn' and 'hell.' Further, Minny makes use of a wider range of both

Figure 6.3 Minny and Aibeleen from *The Help*, Tate Taylor (dir.), 2011, Dreamworks.

pitch (the rising and falling of vocal tone) and amplitude (relative vocal loudness) across the course of the film, while Aibeleen maintains a narrow range for both, even in cases where she is expressing anger. In other words, Aibeleen doesn't yell, but Minny does. Finally, in her interactions with other black characters, Minny makes regular use of the interjection 'mm-hmm' to mean something along the lines of "I am not kidding you." This 'mm-hmm' is frequent in southern varieties of American English and especially AAVE. It differs from the more canonical agreement mm-hmm in terms of having the primary stress on the first syllable, a significantly longer first syllable, high pitch on the first syllable, and rising pitch on the second syllable. The agreement marker, on the other hand, typically has more or less equal length for both syllables, stress (marked with high pitch) on the second syllable, and generally falling pitch. These linguistic differences between the two characters help illustrate their different personalities and provide depth and nuance to the overall narrative.

As discussed in Chapter 5, the film *The Help* was criticized for what some interpreted as being overly stereotypical. Indeed, the film includes a questionable narrative arc concerning the relationships between black and white characters. Given the ways in which race plays a particular role across wide swathes of American history and culture, it is no surprise that the portrayal in both the book and the film met with intense debate. Focusing only on aspects of the characters, though, we can see that things are often a little more complicated than such debates make them out to be. Actors accepted these roles, and Viola Davis in particular was especially critical of the position that these characters were somehow unacceptably stereotypical. As quoted in the *Los Angeles Times*,

> "We weren't just shucking-and-jiving, Ebonics-speaking mammies," says Davis. "I think that *people* actually emerged behind the uniforms, and I think that's something that people haven't recognized. These were our mothers and grandmothers, and these stories are just as emotionally viable as others." – Viola Davis (Sperling 2011)

Davis' quote illustrates exactly what we have been discussing in this chapter. The emergence of characters is a complicated matter involving not only broad social types but also connections to people who live real lives. Authentic characters, like authentic people more generally, compel us to consider our experiences both alone and with other people, what we believe about ourselves and about the world, and why and how we are who we are.

Notes

1 Rather than use the term *identity*, they use the term *intersubjectivity* to account for the fact that we are all simultaneously producers of our own identities as well as produced as certain kinds of people by a host of social factors, pressures, and processes. To avoid too many different terms, though, I'm going to go ahead and use identity.

2 Fan fiction, in which people other than the original author or creator of a character imagine and write about new experiences and relationships for those characters, is a good example of this emotional and creative engagement.

3 This reaction is interesting in and of itself since the Cohen brothers, who wrote and directed the film, were representing a dialect with which they were fairly well acquainted, having grown up in the Twin Cities area. The fact that the film was a comedy may have played a role in the local reactions.

4 There are also differences. For instance, Minny is quite vocal about not trusting white people and not believing that integration is worthwhile. Aibeleen does not express a specific stance toward this issue in the film.

References

Androutsopoulos, Jannis. 2012. Repertoires, Characters and Scenes: Sociolinguistic Difference in Turkish-German Comedy. *Multilingua* 32(2/3).

Atlas, James. 2013. Get a Life? No Thanks. Just Pass the Remote. Retrieved December 4, 2013, from http://www.nytimes.com/2013/05/19/opinion/sunday/get-a-life-no-thanks-just-pass-the-remote.html?pagewanted=all&_r=0.

Bednarek, M. 2012. Constructing "Nerdhood": Characterisation in *The Big Bang Theory. Multilingua* 32(2/3).

Bleichenbacher, Lukas. 2008. *Multilingualism in the Movies: Hollywood Characters and Their Language Choices.* Tübingen: Francke.

Bleichenbacher, Lukas. 2012. Linguicism in Hollywood Movies? Representations of, and Audience Reactions to, Multilingualism in Mainstream Movie Dialogues. *Multilingua* 32(2/3).

Bucholtz, Mary. 1999. "Why Be Normal?": Language and Identity Practices in a Community of Nerd Girls. *Language in Society* 28(2): 203–223.

Bucholtz, Mary, and Kira Hall. 2004. Theorizing Identity in Language and Sexuality. *Language in Society* 34(4): 501–547.

Carey, Stan. 2012. *Fargo* Accent and Dialect Notes. Retrieved November 15, 2012, from http://stancarey.wordpress.com/2012/11/12/fargo-accent-and-dialect-notes/.

Jowett, Lorna. 2007. Lab Coats and Lipstick: Smart Women Reshape. In *Geek Chic: Smart Women in Popular Culture*, ed. S.A. Innes, 31–48. New York: Palgrave.

Labov, William. 1972. The Study of Language in Its Social Context. In *Sociolinguistic Patterns*, ed. W. Labov, 183–259. Philadelphia: University of Pennsylvania Press.

Lippi-Green, Rosina. 2012. *English with an Accent*. New York: Routledge.

Marriott, Stephanie. 1997. Dialect and Dialectic in a British War Film. *Journal of Sociolinguistics* 1(2): 173–193.

Queen, Robin. 2004. "Du hast jar keene Ahnung": African American English Dubbed into German. *Journal of Sociolinguistics* 8(4): 515–537.

Read, Max. 2013. What Is Going on with the Accents in "Game of Thrones"? Retrieved December 2, 2013, from http://gawker.com/what-is-going-on-with-the-accents-in-game-of-thrones-485816507.

Smithsonian. 2013. Why It's O.K. To Be Upset about Yesterday's *Game of Thrones*. Retrieved July 15, 2014, from http://www.smithsonianmag.com/smart-news/why-its-okay-to-be-so-upset-over-yesterdays-game-of-thrones-89113791/.

Sperling, Nicole. 2011. Viola Davis Worked Hard to Get "The Help" Right. Retrieved August 25, 2012, from http://articles.latimes.com/2011/nov/10/news/la-en-viola-davis-20111110/2.

Trawick-Smith, Ben. 2011. The "Fargo" Accent: A Joke that Never Dies. Retrieved September 23, 2012, from http://dialectblog.com/2011/05/29/the-fargo-accent/.

Wright, Jean Ann, and M.J. Lallo. 2009. *Voice-over for Animation*. Burlington, MA: Focal Press.

Chapter 7

Language as Narrative Action

Introduction

In the last chapter, we explored the place of language in constructing characters who are believable. An important component of that believability was for characters to be who they are supposed to be within the narrative context in which they appear. In this chapter, we will think about how language helps situate those characters within that narrative context – in other words, within the overall plot. The plot of a narrative consists both of the set of sequenced events and actions in which characters engage and of the web of relationships that those actions help construct (Booth 2012, 314). According to Thompson (2003), the majority of audiovisual media products organize plots in traditional ways going back to Aristotelian ideas that stories have clear beginnings, middles, and ends that serve to build the various pieces of the narrative into a coherent, entertaining whole. Some audiovisual products tweak that traditional narrative scheme. The series *Seinfeld* (1989–1998), for instance, was well known for being a show about nothing. Still, the more or less straightforward nature of plots in many audiovisual media is one of the reasons that many scholars eschew exploring plot in the pursuit of seemingly meatier elements of analysis.

Although narrative media plotlines may lack a certain degree of complexity, the question of how the plot actually progresses may not be as straightforward as it seems at first glance. Considering just television, for instance, some plotlines may develop over the course of an entire season, or even set of seasons, while others are specific to a given episode. Indeed one of the hallmarks of many of the great television series

Vox Popular: The Surprising Life of Language in the Media, First Edition. Robin Queen.

of the early twenty-first century has been the complexity of plots that develop over the course of the whole series being embedded with plot-lines developed through a single season as well as with episode-specific plots. Dramas like *The Sopranos* (1999–2007), *The Wire* (2002–2008), *Dexter* (2006–2013), *Breaking Bad* (2008–2013), *The Good Wife* (2009–), and *Homeland* (2011–) all embed multiple layers of plot, with each discrete episodic plot typically feeding the plotline of the season as well as the plot trajectory of the whole series. The multilayered nature of the plots is a large part of what makes these series so popular and distinguishes them from films, which typically do not have the temporal luxury of developing plots over such a long period of time (Thompson 2003, 35).

Food for Thought

Compare the plotlines of a single episode, a full season and the full series for a television show. How do the different plots interact with one another? If you were devising a storyline, would you rather work with the plot of a movie or a multi-season television series? What do you see as the challenges and benefits of each type of plot?

Most of us think about the twists and turns in a story as capturing the primary elements of the plot. Often, those twists and turns are captured by specific kinds of events: someone gets shot; the train conductor closes the door and the train pulls out of the station; two people's eyes meet across a crowded room; the gavel comes down. The physical actions of the characters represent one of the most apparent ways in which the plot unfolds, and those actions are typically considered what the characters are "doing." However, often the plot unfolds by virtue of things the characters say. *The Good Wife*, for instance, begins with a political apology on the part of the main character's husband, and that apology sets the whole narrative machinery in motion. Characters professing their love for one another, threatening one another, apologizing to one another, and negotiating with one another enact critical elements of the plot in exactly the same ways as characters running down a street, entering a store, cooking a meal, or buying a train ticket. The main difference is that we typically don't think of language as performing actions in the same ways as we think of it as reflecting and representing actions. But language can perform actions directly by virtue of the different kinds of meanings it points to and by the details of its actual use. If you think back to Chapter 3 where I discussed qualitative methods, you may recall that such methods typically allow for the careful exploration of conversational unfolding. This kind of unfolding represents exactly what it means to say that language can "do" things. In this sense, language functions to link micro-level actions to the macro-level elements in the plot. In this chapter, we focus on exactly this linkage in order to see how language functions as narrative action and in turn how thinking about language as action illustrates some of real creativity and complexity involved with moving a plot from beginning to end.

Performance and Speech Acts

The first step for thinking about language as narrative action requires thinking about action as *performance*. Performance is, of course, a fundamental concept for fictional media generally, and thinking about the similarities and differences between what we can call staged performance and what we can call performed action will set the foundations for thinking about how language serves as action in the context of fictional media. Whenever an actor steps on the stage or in front of a camera, she is entering into a fictional performance of the sort we looked at already in Chapter 6. If we take the staged or fictional sense of performance, what we typically mean is someone stepping outside of him- or herself and enacting a role in order to provide entertainment for an audience. Richard Bauman has articulated fictional performance as central to understanding the relationship of the knowledge of a language (as a particular system) and its use, illustrating the often creative and situated quality of that knowledge as it emerges in moments of staged performance (Bauman and Sherzer 1989; Bauman and Briggs 1990; Bauman 2011). Staged performance arises as this central link because it brings what Roman Jakobson (1960) called the *poetic function of language* into sharp relief. In Jakobson's formulation, the poetic function of language highlights the interrelationships of language form and function. Thus, staged performance creates the space to focus specifically on those interrelationships, which in turn facilitates the recognition of that same relationship in off-stage contexts like regular, everyday life.

The other sense in which we can think of performance is simply in the act of "doing" – 'performing a task' means that that we are carrying out or accomplishing that task. Surprisingly, language itself can be the source of performed actions. In other words, language can do the action it names.

There are some simple examples of how this works linked to individual words. These have been called *performative verbs* (Austin 1961). For instance, if I promise you that you'll enjoy reading this book, then the act of using the verb 'promise' enacts, or performs, itself. Using the verb makes the promise happen. There are of course other ways of making promises, but the point here is to see that if you use the verb 'promise,' you have performed the action captured referentially by the verb itself. There are many verbs whose meanings are directly performative, including 'declare,' 'apologize,' 'swear,' 'pronounce,' and so on.

Food for thought

How many examples of performative verbs can you think of? (Hint: any verb that you can preface with 'hereby' and not really change the meaning is very likely to be a performative verb.) Pay close attention to conversations around you (yes, eavesdrop!). How many different performative verbs do you hear? Which ones?

In Example 7.1, from the film *The Bridges of Madison County*, the performative verb 'apologize' plays an important role in a critical scene in the developing love affair between the two main characters. In this film, Francesca's family has left for the Iowa State Fair, leaving her home to tend the farm alone for a few days. During those days, she meets a photographer and they fall in love. As we see in Example 7.1, the early contours of that affair take shape entirely through the performed actions embedded in the language they use together.

Example 7.1   *The Bridges of Madison County*, Clint Eastwood (dir.), 1995, Warner Bros.

```
1  Robert:     Do you want to leave your husband?
2  [Francesca looks surprised]
3  Francesca:  No. Of course not. [rising from table,
               upset)
4  Robert:     I'm sorry about that. I apologize.
5  Francesca:  What made you ask such a question?
6  Robert:     I thought that's what we were doing [..]
               asking questions. It was stupid, I'm
               sorry.
```

```
 7  Francesca:  <defensive>No, I thought we were just
                having a conversation. You're asking
                me these questions, you're reading all
                these meanings into it. Meanings I
                must be too simple to, understand or
                interpret or something.
 8  Robert:     I'm sorry. I apologize.
 9  [Silence. Robert remains seated. Francesca remains
    at the sink.]
10  Robert:     It's getting late. [rises] Thank you for
                dinner.
11  [Pause. Francesca looks down.]
12  Francesca:  Look, I'm sorry I [
13  Robert:                        [No, I apologize.
                You must forgive me. It was a very
                indiscreet question. It was dumb.
14  Francesca:  [shrugs it off] I feel like something's
                been spoiled now.
15  [Robert smiles and takes her hand.]
16  Robert:     It's been a perfect evening. Just the
                way it is. Thank you.
```

In this scene, Robert says both "I apologize" (lines 4, 8, and 13) and "I'm sorry" (4, 6, and 8) three separate times. Taken together with his other comments, we see that he recognizes that he has done something to upset Francesca and that he feels bad about it and wants to make amends. In others words, he genuinely wishes (intends) to make up for what he said. Interestingly, the verb 'apologize' and the adjective 'sorry' differ in the degree to which they can directly do the work of apologizing. 'Sorry' is an adjective describing a particular state of being, something like feeling remorseful or sorrowful. While its expression can be used to indicate an actual apology, that function is more indexical than embedded in the referential meaning of the adjective itself. This contrasts with 'apologize,' in which the act of apology is embedded in the referential content of the verb. 'Apologize' means what it referentially names. While it's clear that both Robert's utterances are intended to express regret, only the verb 'apologize' can do so directly via its referential meaning. It's this property that led J.L. Austin to focus on the ability of verbs like this to do things. His book on this topic is in fact called *How To Do Things with Words* (Austin 1975).

At some level, all performances (in both the staged and the non-staged sense) are constantly evaluated for whether or not they work. This is true for being believable as a character, as we saw in Chapter 6; it's true for particular activities that characters engage in; and, as we see in Example 7.1, it's true for performative verbs like 'apologize.' The success of a verbal performance has been called *felicity* by Austin and others, and is part of a broader theory known as *Speech Act Theory.* Speech Act Theory attempts to account for how we are able to do things with language beyond simply describing and representing. This can include doing things like apologizing or things like being believable as a certain character or as a certain kind of person. Often these different goals will interact and overlap. For each, though, felicity is one critical mechanism for being able to perform with language because felicity sets the conditions under which speech acts can be interpreted as successful.

Some felicity conditions will be specific to the performance and some will be specific to the performers. For instance, in Example 7.1 involving apologizing, one of the felicity conditions for an apology is that the apologizer wants to make amends. Another condition is that the person being apologized to interprets the apology as sincere. In the scene, Robert keeps repeating his apology because Francesca doesn't immediately accept it. In lines 5 and 7, she contests Robert's initial question in a sign that she recognizes the sincerity of his regret but is not yet willing to forgive him for it. We can thus separate her recognition of the apology as legitimate and her acceptance of it. For his part, Robert interrupts Francesca's apology (lines 12–13), reiterating his own regret strongly and asking specifically for her to forgive him. In line 14, Francesca appears to be apologizing for putting a damper on the evening. Robert's interruption indicates that he understands what she is doing but is still trying to convince her to accept his apology. For words (and language more generally) to be successfully performative, the performative act requires that the listener/audience recognize it as such. In this sense, successful performances depend on the identities of the people involved and on the context in which they find themselves. Additionally, three general felicity conditions hold for all performances and are generally critical to the performance being successful. These are *authority, context,* and *citation.*

The first condition focuses on the authority to do the performance. Authority is often linked specifically to aspects of the identities of the people involved. In order to understand the authority Robert brings to the task of apologizing in Example 7.1, we have to first understand who Robert and Francesca are as characters, much as we discussed in Chapter 6. Robert is a particular kind of man, one who prides himself on not caring what other people think of him and on not being beholden to other people. A second component of authority depends more directly on the action itself. In Example 7.1, for instance, the authority to do the apology depends on Robert having done something that he sincerely wants to make amends for. In this case, he asked an indiscreet question and he feels badly for having done so and wants to make it better. Thus, he has the authority to perform this particular speech act because of who he is as a character and what is required of a successful apology.

Alternatively, an action generally won't be successful if the person doing the act lacks the authority to do it. I can't successfully promise to buy every reader of this book ice cream. If I were to state "I promise to buy you, the readers of this book, ice cream," you wouldn't believe me because you wouldn't believe that I have the ability to fulfill the promise. In other words, I lack the authority for that particular speech act specifically because I do not have the ability to fulfill it. In the case of the act of apology highlighted in Example 7.1, the authority condition for apologies generally is met. Further, the authority of Robert as a character makes the apology felicitous within the specific narrative context of the film and facilitates this micro-interaction being linked to the macro-narrative context of their love affair.

Another condition for a speech act to be successful is that it has to be done in an acceptable context, which means that it has to be done in a context in which it *could* be successful. Robert's apology to Francesca occurs in such a context, namely, a particular interactional situation between the two of them. My promising to buy you ice cream is not performed in an acceptable context for that promise. My promising that you'll enjoy reading this book would an acceptable context since that's what you're doing.[1] In the absence of a context in which the performance could be successful, it will be unsuccessful, or infelicitous. We can see an example of this with Michael Scott from *The Office* (2005–2013).

Example 7.2 *The Office*, "Money," Season 4, Episode 4, Ricky Gervais and Stephen Merchant (creators), NBC, October 18, 2007

```
Michael walks into the office space

1  Michael:   I declare BANKRUPTCY!
2  [later in Michael's office]
3  Oscar:     Hey, I just wanted you to know that you
              can't just say the word "bankruptcy" and
              expect anything to happen.
4  [Michael is sitting at his desk, cutting up a credit
   card]
5  Michael:   I didn't say it, I declared! it.
6  Oscar:     Still. That's, that's not anything.
```

In this case, Michael has the authority to declare bankruptcy; however, the context in which such a declaration is felicitous is generally a court-room or at the very least a context in which one's financial status is relevant. As Oscar points out to him, uttering the words doesn't itself constitute a successful speech act. In line 5, Michael points out that he has used a specifically performative verb to do the action, but the lack of the appropriate context means that the act is nonetheless infelicitous, as Oscar makes clear in the final line.

The final general condition for a successful, or felicitous, performance is that the performance has to be recognized as the action that it is performing. In many ways, this condition is the most critical because it connects the performer with the audience or recipient(s) of the performance, illustrating the importance of the interaction between them for the success of a performance. The recognition of the performance as an example of a previously felicitous performance of the same type is known as citation. Citation is a means of referring to another instance of the same thing. In scholarly writing, citation means that someone else has said something similar to (or, in the case of direct citation, exactly) what the author has just said. Citation in this sense is used to offer support for the validity of what is being said. In the performative sense, it does something similar in that it allows the recipients to do a kind of comparison between other examples of similar acts that they know of and the act that they are currently evaluating. The citations for a felicitous promise, for instance, are examples where that type of promise was made and also fulfilled. My promise to buy all the readers of this book ice cream probably fails most directly as a felicitous promise because of citation. Promises of that type involving lots of unknown people are not only difficult to fulfill, they are also rarely fulfilled. Thus, that promise might be understood as citing previously infelicitous promises and on those grounds isn't likely to be accepted as a true promise.

We can see an example of citation (or, in some sense, its failure) in the British comedy show *Little Britain* (2003–2006). The scene comes from a weight loss meeting where the leader has been berating and making fun of the people there for being overweight. Pat finally has enough and says that she's leaving. The leader, Marjorie, doesn't want anyone to leave, so Pat requests an apology as a condition of staying.

Example 7.3   *Little Britain*, "Hard-Boiled Egg Eating," Season 1, Episode 3, Matt Lucas and David Walliams (creators), September 30, 2003

1	Pat:	I'm waiting [..] for an apology.
2	Marjorie:	I'll come back to you my love.
3	Pat:	I don't see why you can't just say sorry.
4	Male group member:	Yeah, come on.
5	Marjorie:	I can. I can say sorry.
6	Pat:	Well go on then.
7	Marjorie:	Well I'm gonna say it. Any minute now.
8	Male group member:	Well, say it.
9	Marjorie:	I'm about to.
10	Pat:	Go on.
11	Marjorie:	<mumbles inaudibly>
12	Pat:	I didn't hear that.
13	Marjorie:	Well I said it, so

14   Male group   Yeah, well, we didn't hear it either.
      member: Come on, let's go.
15   [Other group members get up.]
16   Marjorie: I'm gonna say it I'm gonna say it I'm
                    gonna say it I'm gonna say it I'm
                    gonna say it I'm gonna say it I'm gonna
                    say it I'm gonna say it I'm gonna say
                    it I'm gonna say it I'm gonna say it
                    [getting quieter every time]
17   [Leader approaches Pat as other group members
      watch on. Leader takes Pat's hands and looks her
      straight in the eye.]
18   Marjorie: I (.) am (.) very (.) sorry (.) That
                    you are so fat!<very fast>Oh no, it
                    just came out!
19   [Group members move to exit]
20   Pat: So rude.

The members of the weight loss group are remarkably willing to allow Marjorie many chances to do a felicitous apology, although we might argue that performing a felicitous apology that has been solicited by others will often have a higher bar since one of the conditions of felicity for apologies is that the apologizer recognize that s/he's done something that has upset the apologizee(s) and that s/he wants to make amends. In Marjorie's case, it is clear enough from each of her turns that she does not really want to apologize. When she finally does apologize in line 18, using the indirect apology form by using the adjective 'sorry,' it begins as if she's sincere. She slows down her speech and pauses between each word. Her voice quality is also contrite, soft, and serious. The pause after 'sorry' along with a lowering of her pitch lead to an interpretation that she has performed the apology since apologies may be judged as infelicitous when there is rationalization or further explanation attached to them and so far, that is absent. However, following the pause she adds exactly such rationalization and does so in a loud, fast, excited manner. That context alone would indicate that the apology probably won't be judged felicitous; however, the content of the relative clause that follows 'sorry' also makes it clear that Marjorie is playing on one of the alternative meanings of 'sorry.' As noted above, 'sorry' can mean both regret and sorrow. In this particular case, what appears to be regret for what Marjorie herself has done (which is what is necessary for an apology) shifts to an expression of sorrow for Pat's state of being fat. Marjorie immediately acknowledges the infelicity of the apology with her final words, "Oh, no, it just came out," which further distance her from taking responsibility for her actions. Pat, of course, also acknowledges the infelicity of the apology in her final line of the scene.

On the one hand, we can see this as a virtuoso staged performance on the part of the actor of a self-obsessed woman who derides people she judges as inferior to herself. The performance is particularly interesting because Marjorie is played by a male actor, Matt Lucas, and this show, *Little Britain*, is known for having male actors animate all of the central characters, including the female characters. So, we have multiple layers of character performance. On the other hand, we see the capability of language to be the source of performed action. The plot of the scene is driven by the performative power of language, the ability of language itself to "do things" (as compared to only being able to reflect things). There is little physical action in the scene and most of the plotline proceeds linguistically, specifically around the felicity of the apology.

Food for Thought

Find a scene in a movie or a television show that involves only conversation (and no other physical actions). What elements of the plot are furthered through that conversation? What specifically gets "done" within the conversation?

Language as a Plot Device

Specific performative words represent only one means through which language can perform actions or events. Language can also perform as a *plot device*. In general, a plot device is an idea, object, situation, or other component that moves the plot forward. Interestingly, the specific details of the device are often not particularly relevant to the story. Some examples of plot devices include: the ring in the *Lord of the Rings* trilogy; James Ryan in *Saving Private Ryan* (1998); and the blue methamphetamine in *Breaking Bad*. Plot devices are sometimes considered a narrative trick and derided; however, we can also think of them as the mechanisms through which narrative action progresses, and, in this sense, many, if not most, narratives will include some kinds of plot devices.

In some ways, language lends itself well to being a plot device, and numerous examples illustrate this. For instance, the stutter found in the character King George in the film *The King's Speech* (2010) is the topic around which the entire film revolves, and in the scene from *Love Actually* (2003) that we explored in the first chapter, language, in the form of the differences between British and American English, serves largely as the plot device moving Colin's storyline forward. Constructed languages can serve as a plot device as well, as is the case with parseltongue in the Harry Potter series or Dothraki in *Game of Thrones* (2011–).

Food for Thought

Make a list of plot devices in movies and television show (you can find many such lists online by searching the keywords "plot device"). For those that you are familiar with, what makes these objects/characteristics plot devices? How do they compare to similar objects or characteristics that aren't plot devices?

In "Little Bo Bleep" of *Modern Family* (2009–), Cameron and Mitchell's daughter, Lily, provides one of the plotlines as she prepares to be the flower girl in a wedding. In Example 7.4, she is practicing strewing the petals, and curses when she makes a mistake (line 7).

Example 7.4   *Modern Family*, "Little Bo Bleep," Season 3, Episode 13, Christopher Lloyd and Steven Levitan (creators), ABC, January 18, 2012

1	Cameron:	Right over here. Okay. There you go. Oh, like you're coming down the aisle!
2	Mitchell:	Yeah. Yeah. Okay.
3	Cameron:	Not too many at once.
4	Mitchell:	That's good. Okay. You're doing great, Lil.
5	Cameron:	Oh, she is, isn't she?
6	Mitchell:	Forget the bride. All the eyes are gonna be on her.
7	Lily:	Oh [bleep]
8	Cameron:	@@@@
9	Mitchell:	I cannot believe you laughed!

10	Cameron:	I am sorry. But you know I have two weaknesses[. . .] children cursing and old people rapping.
11	Mitchell:	Cam, we have to tell her it's a bad word.
12	Cameron:	No. That just gives it more power. The less we make of it, the better. Let's just pretend like it never happened.
13	Mitchell:	Okay. Yeah, maybe it [..] maybe it didn't. Maybe we [..] maybe we misheard.
14	Cameron:	Yeah. Maybe she said "truck." Or, or, "duck." Or "luck." She could have said "yuck."
15	Lily:	Daddy, can I have some ice cream?
16	Mitchell:	No, honey, if you're hungry, you can have some fruit.
17	Lily:	Fruit? [bleep]
18	Cameron:	@@@@@
19	Mitchell:	I have two children.

Later, during the wedding, Cameron is crying as he watches the bride and Lily curses in order to cheer him up, making it clear that she hasn't really understood the word (the episode starts with Cam and Mitchell discussing words Lily understands). The mostly unspecified taboo word is central to this part of the overall narrative, even though it is never actually heard by the audience. Because she doesn't know what the word means (or can mean), Lily can't actually use it to do many of the things that taboo words regularly do, such as curse someone.

The taboo word she uses is a plot device specifically because it doesn't really matter what specific taboo she uses. Interestingly, as a plot device, Lily's taboo words link together the two different ideas of performance that we talked about above. First, the cursing functions as staged performance on the part of the character Lily, particularly in the wedding where she is performing in front of a church full of people. Second, Lily attempts to use the taboo word as a performative action that will cheer up her father. The act is infelicitous based on Lily's lack of authority to use the taboo word and, in the case of the wedding, the inappropriate context in which it is being used. The humor, though, comes specifically from the intertwining of Lily as a character, the form of language involved, and the various functions it fulfills within the narrative context of the episode.

Many scholars have argued that the poetic function as described by Jakobson actually is a part of all acts of using language (Butler 1997; for language, see Bucholtz and Hall 2004). This duality of form and function, also captured in the duality of performing particular kinds of identity while also performing specific actions, has been called *performativity* in the literature. Performativity unites the act of creating some specific kind of social fact (such as a specific kind of identity) with the judgment by an audience (here conceived in broad terms) about how felicitous the performative act is. When an actor like Meryl Streep receives praise for her various portrayals, that praise serves as verification of a successful performance of those characters. Similarly, when someone asks me a question about language because they know I am a linguist, that question serves as an indication that I have performed in a felicitous manner as a linguist. In other words, I am recognizable to the question asker as at least one of the identities I have tried to perform.

These start to be quite heady concepts, and many pages have been written arguing about and refining their details. For thinking about language as action, we can think of performative lexical items (like verbs), performative social acts, and staged performances as related to one another via the three conditions of felicity: authority, context, and citation. In this sense, all (performative) acts are embedded in a social matrix in which "being" is only feasible through "doing," and "doing" is only recognizable through felicity – in other words, through the interpretive evaluation of an audience.

We can think of many of the examples we've looked at in previous chapters as performative in the sense that the variation does broad work in the narrative. In such cases, it's not the semantics of the elements being used that are performative, as is the case with words like 'declare' and 'apologize'; rather, it's often in the juxtaposition of one way of speaking with another that the performative element emerges. In these cases, we can argue that it's language variation specifically that does the performed action, something we see clearly in cases where the actor switches between different styles, dialects, or languages.

Switching as Action

In the *Little Britain* case above, the shift in speaking styles represented the primary means through which the audience (both in-media and outside) recognizes the infelicity of the apology the leader is making. Shifting speaking styles can be a powerful performative action, and speakers frequently use shifting their speech as a primary method for doing all kinds of performative work. Shifting can be between different styles, as is the case in the examples we've discussed so far, or it can involve shifting between conventionally more distinct varieties such as dialects and languages, which we discussed in some detail in Chapter 2. *Code-shifting* (or code-switching) is the term most often used to capture the act of moving back and forth between either different dialects or different languages. Code-shifting can involve single words, small bits of one code being used in the context of another code, or longer stretches, such as whole turns being in one code and then switching to the other. There is a vibrant research tradition that examines code-switching from a wide range of angles (see Gardner-Chloros 2012). Our interest here lies in its connection to performing certain kinds of actions and the degree to which it can function much like the performative verbs we examined in the last section.

Code-shifting minimally involves people who have more or less fluent command of the codes being used; thus, code-switching is a phenomenon that involves either bi- (or multi-) lingualism and/or bi- (or multi-) dialectalism. This means that code-switching can be a part of the linguistic repertoire used to do various kinds of speech acts, and this includes being part of the repertoire available for moving the plot of a narrative along within the fictional media. The following scene from the television show *Weeds* (2005–2012) captures an example of code-shifting involving two different dialects.

Example 7.5   *Weeds*, "Cooking with Jesus," Season 2, Episode 2, Jenji Kojan (creator), Showtime, August 21, 2006

```
1  Conrad:   So I wanna grow hydroponic, gourmet
             organic lettuces.
2  Tyrell:   Come on Conrad, cut the shit, bro.
             Lettuces?
3  Conrad:   Lettuces!<rise in pitch>You see what
             Whole Foods be chargin' for arugula and
             endives and shit?<lower pitch>Tyrell,
             Tyrell, there's money in there, man, I'm
             tellin' you.
4  Tyrell:   Fine, that's how you want to play it?
             I don't see how you could possibly make
             enough to cover your expenses, much less
             make a profit usin' this business model.
             You ain't makin' no fuckin' lettuce.
```

5 Conrad: You talkin' funny right now, dude. This
            how you talk to all your customers?
6 Tyrell: I do when I shared a bunk bed wid 'em at
            the YMCA camp. And even if we didn't go
            way back, bro, any loan officer's gonna
            know you wanna grow some "booyah."
7 Conrad: Can you hold it down?

8 Tyrell: [talking to a white colleague]
            <significant style shift>Hey, Jim,
            ah, I got your email. I'll have those
            loan estimates for you by 3 pm, buddy.
9 Conrad: <shifts to "white" voice, very nasal>
            Hey, Jim, whaddaya say we get together
            after work for like some shrimp poppers
            and a hockey game, dude. Yeah.
10 Tyrell: <style shift back to previous style>
            Look, brother, I'm just doin' what
            I need to be doin'. And I'm not gonna
            risk my job just to give you a grow
            loan. Even if you did keep Antoine Green
            from kickin' the shit out of me at the
            campfire.
11 Conrad: Yeah, well you welcome.
12 Tyrell: I'm sorry, brother. Look, hey, how about
            a free calendar?
13 Conrad: Man, I don't want no damn - Man, can I
            just have my plan, dog?

In this scene, Conrad is being denied a small business loan from his friend, who is a bank officer. The plot proceeds almost entirely linguistically and involves several different kinds of linguistic shifts, including shifts between African American English and Standard English as well as stylistic shifts within both dialects. As such, it provides an excellent illustration of how a plot can progress via language shifting. The first shift comes in line 3 when Conrad responds to Tyrell's implication in line 2 that Conrad is not really planning to grow lettuce. Conrad raises his pitch and amplitude, and shifts the rhythm of the sentence "You see what Whole Foods be chargin' for arugula and endives and shit?" Then he shifts his pitch, amplitude, and rhythm back to what they were in line 1 as he argues that what is important is that he can make money with his plan. In line 4, Tyrell shifts to a more formal style as he addresses the business model directly. While he uses AAVE phonology, the grammar is basically the same as we'd see with Standard American English, until he comes to the final sentence, in which the grammar shifts to AAVE grammar, marked primarily through the use of 'ain't,' the double negative, and the adjectival use of 'fuckin.' While all three of these are found in many dialects of English, Tyrell's pronunciation provides the evidence that this is AAVE.

In lines 5–7, both characters interact in the same style. In line 8, though, Tyrell, speaking to a colleague who is walking by, shifts entirely into Standard American English, and in line 9 Conrad mocks him by doing a similar shift. In Conrad's case, the shift includes phonological, prosodic, and lexical choices that make it clear that he is mocking Tyrell's shift. The accent is very nasal, he uses discourse marking 'like' and references food ('shrimp poppers') and activities ('hockey game') that are widely associated with middle-class white Americans. Mocking Tyrell's language does the work of arguing that Conrad is not getting the loan because Tyrell has sold out culturally. Tyrell rejects that claim in line 10 in which he shifts back to AAVE he used at the end of line 4 and continued with in line 6. Finally, in line 12, he apologizes to Conrad (using a felicitous apology!), shifting again to a style that is closer to Standard American English than what he uses in lines 6 and 10.

The ability of language shifting to work within the narrative is of course contingent on it being part of a repertoire that the audience has sufficient familiarity with that they can recognize the shifting as felicitous. Given that varieties of American English don't typically differ from one another so significantly that a broad range of speakers of this variety have trouble understanding them, dialect variation and dialect switching in the mass media are available as tools to do similar performative work as we see with more general style shifting. If you compare Example 7.3 from *Little Britain* with Example 7.5 from *Weeds*, you can see how this can work. Even though the varieties used in both examples typically contain more significant variation in real-life contexts than is incorporated into the examples, incorporating all the real-world variation might make the interpretation of the acts being performed too difficult for a broad audience.

Food for Thought

Find several examples where characters switch languages or language styles. What does the switching seem to achieve in each case? Which characters are more likely to switch and which rarely or never do? How does switching intertwine characterization with the development of the storyline?

Media producers can use language shifting as a part of the plot even when they assume that the audience will not have access to both (or all) the languages involved. An example of this kind of shifting can be seen in Example 7.6, from the film *Crash* (2004). In this scene, as in the scene from *Weeds*, language switching is the source of narrative conflict and is thus performative. Both scenes are at least partially about attempts by one character to police the language of other characters. In *Weeds*, the switching is about Tyrell feeling like he's doing his job and Conrad feeling like he is being distanced by that language. In the *Crash* scene, the gun seller tries to police both the use of a non-English language and the non-native use of English.

Example 7.6 *Crash*, Paul Haggis (dir.), 2004, Lions Gate Films
Note: Farsi utterances are marked by a different font.

```
1  [Seller sets gun on counter]
2  Seller:  You get one free box of ammunition.
            What kind do you want?
```

3 [Farhad and Dorri at counter speak to one another
   in another language as the seller looks back and
   forth between them. Subtitles are provided]

 4 Farhad: <What did he say, ammunition>
 5 Dorri: <He said, "What kind of bullets?">
 6 Farhad: <The kind that fit>
 7 Dorri: <There's more than one kind>
 8 Farhad: <I don't know anything about guns>
 9 Dorri: <Another good reason not to own one>
10 Farhad: <Don't start with me again>
11 Seller: Yo, Osama. Plan the jihad on your own
             time. What do you want<t in 'want'
             aspirated>?
12 [Man and woman speak to one another again
   before man speaks to seller. Not subtitled]
13 Farhad: Are you making insult at me?
14 Seller: Am I making insult at! you? Is that the
             closest you can come to English?
15 Farhad: Yes I speak English, I am American
             citizen=
16 Seller: =Oh God, here we [go
17 Farhad: [I have right like you
             I have right to buy gun=
18 Seller: =Not in my store you don't, Andy,
             get him outta here now<shift to
             non-rhotic usage>
19 [Another man comes to escort man out]

```
20  Dorri:    [to man] Dad, Go wait in the car
21  Seller:   Now, get out!
22  Farhad:   [speaking in Farsi, not subtitled] You
              are an ignorant man
23  Seller:   Oh, yeah, I'm ignorant? You're liberatin
              my country and I'm flyin' 747s into you:
              mudhuts and incineratin your friends? get
              the fuck outta my sto:e=
24  Farhad:   <increased amplitude>=No you get the fuck
25  Dorri:    Okay
26  [People yelling over one another. Security guard
    takes hold of Farhad]
27  Farhad:   No don't touch me, he cheat me<security
              guard says "all right" quickly
              throughout>
28  [More talking over one another, Farhad and Dorri
    using both Farsi and English. Farhad and security
    guard leave store,]
29  Dorri:    [to father] okay, okay
30  [Dorri turns to seller]
31  Dorri:    You can give me the gun or give me back
              the money and I'm réally hoping for the
              money
32  [Seller stares at woman then sets gun down]
33  Seller:   What kind of ammunition do you want?
              <lower amplitude>
34  Dorri:    Whatever fits
35  Seller:   <style shift, eerily calm and
              threatening>Well we got a lotta kinds.
              We got long colts, short colts, ball
              heads, flat nose, hallow points, wide
              cuts(?), and a dozen more that'll fit
              any size hole. Just depends upon [.]
              how much bang! you can handle
36  Dorri:    [looks at shelf] I'll take the ones in
              the red box
37  Farhad:   [glances over his shoulder] You know what
              those are?
38  Dorri:    Can I have them?<insistent>
39  [Man takes down box and puts it with gun. Woman
    takes gun and ammunition and leaves.]
```

Several points stand out with respect to the alternating use of Farsi and English, beginning with the fact that the initial conversation between Farhad and his daughter is subtitled (lines 4–10) but subsequent uses of Farsi between them are not. Thus, the audience has information that the gun seller doesn't, and this difference is an important part of the plot development in the scene. The audience knows that Farhad is an inexperienced gun buyer and is unlikely to be buying the gun to do anything sinister (though we don't yet know why he's buying the gun). We also know that the man's daughter doesn't think he should buy the gun at all. The gun seller, however, becomes increasingly threatened by his lack of understanding of what is going on between Farhad and Dorri. He appears to be linking this language, which he presumably doesn't know is Farsi, to terrorism. (This film was made in 2004, when the memory of the 9/11 terrorist attacks, and the backlash against people who appeared Middle Eastern, was still quite fresh for many Americans.) The gun seller's lack of understanding of what they are saying, along with his assumptions about Middle Easterners, lead him to decide not to continue doing business with Farhad.

The scene indexes a common American ideology about bilingualism that assumes when people are speaking a language you don't understand, they are talking about you in a problematic way or they are discussing something illegal or otherwise sinister. Farhad's non-native English causes additional concern on the part of the gun seller, as he corrects Farhad's prepositional use (line 14) and rolls his eyes at Farhad's claims to speak English and be an American citizen (line 15). The switching between Farhad and Dorri establishes for the audience what assumptions are in play and constitutes the gun seller's rejection of Farhad as clearly racially motivated. In this sense, the switching between the two languages enacts an important component of the plotline.

Dorri's use of Farsi and English serves as an additional component of the narrative action. Initially, she serves as the translator between the gun seller and her father in a transaction of which she doesn't approve. In the second part of the scene, after Farhad has left, her English accent, primarily a Standard American English that indexes a reasonably high class and educational status, is a surprise to the gun seller. Dorri's English connects to the plot by indicating to the gun seller that she is not what he assumed. This realization is followed by a shift on his part to an overall tone that is highly sexualized and threatening.

The gun seller also engages in style shifting. He shifts in particular between rhotic and non-rhotic pronunciations, something notable since this film is set in Los Angeles, which is generally a rhotic area. Here, lack of rhoticity indexes a social stance and social class in ways that seem intended to transcend region. Lines 11 and 16 are rhotic while the majority of the other lines are non-rhotic. Line 18 is pivotal as he indicates that he will not sell a gun to Farhad. In this line, 'store' is rhotic while 'here' is not (this contrasts with the 'here' in line 16 which is rhotic). In the section of the scene captured by lines 31–38, when he has shifted his style to be more sexually threatening to Dorri, he remains non-rhotic, thereby creating a clear contrast between himself and Dorri. This only adds to the narrative tension as Dorri selects the ammunition to go with the gun. Her choice will later prove crucial, although at this point in the narrative, the specific nature of the ammunition is left unclear with her use of the demonstrative pronoun 'that' rather than one of the different labels for ammunition the seller has listed.

Line 23 represents an especially important moment in the scene as the gun seller's overall frustration, fear, and racism become fully expressed. In reacting to being called ignorant, he launches into an explanation of his own sense of ignorance as related to the terrorist attacks of 9/11. This utterance is fully non-rhotic, involves only '-in' pronunciations ('libera-tin,' 'flyin,' incineratin'), and is otherwise linguistically marked with greater amplitude and vocal tension. This line also includes the taboo word 'fuck,' which underscores the general intensity of the turn overall. These linguistic elements combine to maintain consistent characterization of the gun seller but also to do the performative work of threatening Farhad and to set up Farhad's attempt to counter the gun seller's claims as Farhad tries to mimic that final line but is not successful, presumably due to his own anger and frustration in combination with his non-native command of English.

The two uses of 'fuck' in this scene point to another component of language serving as the performed action in a narrative. When words like 'fuck' are used, they function at several different performative levels, owing in part to their capability as performative verbs to enact curses and in part to the critical social relations created through their use. In the *Crash* scene above, 'fuck' performs an act of both social distancing and social conflict between the gun seller and Farhad. Although neither use recalls the word's referential meaning as linked to sexual activity, the two instances of it help construct the escalating conflict between the two men to dangerous levels. This is achieved largely because the word 'fuck' is tabooed. Since the nature of taboo words is that they should not be uttered, any utterance of one of them necessarily has a performative effect.

Taboo Language as Action

In the *Modern Family*, *Weeds*, and *Crash* examples, *taboo words* were used in several different ways. In each case, though, the performative effect of each instance of a taboo came from the fact of the word being tabooed rather than specifically from the referential meanings of the terms. None of the taboo words in the examples above relate to the relevant referential meanings; however, all of them gain power to varying degrees for being among the terms linked to social offense. Thus, they are performative by invoking the taboo itself (rather than what the word means) and the potential for offense. Taboo words typically express anger, frustration, and surprise, among other affective characteristics. They can also serve grammatically as intensifiers and interjections. They can create both solidarity and distance among characters and be an important component of characterization. The character Frank Booth in the film *Blue Velvet* says the word 'fuck' in the majority of the lines he utters. Frank uses the term in all of the ways mentioned above as well as a few others. In the final scene of the film, for instance, he uses 'fuck' both to refer to the sexual act, "Baby wants to fuck," and as a more general intensifier "don't you fuckin' look at me." This usage captures some of the range that taboo terms can have and shows how their use can be a powerful strategy of developing a narrative.

The word 'taboo' is borrowed from Tongan, the language spoken in Tonga, one of the island nations in the South Pacific. In Tongan, it refers specifically to sacrilege, or religious taboo. The sources of taboo words are fairly consistent cross-culturally and include religion, the body (parts and effluvia), sexuality, disease, death and infirmity, and culturally disfavored groups of people and practices. Taboo words can cause actual physical reactions and are governed by various grammatical rules.[2] One performative function that occurs fairly frequently with taboo words involves condemning or cursing, something we see with the term 'damn,' which specifically means, in the performative verb sense, condemnation.

We can see the condemning function especially clearly in the iconic final scene of the 1968 film *Planet of the Apes*. In this scene, the main character, George Taylor, realizes that the planet he has crash-landed on is in fact a post-apocalyptic Earth in which humans were destroyed through atomic warfare, leaving apes to rise to dominance. On this realization, he shouts in anguish at the sky, "God damn you, God damn you all to hell." This usage is performative in the classic sense, performing an actual curse (here of humans). It differs significantly from another famous use of "damn" in film, that of Rhett Butler telling Scarlett O'Hara in *Gone with the Wind*, "Frankly, my dear, I don't give a damn." Here, 'damn' means something like 'a negligible amount.' The actual utterance of the term, however, is still performative. In this case, though, it is performing an act of dismissal, defiance, and social dominance rather than condemnation. The performative effect derives from the taboo rather than from the primary referential meaning ('condemnation') of the word. Conversely, the performative effect of Taylor's final, agonized curse in *Planet of the Apes* specifically involves the referential meaning of 'damn' because Taylor is condemning his fellow humans.

We can see another example of performative taboo use in Example 7.7, from the film *The Breakfast Club* (1985). In this film, five students from very different social groups within a high school spend the day together in detention. They represent classic high school archetypes, including the 'popular girl' (Claire) and the 'nerd' (Brian), both of whom appear in the example, along with the 'jock,' the 'bad boy,' and the 'emotionally unstable girl.' Over the course of the day, the students come to realize that many of the assumptions they had about each other are inaccurate.

Example 7.7   *The Breakfast Club*, John Hughes (dir.), 1985, Universal Pictures

```
1 Claire:  [teary] I'm not saying that to be
           conceited! I hate it! I hate having to go
           along with everything my friends say!
2 Brian:   Well then why do you do it?
3 Claire:  I don't know, I don't, you don't understand
           [..] you don't. You're not friends with
           the same kind of people that Andy and I
           are friends with! You know, you just don't
           understand the pressure that they can put
           on you!
4 Brian:   I don't understand what? You think I don't
           understand pressure, Claire? Well fuck you!
           Fuck you! [Brian breaks down and begins to
           cry.] Know why I'm here today? Do you?! I'm
           here because Mr. Ryan found a gun in the
           locker
```

In this case, the taboo word, 'fuck' has very different referential content than 'damn'; nonetheless, 'fuck you' functions for Brian to condemn Claire much as 'damn' functions to condemn humanity in the *Planet of the Apes*. It does additional performative work as well, serving (along with other aspects of the scene) to reconfigure the relationships among the characters, providing Brian with new power within the group. This scene occurs near the end of the film after all the other characters have already revealed various secrets to one another. Brian's 'fuck you' serves as condemnation for assumptions being made about him but also allows him to open up and become vulnerable to the others. The heart of the film rests on the power of vulnerability as a means of overcoming generalization and assumption, so this scene stands as one of the central moments to further that aspect of the plot.

Additional performative power of taboos arises specifically from the ways in which some words become tabooed in the first place as well as from the ways in which taboos are formally regulated. Indeed, taboos gain power only by virtue of their regulation (and its violation). One thing we can observe in the United States, for instance, is a decreasing degree of taboo for some terms (for instance, 'damn,' 'shit,' and 'ass') and an increasing level of taboo for others (for instance, racial epithets). One way we know that these have shifted is, in fact, their appearance in mass media. Whereas the former set of terms was virtually unheard in the media of the early part of the twentieth century (Rhett Butler's use of 'damn' was considered highly provocative and potentially worthy of censor), many epithets were in common circulation. In the early part of the twenty-first century, by contrast, this pattern has been largely reversed. The use of the older taboos has become increasingly common. Timothy Jay (2000, 224) notes that the use of taboo terms on television increased sevenfold between 1970 and 1998 (see also Sapolsky and Kaye 2005). The use of racially charged language, on the other hand, has been vigorously contested, and entertainers who use such language open themselves to significant social sanction. This may be true even in cases in which the performer is using terms ironically to critique racism, as was the case in 2014 when Stephen Colbert used 'ching chong ding dong' as a means of critiquing the use of 'redskin' as the mascot of a football team. In this case, the performative power of the taboo was stronger than that of the attempted critique.

Food for Thought

Search Twitter (or a Twitter aggregator) for #CancelColbert. How do the various tweets contest Colbert's use of the racialized language? Can you think of other similar cases where language use is contested and thus highlighted as taboo?

This change in what is tabooed highlights one of the interesting facets of taboo language in the first place. The potential to cause offense in the listener and the regulation of some words as tabooed creates a context in which the taboo can be used performatively to challenge specifically those institutions that have the societal function of policing language use. In the case of the mass media, the use of taboos, particularly since the 1960s, can thus function as an act of political, social, or cultural commentary on the part of the media producers.

Although we'll talk in much more detail about the ways language helps connect media products to the non-media world in Chapter 8, understanding how taboo words are regulated is a critical component of understanding their performative power when they do occur. The producers of audiovisual media have long been subject to various institutionally oriented regulations concerning the use of offensive or strong language. The nature of the regulation differs, however, with broadcast television being regulated via a government agency and film being regulated voluntarily by an internal committee of the Motion Picture Association of America (MPAA). Indeed, the differences in how television and film are regulated help explain many of the differences we find in the use of taboo language across the audiovisual media.

Films are regulated in a system designed to avert specific government action with respect to content. The MPAA voluntarily rates the films produced and distributed in the United States using the findings from the Rating Board of the Classification and Ratings Administration (CARA) (http://www.filmratings.com/). CARA, funded by fees charged to film producers or distributors, determines movie ratings for theatrical releases. According to the MPAA, each rater is a parent who has no affiliation with the entertainment industry outside his or her employment with CARA. By design, none of the raters has any particular expertise in child psychology or child development. The explicit goal of the ratings system is to provide parents with "tools to decide what movies are suitable for their children to watch" (Motion Picture Association of America 2013). Raters' main considerations include "the intensity of the themes in the motion picture, language, depictions of violence, nudity, sensuality, depictions of sexual activity and drug use" (Federal Trade Commission 2000, 2). In a study of parents' preferences concerning information about films (Gentile et al. 2011), offensive language ranked behind sexual behavior, nudity, illegal substance use, and physical violence as something parents wanted indicated, yet 70 percent of parents nonetheless said they'd like an indication of offensive language.

Language is thus one of the primary determinants of how a film is rated, though most often certain types of activities and language co-occur. As detailed in a Federal Trade Commission report to Congress, language is assessed as follows: A G-rated motion picture "contains nothing in theme, language, nudity, sex, violence or other matters that, in the view of the Rating Board, would offend parents whose younger children view the motion picture. . . . Some snippets of language may go beyond polite conversation but they are common everyday expressions. No stronger words are present in G-rated motion pictures" (Federal Trade Commission 2000, 7). A PG rating occurs when there is profanity in the film. PG-13 is used if a film has a single use of one of the "harsher sexually derived words, though only as an expletive." More than one such expletive requires an R rating, as must even one of those words used in a sexual context (2000, 9). The Rating Board may rate a motion picture differently than suggested in the guidelines if, based on a special vote by a two-thirds majority, the raters feel that most American parents would believe that a PG-13 or R rating is appropriate because of the context or manner in which the words are used or because the use of those words in the motion picture is inconspicuous. NC-17 ratings do not take language into consideration.

The intention to protect children from the potentially harmful effects of speech presents an interesting challenge because a host of ways of speaking could be potentially harmful, including challenging the authority of parents or other adults, bullying and being mean to another child, discussing potentially frightening topics, using blasphemy, and so on. Indeed, these types of speech are the focus of an alternative ratings site, Kids-in-Mind (http:// www.kids-in-mind.com/). Whereas CARA uses largely age-based criteria to determine how to rate a film (the PG-13 rating means that people under the age of 13 can't be admitted without an adult; the R rating means that people under the age of 17 can't be admitted without an adult), the approach taken by Kids-in-Mind is content-based for sex/nudity, violence/gore, and profanity. Kids-in-Mind claims that their ratings allow parents to decide for themselves whether a film is or isn't appropriate for their children based on the content in the film. Kids-in-Mind relies on "quantity" and "context" to determine the level at which a movie will be assessed for profanity (by which they seem to mean terms related to canonical areas of taboo as explained in their profanity glossary: http://www.kids-in-mind.com/help/glossary. htm). Here again, the assessment of the word as taboo is entirely based on the response of an audience. In other words, a taboo is felicitous as a taboo if the viewer judges it to be so. Indeed, the majority of the films (80 percent or 331/416 films as analyzed in November 2013) that receive a 10 rating on anything at Kids-in-Mind receive a 10 for profanity.

The documentary film *The Aristocrats* (2005) presents a fascinating case of a film that was not submitted to the MPAA for a rating ostensibly because the producers feared an NC-17 rating for language alone. In the documentary, 100 comedians discuss and perform a joke famous among comedians but typically performed only backstage for other comedians. The joke has a fairly mundane setup in which someone pitches an act to a talent agent. The nature of the act is subject to improvisation and is supposed to be as graphically sexual, profane, violent, disgusting, and/or otherwise tabooed as the comedian can make it. The end of the joke is always the same in that the talent agent, full of disgust, asks the title of the act and the person pitching it replies, "The Aristocrats." In this case, the entire premise of the film rests on the ability of language to do the performative work of inviting disgust and offense. The performativity rests specifically on the level of taboo that the entertainer is able to break. In the case of *The Aristocrats*, each telling of the joke also serves to perform the insider status of the entertainer since this is a joke told by entertainers to other entertainers (rather than to a traditional audience). In this sense, the taboo language constitutes both staged performance and performed action, and the performative potential for both types of performance can only be realized when the felicity of the taboo as a taboo is recognized by its audience.

Unlike the voluntary regulation of films, the regulation of television occurs under the auspices of federal law. The Federal Communications Commission (FCC) largely polices television and radio, specifically material broadcast over public airways, for example programs on the national networks. The FCC has specific rules concerning the broadcasting of taboo terms. While these rules have changed as social norms around the use of taboo terms have changed, taboos are nonetheless regulated in particular ways. Subscription-based television, such as cable and satellite television, is not subject to many of the restrictions on language that broadcast television is, and many of the social changes regarding the broadcast of taboo language are connected to competition between broadcast and subscription networks. For instance, when HBO, a subscription-based cable network, launched in 1975, the comedian Robert Klein exclaimed "It's subscription . . . we can say anything. Shit! How'd you like that? Shit!"

Throughout the thirty-year period 1970–2000, many of the conventions that had been in place before the 1970s began to fall away, both as a result of changing social norms and of the intense competitive pressure coming from subscription-based television. For instance, in 1981 when Charles Rocket used the word 'fuck' during a live broadcast of *Saturday*

Night Live (now called just *SNL*) he was fired from the show. Sixteen years later in 1997, when Norm McDonald did something similar, he wasn't fired (Saturday Night Live Trivia).[3] Social norms had changed somewhat, though of course not entirely. In 2009, when Jenny Slate accidently used the term on the live broadcast even though the sketch called for her to use the euphemism 'frig/frick,' the term was overdubbed with 'frickin' for the rebroadcast in western time zones (Schreffler and Hays 2009).

Federal law prohibits the broadcast of obscene speech and restricts the broadcast of indecent and profane speech to between 10 pm and 6 am (Federal Communications Commission n.d.). Like the film ratings system, these regulations are largely intended to protect children from the "harmful effects of pornography, obscenity, and indecency." Although these laws have been challenged as an unconstitutional censoring of the First Amendment, "obscenity" has repeatedly been ruled to fall outside the category of protected speech (*Miller v. California* 1973). "Obscenity" for the purposes of broadcast regulation is defined as follows:

- An average person, applying contemporary community standards, must find that the material, as a whole, appeals to the prurient interest;
- The material must depict or describe, in a patently offensive way, sexual conduct specifically defined by applicable law; and
- The material, taken as a whole, must lack serious literary, artistic, political, or scientific value.

Indecent speech, on the other hand, refers to language or material that, in context, depicts or describes, in terms patently offensive as measured by contemporary community broadcast standards for the broadcast medium, sexual or excretory organs or activities. Indecent programming contains patently offensive sexual or excretory references that do not rise to the level of obscenity (*FCC v. Pacifica Foundation* 1978). Finally, profane speech refers to language that "denote[s] language so grossly offensive to members of the public who actually hear it as to amount to a nuisance." These explanations themselves capture exactly the performative nature of language that has been discussed thus far. The evaluation of any given instance of language use as offensive, indecent, or profane depends wholly on the interpretation of the audience (which specific audience members are allowed to make these determinations is remarkably undefined).

In 2001, the FCC issued an industry guideline noting that indecency depended on whether the broadcast material described sexual or excretory

Figure 7.1   Taboo word counter from "It Hits the Fan," *South Park*, Season 5, Episode 1, Trey Parker and Matt Stone (creators), Comedy Central, June 20, 2001.

activities and whether it was deemed patently offensive by contemporary community standards (Federal Communications Commission 2001). Following that guideline and the use of several instances of 'shit' and 'bullshit' on prime-time broadcast television, the Comedy Central show *South Park* (1997–) aired an episode called "It hits the fan." In the episode, the term 'shit' is used repeatedly with a counter in the bottom left corner, as illustrated by Figure 7.1.

The episode essentially parodies the idea that indecent language can be regulated in a straightforward way, as shown in Example 7.8.

Example 7.8   *South Park*, "It hits the fan," Season 5, Episode 1, Trey Parker and Matt Stone (creators), Comedy Central, June 20, 2001

```
1  Mr. Garrison:   And so, children, instead of
                   saying "Hand in your papers."
                   I may now say "Hand in your shit."
                   Any questions?
2  Filmore:        What about "I have to take a shit."
3  Mr. Garrison:   No, no, Filmore. You can say "I have
                   to poop and shit." Or "Oh shit, I
                   have to poop." but not "I have to
                   shit," are we all clear?
```

```
4  Children:     No.
5  Mr. Garrison:  Look, it's all about context.
                  For example, recently I have come
                  out and admitted that I was a
                  homosexual. I'm gay. That means
                  that now I can say the word "fag."
                  On television, they usually don't
                  allow "fag." But because I'm gay
                  it's alright. And with the new
                  approval of the word "shit," that
                  means that finally I am free to
                  say (sings) "Hey, there, shitty
                  shitty fag fag, shitty shitty fag
                  fag, how do you do? Hey, there,
                  shitty shitty fag fag, shitty
                  shitty fag fag, how do you do?"
                  This is great!
```

In the case of taboo language use in the examples discussed so far in this chapter (Lily's cursing on *Modern Family*, Brian's curse in *The Breakfast Club*, the gun seller and Farhad exchanging 'fuck' in *Crash*, and the interaction between Conrad and Tyrell in *Weeds*), the tabooed nature of the terms being used is critical to their interpretation, and the work they are doing for the plot is directly tied to their tabooed status. This need not always be the case, however. The *South Park* example highlights the distinction between the tabooed term being used in connection to its tabooed meaning and being used in connection to non-tabooed meanings as clarified by Mr. Garrison in line 3. Additionally, we have also seen that the referential meaning of a taboo word can be a source of its performativity – for instance, in the discussion of Frank Booth's use of 'fuck' in *Blue Velvet* or the comparison of George Taylor's and Rhett Butler's use of 'damn.' We have also seen that the referential meaning may be irrelevant to the functioning of the taboo, a fact that calls into question at least some of the regulatory reasoning behind rules about taboo language use in the mass media.

In Example 7.9, from the television series *The Wire* (2002–2008), we see a case where none of the instances of the tabooed word are linked to the referential meaning tied to the word.

Example 7.9a   *The Wire,* "Old Cases," Season 1, Episode 4, David
Simon (creator), HBO, June 23, 2002

```
1    Bunk:      Aw:: fuck [looking at picture]
                [3.97]
2    McNulty:   Motherfucker
3    [Both move to kitchen and start laying the
     pictures in the places they were taken] [9.36]
4    Bunk:      fuck, fuck, fuckin' fuck....fuck ....
                mmm. fuck. Fuck fuck fuck [5.9]
5    McNulty:   Wh' the fuck? [9.04]
6    Bunk:      [drawing circle on floor] Fuck
                [7.85]
7    McNulty:   [measuring tape gets his finger] Fuck
                [Trying to set up height of shooter.]
                [28.97]
8    Bunk:      Hmm [.] mmm
9    McNulty:   Aw fuck [kneels and holds gun up to
                see if that could be how she was shot]
                [10.09]
10   McNulty:   [looking around on the floor] Fuckin.
                [2.6] the fuck [7.29]
11   Bunk:      [looks at wall and then looks at where
                the bullet came through the window].
                Mother fuck.[6.8]
12   McNulty:   Aw fuck, aw: fuck
13   [They figure out that the woman was shot through
     the window. McNulty points to place in chest and
     place in back where bullet entered and exited.
     Bunk nods] [14.43]
14   McNulty:   Fuckity fuck fuck fuck fuck.[Looks at
                pictures on floor] [.46]
15   McNulty:   Fucker. [Checks the wall] [4.25]
16   McNulty:   Aw fuck.[checking for bullet mark in the
                wall] [1.5] fuck, fuck[fuck
17   Bunk:      [glottalized] [Fuck fuck. Fuck
                fuck
18   [McNulty points out glass on the floor in one
     of the photos][9.87]
19   Bunk:      Motherfucker
```

20 [McNulty finds a spot in the fridge] [3.5]

```
21  McNulty:  Fuckin' A.
22  Bunk:     mm-hmmm [14.9]
23  McNulty:  Fuck [removes plaster from fridge hole
                and pulls out bullet. Shows it to Bunk]
                [14.43] Mother fucker.[3.7]
24  Bunk:     [takes bullet] Fuck me.
```

In many ways, this scene is unremarkable, illustrating two detectives who have worked together frequently piecing together a crime scene while the building manager looks on. The crime itself is the murder of a young woman that has gone unsolved (and unattended) for several months and the two detectives assume that this has nothing to do with the larger case they are investigating, but rather is busy work (something they discuss just prior to this scene). The images of the crime scene are grisly, showing the murdered woman, naked, lying on the floor with blood all around and a large bullet wound in the chest with an exit wound in her back. Other than that, however, the scene is like dozens of others you might find in any police procedural. The plot proceeds as a crime puzzle to be solved, and the two detectives go about the process of solving it.

The scene becomes something noteworthy in how the two detectives use language, specifically the lexeme "fuck" and variations on it. The twenty-one lines of dialogue contain thirty-eight different examples of a version of the term, not one of which makes clear reference to its primary referential meaning. The meanings are wide-ranging, including interjections, filler, and markers of frustration and congratulation, among others. A rough translation looks as follows:

Example 7.9b   Loose translation of Example 7.9a
Translated lines are enclosed in < >.

```
1   Bunk:      [looking at picture] <this is awful>
               [3.97]
2   McNulty:   [looking at picture] <what a jerk>
3   [Both move to kitchen and start laying the
    pictures in the places they were taken] [9.36]
4   Bunk:      <what happened here> [5.9]
5   McNulty:   <This is odd> [9.04]
6   Bunk:      [drawing circle on floor] <here's where
               a bullet hit> [7.85]
7   McNulty:   [measuring tape gets his
               finger] <ouch> [Trying to set up height of
               shooter.] [28.97]
8   Bunk:      hmm - mmm
9   McNulty:   <this is more complicated than reported.
               She wasn't shot while standing at
               the fridge> [10.09] [kneels and holds
               gun up to see if that could be how
               she was shot]
10  McNulty:   [looking around on the floor] <where's
               the evidence of the bullet if she was
               shot while kneeling> [7.29]
11  Bunk:      [looks at wall and then looks at where
               the bullet came through the window].
               <I don't believe it. Look at this.>
               [6.8]
12  McNulty:   <we're figuring it out > 
13  McNulty points to place in chest and place
    in back where bullet entered and exited.
    B nods [14.43]
14  McNulty:   <now we're getting somewhere> [looks at
               pictures on floor] [.46]
15  McNulty:   <Jerk> [Checks the wall] [4.25]
16  McNulty:   <getting closer>. [checking wall]
               [1.5] <where's the bullet>
```

```
17  Bunk:      <what happened? How was she shot? Where's
                the bullet?>
18  [McNulty points out glass on the floor in one
    of the photos]-[9.87]
19  Bunk:      <You're right. You got it. It's the
                fridge>
20  [McNulty finds a spot in the fridge] [3.5]
21  McNulty:   <Found it>
22  Bunk:      mm-hmmm [14.9]
23  McNulty:   <I think we got it>(removes plaster from
                fridge hole and pulls out bullet. Shows
                it to Bunk).[14.43]<We solved it. That
                jerk>[3.7]
24  Bunk:      (takes bullet)<Unbelievable>
```

Comparing the original version with the rough translation highlights the performative power of the expletive for helping the narrative progress. Most of the instances of 'fuck' involve variations in pitch, loudness, and overall pausing, which indicate the different functions they fulfill. For instance, the use in line 7, when the tape measure snaps McNulty's finger, is low-pitched, with a tense vocal tract and a relatively short vowel, all of which indicate that here, the meaning is a general interjection. By contrast, in line 12, when Bunk and McNulty figure out that the woman was shot while standing in front of the window instead of in front of the refrigerator as they'd initially thought, McNulty's pronunciation of the term is louder, with a longer vowel, laxer vocal tract, and generally more excited tone. Each different function co-occurs with variation in pronunciation involving pitch, amplitude, vowel length, and overall rhythm, creating a textured dialogue in a creative and surprising way.

While the two detectives are also engaged in physical actions that help make sense of what's going on and thus take some of the interpretive pressure off the language, certain instances of the term constitute aspects of the narrative action. For instance, in line 11, Bunk's use of 'mother fuck' serves as a type of imperative, calling McNulty away from the line of reasoning he's pursuing (looking for evidence that the woman was shot in front of the fridge) and toward a new argument, namely, that she was shot through the window. A rising and falling pitch on the first syllable ('mo-') does the work of indicating that this use differs from some of the others. Similarly, McNulty's 'mother fucker' at the end of line 23 provides the declarative that the puzzle has been solved, and Bunk's final line links this murder to the larger investigation that serves as the primary plotline for the entire first season. This scene will turn out to be a pivot point because it starts the process of connecting seemingly unrelated crimes to the larger drug organization the police are investigating. Thus, the use of 'fuck me' in the final line also foreshadows much of the plot that will unfold throughout the season in that the police will be involved in a cat and mouse game with the group of people they now know to be responsible for this murder.

Food for Thought

Examine what each use of 'fuck' seems to be doing in this listing for the top 10 F-Bombs in movie history, http://goo.gl/0ELGwW (Alternative Reel 2008). How do the uses on that video compare to the one in the scene from *The Wire* above?

Throughout this chapter, we've seen different instances of the term 'fuck' being used. In the *Modern Family* scene that occurs early in the chapter, a child's lack of referential knowledge serves as a plot device for the episode as a whole, allowing the adults (and the audience) to react to the utterance itself (which is bleeped out in the episode but is known by virtue of the words it rhymes with). Part of their (and our) reaction is tied to the complexity involved in understanding the tabooed nature of the term in the face of its frequent expression and also in the face of the fact that, while nearly always tabooed, it has many meanings that have nothing to do with its primary reference to a sexual act. In Example 7.5 from *Weeds*, it occurs again as Tyrell tries to navigate his friendship with Conrad along with the fiduciary responsibilities of his job. In his case, the term functions to intensify his utterances and also to mark some of his speech stylistically. In Example 7.6 from *Crash*, the term connects again to intensification on the part of the gun seller, demanding that Farhad leave his store, and Farhad's disempowered attempt to combat his unfair treatment from the gun seller by mimicking what the seller has said. In Example 7.7 from *The Breakfast Club*, it occurs performatively as a curse. Finally, we have the many varied uses in Example 7.9 from *The Wire*. Each of these cases focuses the capability of this term to actually do things in the plot and to work as the source of ongoing narrative progress, just as performative verbs and switching between different styles, dialects, or language can. In the final chapter of the book, we will examine another facet of linguistic performativity by turning our analytic lens on the mechanisms through which language variation helps connect media producers, media products, and media audiences.

Notes

1 That promise might still be infelicitous because I don't really have the authority to fulfill that particular promise either.

2 In English, the only terms that can be infixed are a small number of taboo words. An infix is like a prefix or a suffix except that the morpheme occurs in the middle of the word. Many languages rely on infixation as a productive process for making words, but in English, the only morphemes that can be infixed are a small number of taboo words in their participial or adjectival forms, such as in "un-fucking-believable." Additionally, taboo words (or their euphemisms) are also the only ones that can fit in the syntactic frames "too ___ bad" and "what the ___ are you doing?" The function of the taboo terms in both cases is generally intensification.

3 McDonald was eventually fired; however, his use of 'fuck' doesn't appear to have been the catalyst the way it was for Rocket.

References

Alternative Reel. 2008. Top 10 Most Creative Uses of the F-Bomb in Movie History. Retrieved August 22, 2013, from http://alternativereel.com/cult_movies/display_article.php?id=0000000054.

Austin, J.L. 1961. Performative Utterances. In *Philosophical Papers*, ed. J.O. Umson and G.J. Warnock, 220–239. London: Oxford University Press.

Austin, J.L. 1975. *How To Do Things with Words*. Cambridge, MA: Harvard University Press.

Bauman, Richard. 2011. Commentary: Foundations in Performance. *Journal of Sociolinguistics* 15(5): 707–720.

Bauman, Richard, and Charles L. Briggs. 1990. Poetics and Performance as Critical Perspectives on Language and Social Life. *Annual Review of Anthropology* 19: 59–88.

Bauman, Richard, and Joel Sherzer. 1989. *Explorations in the Ethnography of Speaking*. Cambridge: Cambridge University Press.

Booth, Paul. 2012. The Television Social Network: Exploring TV Characters. *Communication Studies* 63(3): 309–327.

Bucholtz, Mary, and Kira Hall. 2004. Theorizing Identity in Language and Sexuality. *Language in Society* 34(4): 501–547.

Butler, Judith. 1997. *Excitable Speech: A Politics of the Performative*. New York: Routledge.

Federal Communications Commission. n.d. Obscene, Indecent and Profane Broadcasts. Retrieved August 20, 2013, from http://www.fcc.gov/guides/obscenity-indecency-and-profanity.

Federal Communications Commission. 2001. Policy Statement. Retrieved August 20, 2013, from http://transition.fcc.gov/eb/Orders/2001/fcc01090.html.

Federal Trade Commission. 2000. *Marketing Violent Entertainment to Children: A Review of Self-Regulation and Industry Practices in the Motion Picture, Music Recording and Electronic Game Industries.* Federal Trade Commission.

Gardner-Chloros, Penelope. 2012. Sociolinguistic Factors in Code-Switching. In *The Cambridge Handbook of Linguistic Code-Switching*, ed. B.E. Bullock and A.J. Toribio, 97–113. Cambridge: Cambridge University Press.

Gentile, Douglas, Julia Maier, Mary Rice Hasson, and Beatriz Lopez de Bonetti. 2011. Parents' Evaluation of Media Ratings a Decade after the Television Ratings Were Introduced. *Pediatrics* 128(1): 36–44.

Jakobson, Roman. 1960. Closing statement: Lingusitics and Poetics. In *Style in Language*, ed. T.A. Sebeok, 350–359. Cambridge, MA: MIT Press.

Jay, Timothy. 2000. *Why We Curse.* Amsterdam: Benjamins.

Motion Picture Association of America. 2013. Film Ratings. Retrieved November 21, 2014, from http://www.mpaa.org/film-ratings/.

Sapolsky, Barry, and Barbara Kaye. 2005. The Use of Offensive Language by Males and Females in Prime Time Television Entertainment. *Atlantic Journal of Communication* 13(4): 292–303.

Saturday Night Live Trivia. Retrieved August 15, 2013, from http://www.imdb.com/title/tt0072562/trivia.

Schreffler, Laura, and Elizabeth Hays. 2009. "Saturday Night Live" Cast Member Jenny Slate Drops F-Bomb in Premiere Episode Hosted by Megan Fox. Retrieved August 20, 2013, from http://www.nydailynews.com/entertainment/tv-movies/saturday-night-live-cast-member-jenny-slate-drops-f-bomb-premiere-episode-hosted-megan-fox-article-1.383203.

Thompson, Kristin. 2003. *Storytelling in Film and Television.* Cambridge, MA: Harvard University Press.

Chapter 8

Connecting to the Audience

Introduction

We've now looked at two different ways in which language variation does particular kinds of work – or fulfills particular kinds of functions – within the narrative mass media. On the one hand, language variation is part of what sustains the overall backstory, especially in terms of characterization. On the other hand, language variation is part of what moves the plot along in terms of being an actual set of actions. Sometimes, of course, these two functions overlap, as we saw with the discussion of *Love Actually* (Chapter 1), the example of the final scene of *The Help* (Chapter 5), and the scene in *Crash* (Chapter 7). Additionally, we've discussed not only what constitutes language variation but also how to link that variation to meaning via ideologies and indexicality. What we haven't entirely explored, however, is the role of the audience for these various functions.

There is always an implicit interaction between the production and reception of language and language variation, and I've argued in different places that that interaction is fundamental to the ability of language variation to do a particular kind of work. I've also claimed that the interaction is critical for defining and constraining the work language variation can do. Much of what we have looked at throughout the book has been about interaction within a given media product – what we might consider the representation or performance of interaction. In this chapter, we will turn more directly to the interaction between language variation that occurs on the screen and the audience for whom it is generally created.

Vox Popular: The Surprising Life of Language in the Media, First Edition. Robin Queen.

Audiences

Attracting an audience exists as one of the critical drivers of most narrative media. Even when media producers are not primarily focused on commercial success, they typically create their work with the hope that it will be experienced and enjoyed by other people. For the most part, media exist in a complex marketplace that depends on audiences for its continued existence. While there has been quite a bit of research on audiences over the past several decades, very little of it has focused on questions of language. This is of course not surprising, given how little research there is about language in the media more generally. Still, since so much of a media work's form is tied to connecting in some way or another with an audience, and since language is such an important component of how people connect to each other, it is useful to consider what the audience brings to the matter of thinking about language variation in the media. We can think of the audience of a media work as analogous to a "listener" in everyday conversation and the media producers as metaphorical "speakers."

Throughout this book, I have used terms like 'speaker' and 'listener' without discussing the fact that in virtually all face-to-face-type interactions, a given individual inhabits both roles at different points, sometimes inhabiting both at once. When someone is listening to someone else talk, the listener often gives cues that they are listening, with utterances such as 'right' or 'mm-hmm.' This is obviously speaking, but it's speaking as an indication of listening. For most analytic purposes, though, it's important to abstract away from our knowledge that speakers and listeners are not as clearly distinct from one another as our models might suggest. The relationship between fictional media products and their audiences reveals one place where that abstraction connects more concretely to the observable dynamics between "speakers" and "listeners."

When we begin talking about "listeners" and "audiences," we are talking about users of language just as concretely as when we focus on "speakers" or "characters." It's the interaction between these different user roles that helps connect people with language generally and with language variation specifically. In the discussions of indexical meaning in Chapter 5 and felicity conditions in Chapter 7, the listener emerged as the critical element for the constitution of successful moments of language use, and in particular successful articulations of language variation as itself meaningful. Once the listener is given an equal role in the communicative exchange, the place of individuals for understanding language and language variation requires a degree more nuance and thought. The fact that users of language are constantly shifting between being producers and perceivers highlights the fundamentally communal nature of language. In short, language is as much a property of groups of individuals as it is a property of individuals alone.

Modeling language as a property of groups of people can be a little bit tricky, though. For instance, some characteristic can be used to create categories of people and then to link those categories to language. This is what is often done with social demographics. People are grouped based on characteristics such as their sex, where they are from, their age, their education level, their ethnicity, or their social class. While each of these might capture a variety of elements about the people in question, the assumption behind such categorization is that these demographic features represent something that is shared among those within a category and that differs across categories.

Demographic features have long been associated with audience research, with media products being targeted to particular demographic groups, such as women between the ages of 18 and 35. Because language variation may be similarly linked to demographic groups, fictional media products aiming at such a target take that target into account as the product is created. The genre of "chick flicks," for instance, often has this demographic group as its target, and the language found in chick flicks has several generic qualities. For instance, there tends to be very little use of regional or other kinds of dialect variation, at least as compared to some other genres, and the romantic leads frequently speak using a relatively unmarked version of American English (at least for chick flicks produced by the American film industry).

Demography has some clear limits, however, in that it is not at all certain what people who are categorized in a particular demographic group actually have in common or how they clearly differ from those in other demographic groups. Increasingly within media audience research, people focused on marketing media products to particular audiences rely on what are known as psychographic measures such as general beliefs, activities, attitudes, opinions, and interests rather than specifically on demographic characteristics, though of course these may overlap in many cases (Abzug 2011). As more audience members participate directly, and quickly, with media products, these psychographic measures facilitate much more nuance with respect to targeting the products. Within language studies, too, researchers are increasingly turning away from correlating language variation with demographic features and instead linking it more to shared activities in which people engage. Focusing on activities provides a more obvious means through which to link broad ideas about linguistic variation to the people engaging with that variation.

When people come together around some kind of shared notion – a place, an activity, a faith, a love, an interest – the thing they share forms the basis of a community. These types of communities have been called *communities of practice* (Eckert and Wenger 2005). The community of practice captures an important component of communities generally because it invokes some degree of choice and agency on the part of those embedded in such communities. Further, it captures an important way that people typically think of themselves as belonging to communities. Although we can talk about speech communities as collections of people who share both a linguistic system and a sense of how to use that system, people don't typically perceive themselves as belonging to speech communities. Instead, they perceive themselves as belonging to communities tied to other entities, such as a nation, a region, a family, a tribe, an ethnicity, or an activity.

Audiovisual media, of course, are frequently the source of communities in which audiences and media producers interact primarily around the media product. But even the communities that form around constructed languages like Klingon or Na'avi are primarily tied to the cultures linked to the languages. Active fan communities exist for virtually every television series and many movies, often found on Internet discussion boards and groups convened through social media. Characters (and the actors who animate them) may appear in these venues to interact with fans, creating a simulacrum of the kind of interaction that occurs in regular conversation, on or offline. In this sense, media products can be the locus of a community of practice.

Food for Thought

What different kinds of communities do you think of yourself as belonging to? What is the basis of the community? Do you feel like you belong to a community that's tied in some way to a media product? If so, what shape does that community have and how do you participate in it?

Another kind of community that forms in connection with audiovisual narrative media is the community created internal to the work itself. In the television series *The Wire* (2002–2008), for instance, the police officers and the various street organizations they are working to bring down exist in a complex community with one another, and this community is captured in part by language. The series is set in Baltimore, a city with a distinct urban dialect that is distributed in different ways among different groups of people. The audience can thus hear the differences in the different groups of people involved in that small microcosm, including the police and local street organizations as well as politicians, journalists, and educators. Each of these groups uses language slightly differently, as do the different street organizations. The lone wolf character in the series, Omar Little, speaks differently from everyone else.

This kind of dynamic occurs in virtually any television series and is part of what makes looking at the language component so fascinating. Communities that exist within a media world and those in the non-media world frequently rely on very similar linguistic repertoires. Outside the media product, language variation functions as indirect glue between media producers, media product, and media audience. Within a given media product, it functions as the (staged) glue among the characters. The dual nature of community within narrative media represents one of the media's more intriguing characteristics. The communities being represented in a media product are designed specifically to appeal to an audience that exists outside that product and that can often only be imagined during the process of production.

Fewer and fewer television shows and no films at all are produced in front of a live audience, which has both benefits and costs. As Bauman (2011b, 40) notes for early sound recordings, there is an intentional tension between the performer's interaction with the known live audience and with the unknown distributed audience that experiences the performance via recording. With a live audience, the media producers can alter what is happening if they notice the audience is not responding as planned. Test audiences can play an intermediate role of providing more immediate feedback; however, for most narrative audiovisual media the audience isn't known until after the work is produced and distributed. For films, the audience can only interact with the finished product; for television series, the audience has more potential for direct interaction provided the series is ongoing. We can see this kind of interaction in the comments of *The Closer* (2005–2012) fans and the response by the series' creator concerning the main character's accent, with many fans expressing extreme dislike (about 60 percent of the comments from fans were negative, based on informal counts I did of several sites). The media producers were aware of this dislike and engaged with it directly; however, they did not alter the character's accent.

Since the actual audience for a show can't be known with any accuracy, media producers must imagine their ideal audience. Typical components of imagining the audience will be aspects of their demographics, their overall personae or stance (the kinds of role relationships we looked at in Chapter 6), and aspects of their overall habits – what things inspire them and what things turn them off, what kinds of voters they are, what kinds of emotional experiences they like and how they like to get them, what they like and dislike about particular genres. We can imagine that media producers may use a variety of methods, from very specific to very vague, in constructing their ideal audience. For language and language variation within the media product, this means that media producers will target the language used to the specific linguistic competence of their target audience, and the ideologies about language they believe that audience holds. As Weldon (2013, 230) writes, "Because scripted speech typically has a predetermined target audience, it can also be ideal for examining linguistic style via accommodation and audience design. For example, in my research I found that smaller-grossing films aimed at primarily African American audiences presented more nuanced (and perhaps more authentic) portrayals of AAVE and its speakers than larger-grossing films aimed at more mainstream audiences."

Audience Design

Allan Bell developed a particularly influential model for thinking about the relationship of an audience to language variation, which he first called the Audience Design Model (Bell 1984) and later renamed the Audience and Referee Design Model (Bell 1999). The idea behind both of these versions of the model is that speakers adapt their linguistic output largely in relation to their audience. The *audience design* component of the model captures linguistic variation used in response to aspects of the audience, and the *referee design* component captures linguistic styles used to index groups not directly present. Changing from a formal to an informal style of speaking when moving from speaking with a work supervisor to a friend illustrates the audience design component, with the idea being that the shift in styles occurs as a response to different properties of the audience (here, either the boss or the friend). As for the referee design component, a good example of this can be found in music genres. Before they became popular, the Beatles (as did, and do, many pop singers who aren't Americans) sang using an American accent rather than their native British accent (see Trudgill 1983 and Beal 2009 for discussions of this phenomenon). In this case, it wasn't some specific listener that they were responding to in shifting to an American accent. They were, in a sense, creating the context of being authentic pop/rock singers by virtue of making the shift. As Bell writes:

> We need a framework which acknowledges that much of our interpersonal linguistic behaviour displays a pattern which can be systematized, and that we are also continually making creative, dynamic choices on the linguistic representation of our identities. These are to be seen as two co-existent but distinct dimensions of style, which operate simultaneously in all speech events, just as structure and agency are present in all social actions. (1984, 526)

These two design components, audience and referee, are meant to capture the ongoing dynamic between structure and agency by tapping into existing indexical associations (audience design/responsive shifting) and creating new ones (referee design/initiative shifting).

A further component of this model, which is useful for thinking about language variation in the media, concerns the conception of the audience. In the Audience and Referee Design model, the audience is conceived in layered parts that include the direct participants in a conversation as well as various other people who may experience the conversation. When we interact, a whole variety of different kinds of people may be either directly or indirectly involved in the interaction. For instance, you may be talking directly to one specific person in a group of people. That person is your *addressee*. The other people who are present are also part of the audience, even though they are not being addressed directly. In the Audience and Referee Design model, these people are known as *auditors*. In addition, there may be people who can hear you (and who you know can hear you) but who aren't otherwise part of the conversation. The Audience and Referee Design model captures this layer of the audience as *overhearers*. Finally, there may be people who are present but who aren't known to the participants or otherwise involved in the conversation, referenced in the model as *eavesdroppers*.

Food for Thought

Think about creating a film that involves a Chinese immigrant living in a large urban area. How might you construct that character's language output differently depending on different characteristics your target audience has? How might different media producers think about that issue differently – e.g., the writer, the actor, the directors, the film's marketers?

Bell based his original formulation of the model on radio announcers who worked for stations that catered to different target audiences, and he noted that the shifts in how they did the announcing were best captured by considering them as a response to those different audiences. This makes intuitive sense; however, modeling the audience for narrative fictional media is a somewhat more complex task since the audience is both internal to the performance in the form of the direct interaction among characters and external to the performance in the form of the people who watch the performance after it's been created. (The people who write, direct, and capture the performance are also a part of the audience, but we won't pay a lot of attention to them at this point.) The second audience functions simultaneously as a set of auditors, overhearers, and eavesdroppers.

Example 8.1 illustrates these layers of audience. The scene involves speakers who are talking to someone on the phone while reacting to an overhearer to the conversation.

Example 8.1   *Key and Peele*, "Phone Call," Keegan-Michael Key and Jordan Peele (creators), Comedy Central, promotional video released online November 15, 2011

```
Key, talking on his cell phone standing on a street
corner
```

```
1  Key:    Cause you're my wife and you love the
           theater and uh it's your birthday, huh [..]
           Great. Unfortunately the um [another man,
           Peele, walks towards street corner calling
           someone on his cell phone] the orchestra's
           already filled up but they do have seats.
```

2   [Key notices Peele as he stops at street
    corner waiting for the light to change
    so he can cross. Both continue their
    separate conversations.]

3   Key: That are still left in the<voice shifts
             from upbeat and standard to a bit lower
             and more vernacular>dress circle so if
             you want um me to get them theáter tickets
             right now Imma do it right now

4   Peele: <deep voice, vernacular>Wassup dog. 'm
             about five minutes away.

5   Key: Yeah, okay, yeah, cool, no dey all good
             singers, dey all good singers

6   Peele: Yeah son [..] Nah man I'm 'bout [..] I'm
             tellin' you man I'm about to cross the
             street.

7   Key: Naw dey got dat one dude in it datchu love,
             man, he gon' be in it.

8   Peele: Oh come on man you know I'm almost there
             a'ight?

9   Key: Right, nah, Imma pick yo' ass up at six
             thirty then. Coo'

10 [Peele looks at Key. Key nods back at Peele,
    who looks back to the street.]

11 Peele: Coo', coo'

12 Key: Yeah, yeah, yeah, yeah, de parking is uh
             the parking's free

13 [Peele starts crossing the street leaving Key behind.]

14 Peele: Oh my God Christian I almost totally just
             got mugged right now?

This scene was released as a preview in advance of the start of the sketch comedy series, *Key and Peele* (2012–), so it is directly intended to create an audience for the show. The humor in this scene comes from the erroneous assumptions of danger on the part of both Key and Peele, assumptions linked to broader ideologies about black men in urban areas. Within the scene, these assumptions are reinforced largely through the shift in language from a standard version of American English that is indexed to higher social classes and/or education levels to a version of AAVE that is highly indexed to urban masculinity. Peele also shifts further to a style that is indexical of American gay men at the end of the scene.

In the interaction, the person on the telephone in each case is the addressee; however, the first shift (line 3) occurs in response to Peele's character, an overhearer in this case because he is not part of Key's audience. Peele's switch in line 14 to a different style shifts the context entirely for us, the viewing audience, since we have only heard him using the more urban style to this point. In that sense, his shift is initiative. The joke carries through the scene in that Key's initial shift in line 3 creates an assumption about the danger Key perceives is presented by Peele, while Peele's shift in line 14 changes the entire context to show that he made the same assumptions from the beginning.

The first shift the audience hears is clearly responsive, while the second is initiative. Though both are undoubtedly created for the viewing audience, the first is much more contextually bound to the interaction in the scene itself, while the second engages the audience, as overhearers, more directly as the punchline of the sketch. In this case, the switch also achieves the overall plot resolution for the sketch.

The preview sets expectations for the viewing audience about what kind of show *Key and Peele* is likely to be. In less than four minutes, the viewing audience can deduce that *Key and Peele* will be a sketch comedy and that the actors involved will use their abilities to change their language for various situational and humorous effects. From the shifts they make, we also know that the show will probably use ethnicity as a primary focal point for much of the humor (and possibly social critique), and we can see that that focal point will include intersections with other major social categories, such as gender and social class. For viewers familiar with sketch comedies that use ethnicity as a focal point, the preview also recalls other similar shows, especially *In Living Color* (1990–1994) and *Chappelle's Show* (2003–2005).

Given what we now understand about how language variation helps "design" the experience of audiovisual media for the viewing audience, including the many ways that such variation is meaningful, the *Key and Peele* example encourages us to shift our analytic lens from the kinds of micro-interactional details that we focused on in Chapter 7 and from the details of character exposition that we covered in Chapter 6. Instead, *Key and Peele* pushes us to think more directly about how the language variation used in character exposition and that used in an unfolding plot interact to create an overall language form that helps the viewers anchor a given media product in the more general media environment.

Setting Expectations for Viewers

Using categories of audiovisual media represents an important mechanism that consumers of media can use for deciding how a specific television show or film might fit their own particular interests and media landscape.

I know, for instance, that it is a rare kind of science fiction that will both capture and retain my interest. I can take or leave romantic comedies, although I will usually be drawn to those involving some of my favorite actors. Like many other viewers, I derive true pleasure watching Meryl Streep or Jennifer Lawrence transform themselves chameleon-like into a wide range of different characters. However, for as much as I enjoy their acting prowess, I typically skip their movies if my understanding of the general situation of the story involves something I find creepy, scary, or gross. I stopped watching *Mad Men* (2007–) regularly when I began to find the sexism and racism, however realistic for the time period, unbearable, and, similarly, when the taboo language use in *Deadwood* (2004–2006) started to seem unrealistic for the situations in which it was being used, I stopped watching. What these examples have in common is their connection to my expectations of what I would experience. Connecting a media product to a pre-existing set of recognizable types of media signifies one of the most critical means for setting audience expectations.

For centuries, going at least as far back as the ancient Greeks, people have used heuristics (i.e., general rules of thumb) to categorize different types of events, including language events, in ways that make them recognizable. In Chapter 2 we discussed the basic categorization of bundles of features into "languages" and "dialects" and noted that the distinction largely rests on users' own beliefs about how bundles of features should be categorized. As we've seen throughout this book, variation within languages and dialects proves to be critical for achieving many of the effects we find in the audiovisual media. Those effects are tied broadly to three intersecting elements: (a) the linguistic material, (b) the context of use, and (c) the users of language. The anchoring work that linguistic variation may do involves all three of these, and, critically, it's their interaction that does the work of "designing" the linguistic *gestalt* (or whole system) of a media product for the viewing audience.

Although the three components are always interacting with one another, it can sometimes make sense to highlight one or the other element to better understand how the viewing audience may be engaged. In linguistics, the most common terms for these different elements are genre, register, and style. Broadly, *genre* captures systems related to one another by virtue of shared elements (linguistic or other aspects) of form; *register* captures systems related to one another by virtue of shared aspects of their situation of use; and *style* captures systems related on another by virtue of shared aspects of users. Although each of these terms provides a slightly different angle on the basic phenomena of systematic variation, it will not always be clear-cut or easy to distinguish between them. Just as we saw in our discussion of dimensions of variation in Chapter 4, the terms used to capture an overall linguistic gestalt are best understood in gradient rather than categorical terms.

Genres are typically named (think here of "Westerns," "fiction," "rom-coms," "sitcoms," and so on), while registers and styles typically are not (though think of "Gangnam style"). A genre is a way of categorizing texts (where that can be used quite broadly to include films or television shows) based on a property or set of properties that they share. Language will often be one of those properties, though rarely the only one. Genres are in every sense tied to the concept of the generic, and they typically organize texts or performances based on those generic properties (see Briggs and Bauman 1992). Media products are frequently organized in terms of genres. Consider how Amazon.com or NetFlix categorize their media products, and you'll see a very broad categorization based on genre at work. Speech genres relevant to the audiovisual media include many of the different forms connected to unscripted media, such as those used by newscasters, sports announcers, and talk show hosts. Within the audiovisual narrative media, film genres themselves are often marked by different speech genres. For instance, the forms of language found in dramas tend to differ considerably from those found in comedies.

Food for Thought

Watch (or think about) two comedies and two dramas (or pick two other genres that you think contrast with one another). Can you name three ways that the language use seems similar within the genres? How about three ways that the language differs across the two genres?

Register, on the other hand, seeks to categorize variation based on differences in situations of use. As Anna Babel explains,

The term register was first developed in sociolinguistics to describe special types of language that seem to be set apart from ordinary speech in some way (Halliday 1964, 1978). These types of language are often related to a professional jargon, such as sports broadcaster talk or legalese. Register is also associated with formality scales, ranging from very informal, conversational speech to reading or reciting styles (Joos 1961). The term register is often used in connection with languages such as Javanese (Errington 1988), which have a variety of named registers that are appropriate for certain types of interlocutors. A central property of these theories of register involves linking language varieties to situations rather than to speakers. (2010, 10)

The concept of registers is not as widely known outside of linguistics as the concept of genre; however, people frequently notice language variation when it occurs unexpectedly in some situation or another, which is essentially noticing register variation. For instance, the use of conventional taboo words like those we discussed in Chapter 7 is highly linked to registers, with the taboo being culturally strongest in situations that are more public, more formal, and otherwise more serious or grave. Part of the humor in Example 8.2 comes from the prince's misunderstanding of the register.

Example 8.2   *Coming to America*, John Landis (dir.), 1988, Eddie Murphy Productions

```
Prince Akeem stands on rickety balcony in a seedy
area of town but is full of cheer and delight.
Sami, his servant, opens the window and looks at him
skeptically.

1 Akeem:      Behold Sami, life, real life. The thing
              that we have been denied for far too long.
              [He grins and looks around]. Good Morning,
              my neighbors.
2 Someone:    Hey, fuck you
3 Akeem:      <happily> Yes, Yes, fuck you too!
```

In this scene, Prince Akeem, who has arrived in Queens, New York, to search for a marriage partner, takes in his new surroundings with a sense of adventure. The surroundings are decidedly less posh than those he is used to being in, and his servant, Sami, is deeply unhappy to be in such humble accommodations. When the Prince's "Good Morning" is met with a curse, he misunderstands what has happened, assuming based on the register variation associated with well-intentioned greetings that "fuck you" is a return greeting of some kind. Thus, he says it back to the neighborhood. The humor comes from the mismatch of situation with particular linguistic material.

The remaining component relevant for thinking about how to categorize shifts between different systems has to do with aspects of users, which is often referred to as style. Different scholars have defined style in different

Food for Thought

How might you change the way you greeted someone if you met them at a football game versus at a business meeting versus unexpectedly while on a walk in the woods?

ways. Labov (1972) provided one of the simplest definitions of style, namely, as attention paid to speech. Others (Coupland 1980, 2007; Bell 1984) have argued that style is variation as tied to individuals (compared with whole populations) or to systems of co-occurring elements (Irvine 2001). For our purposes, we can think of style as a form of language that has meaning beyond the basic referential meaning of the words and syntax. Coupland (2007, 69) has argued that styles are the meanings that get linked to variation in language when it is put into action as part of people interacting with one another (see also Eckert 2008). The critical component here is that style is generally variation that is focused on aspects of users (as compared to situations of use or the shared characteristics of the formal elements in use).

On the one hand, we can think of style as a kind of individual linguistic signature – as a way of marking something as originating from a specific person. My personal style might include sarcasm or asking many questions. Every time I use sarcasm or ask a question, I mark that occasion as "mine" in a sense. It's a bit like fashion in which different designers come to have recognizable design styles, and you can point to specific elements as well as combinations of elements to distinguish one designer from another. In the case of language, an individual's style can include elements from all parts of the grammar. A friend of mine, for instance, has a distinct accent that differs from all of his family members' and friends' accents and from the region where he has lived for his entire life. Many people assume he immigrated to the place where he lives; however, this is not the case. It is simply that his personal style is particularly distinctive.

Thinking about style beyond individuals' idiosyncratic uses leads us to a different set of considerations, a set that depends more directly on the interaction between producing and interpreting styles. This orientation to style relies on conventionalized meanings, or indexicalities (see Chapter 5), that become attached to groups of linguistic features that typically co-occur. For instance, if I say, "I ain't got no money" (as Bob Seger did in his eponymous song), I have used two different linguistic features that often go together, 'ain't' and double negation. Stylistically, this is quite different than if I say, "I don't have any money," even though the referential meaning is the same. The difference is not idiosyncratic to me; rather, it is something that most speakers of English understand as meaningful regardless of who utters it. Although we don't entirely understand the process through which people come to interpret the differences between these two sentences in a very similar way, we do know that they do interpret them similarly. In talking about "conventionalized meanings," that similarity in interpretation is what is at stake.

Food for Thought

List some of the differences in meaning between the two versions of the sentence about money in the paragraph above. If you have access to the Bob Seger song, listen to it for other features that might go along with 'ain't' and 'double negation.' For instance, how many times does he use the [IN] pronunciation of the progressive morpheme?

People shift between different styles for all kinds of reasons; however, most of those reasons can be captured by the two broad explanations offered in the audience design framework. First, people may shift their style as a reaction to something in the situation or general context. In the last chapter, we looked at an example from the television series *Weeds* where one character is trying to get a bank loan from another character. The pivotal point in the scene involves the bank manager completely switching his speaking style when he makes a comment to his colleague; something the other character mocks him for with a style shift of his own. Both of these shifts occur as a reaction to something in the scene: in the first instance, the appearance of the colleague, and in the second, the style shift of the bank manager. While the shifts themselves function to further an element of the narrative, and in that sense alter the context from what it was, the shifting per se doesn't create a new context. This is responsive shifting.

Creating a new context represents the second broad explanation for style shifting. Actors shift to new styles and accents as a means of creating new characters. Indeed, the ability to do so represents a large part of the craft of acting. Meryl Streep creates Julia Child and Margaret Thatcher (two award-winning roles she's played) in large part by stylistic shifts in language that correspond to other shifts in general style. Further, many narratives that use the plot device of dual or hidden identities rely on style shifts to create the contexts in which one or another of the identities is activated. You can see this type of shifting in films like *Big* (1988) or *Freaky Friday* (1976 and 2003), in which a child lives as an adult, and in films like *Victor/Victoria* (1982) *Tootsie* (1982), and *She's the Man* (2006), in which a person of one conventional gender pretends to be the other. In these cases, stylistic variation often serves as the linchpin for creating the different character identities. We can think of this type of shifting as creative shifting.

As is true for most categorization schemes, it is not always easy to determine whether you are working with a creative or responsive type of shifting. It's also not always easy to know if the shifting is tied to register, genre, style, or some combination of these. For instance, a specific doctor might have a largely informal style within the register of doctor–patient interaction and the nature of that style will likely differ from the same speaker's informal style in the situation of speaking to the non-profit club she works with after hours. Similarly, the components of one doctor's informal style may differ from the components of another doctor's informal style, even within the same contexts. In this way, we see that the linguistic elements involved can be simultaneously linked to aspects of the individual users (style), the situations of use (register), and the similarities of form across different instances (genre). Determining whether to focus more on genre, register, or style often depends on the relative weight of one of the three components, although in actuality all three will generally be relevant.

Enregisterment

In the discussion so far of different ways of talking about linguistic systems, I purposively glossed over the question of where these systems come from in the first place, a question that is critical for understanding their ability to do the kinds of work that we have explored them doing throughout this book. Asif Agha (2007) has called the process of how systems emerge as recognizable wholes *enregisterment*. Agha describes this as the process by which a set of linguistic variables or features becomes interpretable as belonging to a distinguishable code or variety (2007, 231). The key element for enregisterment is the relationship between distinguishing one linguistic form from another and linking linguistic forms to language users in an indexical way. It is how we know what we are talking about when we say something like "English" or "southern" or "child-language." Especially useful for our purposes in thinking about language variation in the fictional media is that you can use the features that show up in the media to understand more about how groups of linguistic forms have been enregistered as distinctive. Lauren Squires explains enregisterment as

> An ideological process whereby speakers' perceptions of linguistic variation, social structure, and other pertinent concepts are put to use in construing practices as group- and/or variety-specific. Ideologies of language are subconscious heuristics through which speakers perceive and explain patterns of linguistic structure and use (Silverstein 1979, Mertz 1998, Woolard 1998, Irvine and Gal 2000, Kroskrity 2000), and an enregistered variety brings those heuristics into observable and conscious focus, sharpening them into a central organizing concept that specifies (to varying degree) the parameters of a variety and its speakers (or nonspeakers). (2011, 460)

Enregisterment provides a set of guideposts for focusing in particular on how discussions of language specify a principle for organizing linguistic features into larger conceptual groupings like dialects, registers, styles, or languages that can be interpreted by an audience. Enregisterment models the process through which ideology and indexicality become linked, and that process turns out to be heavily dependent on the dynamic interaction between "speakers" and "listeners" (or producers and audiences) and the mechanisms of interpretation at work within that dynamic.

In the media, these mechanisms frequently take the form of *metalanguage*, or language about language. Metalanguage can be from fans about the language(s) of characters, from actors (or directors/writers) who discuss how they have those characters speak, or from the characters themselves in the context of direct interaction in the media product. In Example 8.3, we see an example of metalanguage between characters.

Example 8.3 *Mean Girls,* Mark Waters (dir.), 2004, Paramount Pictures

```
1  Regina:    Oh my god?, I love your bracelet. Where
              did you get it?
2  Cady:      My mom made it for me.
3  Regina:    It's adorable.
4  Gretchen:  Oh, it's so fetch!
5  Regina:    What is fetch?
6  Gretchen:  Oh, it's like slang, from England.
7  [Later in film]
```

```
8  Gretchen:   Look how red she is. You love him, and
                he totally complimented you. That is so
                fetch.
9  Regina:     Gretchen, stop trying to make "fetch"
                happen. It's not going to happen
```

In Example 8.3, Gretchen uses a new term that the others don't know (line 4), using it directly after Regina has said that the bracelet is 'adorable.' When Regina asks Gretchen what the term means, Gretchen doesn't actually define it. She explains instead that 'it's like slang, from England.' This is exactly the kind of metalanguage that helps create namable linguistic varieties. In this case, the metalanguage about 'fetch' connects it to teenagers and the kinds of novel words they typically introduce. While the majority of those words don't make it into adulthood with the teenagers who introduce them, some of them do. Words like 'cool,' 'hang out,' and 'psych' all survived their initial period as teenage slang to become a part of the American English lexicon, albeit as part of a more colloquial, informal style. Further evidence of enregisterment in action occurs in lines 8–9, from much later in the film when Gretchen uses the term again. This is in fact the third use of the term, and Gretchen is following the typical procedure for introducing new words, using them until others pick them up. Regina, however, calls her on this attempt, telling her that it's not going to work. Regina's comment not only critiques Gretchen's use, it also provides direct insight into the process, in this case presumably failed, of incorporating new terms into the lexicon.

We also find enregisterment when actors or directors talk about language. For instance, the creator of *The Closer* discusses reactions to Kyra Sedgwick's southern accent:

> Southern accents, like the Georgia twang that New York-raised Kyra Sedgwick drawls on "The Closer," are rare for lead characters on TV. Critics and fans have been vocal about their love-it-or-hate-it relationship with Sedgwick's thick delivery, but series creator James Duff says neither he nor TNT execs ever considered losing the accent... . "There was never any question at all, because the character of Brenda Johnson was complete with that accent," Duff says. "TNT was interested in a complete character, and I think the accent was the finishing touch. I always felt like, "If people hear her authenticity, they'll hang out more with the show." Hang out they have, with improved ratings, according to Nielsen, over the course of four seasons. Not that Duff doesn't still read accent bashing online. "Most of the people who say it's not quite right are definitely from the North," says Duff, who sports his own distinctive Texas twang... .

Duff admires the accent for similar story-value reasons and personal ones as well. "I grew up in the South with really smart people who had that accent, and every time I saw them on television, they seemed like the stupidest people on the face of the earth. Like the accent was a badge of inferiority," he explains. "I thought, as long as we're doing something different, how about if the woman lead with the Southern accent is the smartest person in the room instead of the most ignorant?" (Boyd 2009)

Duff explicitly discusses the well-trodden connections between southern American accents and being dumb in the last line of the quote above, noting that he specifically wanted the person with the southern accent to be the smartest person in the room. He also notes that it is most likely people unfamiliar with the accent, "from the North," who find it inaccurate or inauthentic. Judging from fans who identify where they are from, Duff is probably not entirely accurate with his comment; however, saying that people from the north are criticizing because they are unfamiliar with the dialect is part of the ongoing metalanguage that helps constitute southern American English as a variety in the first place. Thus, this is another example of the process of enregisterment.

Indeed, when fans discuss the language of characters, they, too, engage in the process of enregisterment. Below are some of the fan comments from an *Entertainment Weekly* article on *Life* naming the worst accents in movie history (Semigran 2011):

1   Since you didn't limit the selections to movies, I nominate Kyra Sedgewick [sic] in "The Closer". Her "Southern" accent is so over the top and farcical I am embarrassed for her. I can't believe this show is supposedly top rated in any universe because listening to her butcher a southern accent makes me sick and I turn the channel.

2   But the REAL award def goes to Kyra Sedgewick [sic] in The Closer. No educated, professional Southerner speaks like that.

3   TM, if you'll notice she really turns it up when she's trying to get her way (especially with Fritz)!! Every good Southern woman knows how to lay it on thick to get what we want!! LOL!! 😊

4   I love the show but Kyra Sedgwick on The Closer. She supposed to be from Atlanta, which is where I'm from, but no one here speaks that way. It's a little grating …

5   I live in Alabama and compared to most Hollywood "Southern" accents, hers really isn't that bad. There are definitely women here who can make a "thank you" sound like a "go screw yourself" like she does. Yes, it's a touch over-exaggerated & overly gracious but I do know people who do that. I had a professor from Georgia who did that when he was excited or trying to make a point.

6   Brenda's "over-exaggerated & overly gracious" accent, along with her floral prints and pink coat, are used to disarm people into underestimating Brenda. It's a persona developed by the character. No matter who played the role, Brenda would have that over done accent.

The various comments from the site reference both the actor Kyra Sedgwick and the character she animates, Brenda Johnson, disagreeing on whether or not the accent is a "good" accent. The fans identify themselves in some cases as from the south (comments 3, 4, and 5), belying the series' creator's claims that it is northerners who critique the accent. Some of them also note that the character uses the accent for effect. This is the stance taken in comments 3, 5, and 6, in particular.

What we see by looking at the fan comments is another facet of enregisterment as the viewers react to the media products they experience. In this case, all of the comments reference the dialect in question as if it is a clearly delineated object, and none make any attempt to tease apart the various components of the different dialects being compared (the series creator James Duff, discussed above, doesn't either). Rather, they accept the "accent" as a namable, specified system. In other words, the fans calling the system the "accent" engages the process of enregisterment.

Most discussions of enregisterment consider mass media one of the primary institutions involved in the process on the assumption that the media have a clear influence on how language variation is perceived and produced outside the media. Indeed, the diffusion of linguistic forms across communities that are otherwise disconnected from one another exemplifies one of the primary influences ascribed to the media in linguistic research. Jane Stuart-Smith and her colleagues (2013) have shown, for instance, that adolescents in Glasgow use features of the sound system more characteristic of London, even though they have little connection to London as a place or to people from London. In her work, those adolescents who are avid viewers of the long-running soap opera *EastEnders* show the most pronounced use of the London sounds (for instance pronouncing the < th > sound in words like 'thing' with an < f > as in 'fing'). Thus, despite virtually no direct connection to London, these features are starting to be enregistered as part of Glaswegian, and the path of that enregisterment moves through the fictional media.

Jane Stuart-Smith's work demonstrates one way in which a media product can engage its viewing audience linguistically, such that language variation experienced through the media serves as a source for enregisterment. A further mechanism of enregisterment that we encounter in the media occurs with the use (and subsequent recognition by viewers) of variation that may not specifically be linked to variation outside the media. This kind of variation may be referred to in different ways, such as 'cinema speech,' 'film dialogue,' and 'movie accent,' and captures exactly the systems that voice coaches and teachers work with actors on perfecting. In film traditions linked to dubbing, such as those in much of western Europe, the style of dubbing is typically recognized as a sub-genre of the 'movie accent' (see Queen 2004, 521).

Food for Thought

It is not easy to find clear examples of enregisterment because the process of enregisterment is typically normalized so that it seems unremarkable. Still, it can be worth looking for examples. Can you think of any cases in the media in which a dialect or accent is discussed as a specific thing within the media? Do those discussions differ in particular ways from how standard varieties are discussed?

One accent that was specifically enregistered for fictional media purposes within English-speaking media is the *transatlantic accent*. Nan Withers-Wilson, cited in Kozloff (2000, 240), explains this accent as representing "a neutral dialect that borrowed from both Standard British and Standard American pronunciations." It was particularly prevalent from the 1930s through the late 1950s, falling out of favor as the film industry moved away from studio control of actors, directors, and writers. The transatlantic accent was specifically taught to actors and involved stylistic variation of its own, primarily to distinguish higher-class and lower-class characters or to distinguish regional origins of characters. It very clearly indexes overtly staged performance.

Although current narrative films and television series are characterized by approximations of more realistic accents, they still follow some of the conventions of the transatlantic in certain circumstances. This creates an interpretive loop for audience members, who can use their knowledge of the transatlantic in older films to anchor their experience with more contemporary media. Films in English but set in non-English-speaking places often use a variety of English that has characteristics of the transatlantic. For instance, in the American remake of *The Girl with the Dragon Tattoo* (2011) most of the actors use this style. You can also hear it in the accents found in *The Hunger Games* (2012). Elizabeth Banks, who plays the character Effie in *The Hunger Games*, notes specifically that she crafted the character's accent as a "combination of *The Philadelphia Story* (1940) and Rosaline Russell in *Auntie Mame* (1958)" (Orange 2012). Both of those films contain canonical examples of the transatlantic accent.

Another context in which a modern version of the transatlantic appears is films set in the time period when the transatlantic was in full force. This includes films like *Hugo* (2011), *The Artist* (2011), and *Chicago* (2002). In these films, the accent creates the setting of the earlier film era even as it keeps the film grounded in a contemporary setting. *Hugo* is especially interesting because it illustrates both of the contemporary uses of the transatlantic accent, as the film is in English but set in 1930s Paris. The narrative focuses on the silent film era and thus is a movie about movies and making movies. As a movie about movies, *Hugo* simultaneously connects the time frame of its production (early part of the twenty-first century) and the time frame it represents (early part of the twentieth century). The accent of the characters plays an important role in this framing. The main characters all use the modern transatlantic; however, minor characters use French-accented English and Cockney in addition to the transatlantic.

One of the key mechanisms of enregisterment involves language that calls attention to itself in some fashion, and, in many ways, this is exactly what the transatlantic does because it is a variety of English that has no connection to real-world varieties of English. In calling attention to itself, the transatlantic creates complex ties between media producers, media products, and their viewing audiences. In this sense, the transatlantic may be seen as a representative of much of the language variation that occurs in the audiovisual narrative media, in which media producers specifically highlight conventions of genre, register, and style in their efforts to connect to their audience. Most scholars who work on language in the media have referred to this highlighting as stylization.

Stylization

Stylization in language refers to speaking in a voice other than one's own in an overtly noticeable manner (Bell and Gibson 2011, 560). A simple example where we see stylized language occurs when someone (S1) mimics another person (S2). In that instance, S1 is simultaneously acting as herself as well as S2. If S1 directly quotes S2, she may well try to perform S2's own vocal style. Indeed one of the ways to indicate a direct quotation without using a quotative verb is to stylize the speaker being quoted. In this sense, stylization can be understood as embedded directly within grammars.

Stylization is both an act of authentication (making yourself believable as yourself) and deauthentication (making yourself believable as not yourself), making it a curiously reflexive method of speaking. Coupland (2007) refers to stylization as *strategic inauthenticity* and sketches it as a manner of speaking that projects personae and situations other than those current in the speech event into the speech event, thereby embedding one layer of social context into another. He further notes that stylization is a creative skill of performance that requires some degree of aptitude and learning. As such, it is often hyperbolic and overly emphatic, which adds to the effect of calling attention to itself (2007, 154). Bakhtin (1986) referred to this aspect of language use as *double voicing*.

Stylization differs somewhat from the work that actors do when they create a character, which we discussed in depth in Chapter 6. While it is certainly true that creating a character is a simultaneous act of authentication and deauthentication, the critical component distinguishing characterization generally from stylization is the layers of embedding of social contexts. When a character stylizes, he or she adds an extra layer of social embedding to the performance. Thus, we have the first layer, in which the actor performs the character, and a second layer, in which the character performs as yet a different character. This added layer requires a different kind of interpretive engagement from the audience than does the initial characterization.

A nice example of stylization occurs in the film *Wanderlust* (2012), in which two characters find themselves living in a very different context than they are used to. One of the different facets of this new community is a much more open approach to sexuality and sexual relationships, and, in Example 8.4, George tries to prepare himself to have sex with someone other than his wife (at the prompting of his wife, who is interested in doing the same). As he speaks to himself in the mirror, he increasingly shifts his language into a stylized version of a hypersexualized persona.

Example 8.4   *Wanderlust*, David Wain (dir.), 2012, Apatow Productions

```
1  Linda:   You gotta do this
2  [George walks to other room where there is a
   bathroom]
3  George:  Oh, God.
4  [George moves to mirror and talks to himself]
5  George:  This was your idea, George. It's a good
            idea, right? It's a good idea, monogamy is
            sexual slavery. <Style shift> She
            got an exquisite pussy well how 'bout my
            exquisite erection, huh? <deeper pitch> Eva,
            whaddya think? You like my exqui%exquisite
            erection? Mmmm? You like my, erection
```

selection? [Hand gesture like a waiter
offering tea] Whaddya think,
Eva? Yeah? <breathy><Style shift again>
you 'onna take it? You 'onna take that
dick? <lips stretched over teeth; slower,
lower pitch, heavy release of /k/>You gonna
take that dick<diphthongized vowel and
heavy release of k>I'm'na pop off a piece
of my dick [monophthongized /ay/ on<my>].
Oh yea, I'm fixin's ta fuck ya. I 'ona fuck
ya. Mm. Hmm-hmm. I'm gonna git it all up
in yo vag<long vowel, diphthongized>Git
it up in yo vag with my dick. Wif my
dick<monophthongize /ai/, diphthongized
/I/ and heavy release of /k/. Lower pitch
again.>Gonna put it in, wif my dick<same
as above, lower pitch on 'wif my dick'>I'm
gonna puts my dick in<higher pitch,
monophthongized<my>]. I'm gon' puts my
dick i:::n<Style shift: louder,
higher-pitched>

6 [Rodney walks by]
7 Rodney: What's up man, you all [right?
8 George: <Normal voice>   [hey man What's up?

According to an interview with Paul Rudd, who plays George in the
film, this scene was the second scene they filmed and is entirely ad-libbed
(Ain't It Cool News 2012). It is difficult to capture the noticeable style
shifts that occur in the film in a transcript; however, indicators to some of

the features of the shift are noted in the transcript itself. In the scene, George stylizes a character with a particular kind of sexual prowess, and, as he does so, he uses a range of linguistic features that are indexical of sexualized masculinity, lack of education, lower social class status, and both urban and rural masculinity. As he begins his monologue in turn 5, he shifts his style to a stylized formal style, captured in particular with the word 'exquisite' and the poetic 'erection selection.' Following that, he style shifts again and begins using the more colloquial and vulgar term 'dick.' This shift includes a much lower pitch as well as vowel and consonant pronunciations indexical of the rural south, including the auxiliary verb 'fixin' to.' As he continues to try and convince himself to have sex with another women, he begins using some stylized grammatical features that are found both in urban and rural areas of the United States, including an added '-s' on 'fixin' and 'put,' 'I'ma' as a marker of future tense, and the pronunciation of 'with' as 'wif.' It is clear throughout the monologue that George is stylizing a very specific kind of man, a man more or less the opposite of himself.

In considering this scene, there are also several identities to keep in mind. There is the actor himself, Paul Rudd, as well as the character, George. Paul creates George in a more or less stylized manner, and George stylizes a different, more idealized persona in order to try and shift himself toward activities that he would otherwise not engage in and about which he is profoundly uncomfortable (and when he uses this stylized persona with the woman he wants to have sex with, she is completely turned off and rejects him, even though she had propositioned him earlier). In a discussion about white characters shifting into AAVE, Quina Lopez and Mary Bucholtz make a distinction between 'styling' and 'stylizing' to capture specifically the difference between Paul Rudd performing George (*styling*) and George performing as a very different persona than his 'normal' one (stylizing) (Bucholtz and Lopez 2011, 151).

Food for Thought

Find three examples in which a character stylizes either another character or some other kind of persona. What linguistic distinctions can you find between how the actor styles the character and how the character stylizes the Other?

Another way to capture this kind of stylization is to consider it in terms of indexical ordering like we discussed back in Chapter 5. In this case, we could simply think of stylization as recursive in which one moment of stylization opens a path for additional ones that are linked in some way or another to the first. While this is quite common in the media since characters can stylize as much as actors can, we can assume that it is also available outside the media. Indeed, Elaine Chun (2009) illustrates exactly such a case when she describes a high school student doing an imitation of a friend doing an imitation of someone outside the friend group. Thinking about stylization as recursive (as well as reflexive) helps provide a model for how and why stylization connects media producers, media products, and media audiences.

Interacting with Audiovisual Media

Throughout the book, we've talked about different components of language as well as different ways of understanding the kind of work that language does beyond relaying content. In this chapter, we've looked specifically at the interrelationships between features of language, features of situations of use, and features of users. In thinking about those interrelationships, we've focused simultaneously on the interactions that occur among characters as well as those that function outside the media product, namely, among those who create the product and those who experience it as part of the audience. One important connection between these two layers of interaction is language. While the language variation found in a media product may differ in both qualitative and quantitative ways from the language variation found off-media, the basic patterns and contours of variation are quite similar. This similarity comes from the fact that creators and the viewers draw on and have access to the same basic repertoires, including codes that are linked specifically to media, such as the transatlantic accent. The processes of enregisterment and stylization that we discussed above provide the mechanisms by which these repertoires are shared and facilitate the believability of characters and their actions. That believability creates a narrative coherence that in turn helps maintain viewers' connections to the media product.

Media studies scholars have explored what is known as *parasocial activity* since the 1970s. Parasocial activity captures the real affective, emotional, and cognitive relationship that someone experiencing a media product has with the characters and activities shown within the product (Perse and Rubin 1989). Because audience members are not generally in a position to interact directly with media characters, the relationships are considered parasocial. Parasocial activity has been evaluated in a variety of ways, including in terms of tourism (Kim 2012), cognitive engagement (Giles 2012), and identification and interaction (Auter and Palmgreen 2000). Audience members come to care about fictional characters, and the degree of interest in characters' lives extends similarly to characters who are embodied by actual humans actors as well as those who are represented in other ways (Giles 2012).

One of the ways that all relationships proceed is of course through language, and parasocial relationships in particular depend on language for their expression, given the general unlikelihood of face-to-face interaction between the audience and characters. In a very interesting study examining converging linguistic styles, Goode and Robinson showed that fans who commented on blog posts ostensibly written by favorite soap opera characters used similar linguistic features as the authors of the blog. They argued that this illustrates that parasocial interaction is not "something that resembles interpersonal interaction" but that it is interpersonal interaction (2013, 463).

Richard Bauman (2011a, 710–711) has argued that "the poetic organization of performance sets up patterns of expectation and fulfillment in an audience that serves as a powerful means of eliciting their participatory involvement." In parasocial activities, we are able to observe somewhat directly how that involvement unfolds. Further, through stylization and enregisterment, we have a model for how language can help construct and maintain parasocial relationships and participatory involvement (see also Zubair 2011). We also see particular roadmaps for evaluating authenticity. In Chapter 6, we explored the notion of authenticity, and I argued that authenticity captures the relationship between ideological generalization and lived sensory experience. The particular codes and combination of codes and features used by media producers provide a powerful means for triggering assessments of authenticity.

Food for Thought

Find a discussion board, Twitter thread, or blog that appears to be maintained by a character (or set of characters) from a television series. Examine the interaction between the characters and the fans. Do you see evidence there of parasocial activity? What aspects of language seem to be involved?

Such triggering may help explain the role of *EastEnders* in the diffusion of certain sounds into Glaswegian (described a few pages ago). Jane Stuart-Smith and her colleagues (2013) argue that the diffusion of these forms to Glaswegian comes partially through the specific ways that adolescents consume and participate in the soap drama. They demonstrate through regression modeling that passively viewing *EastEnders* is not sufficient to exert a linguistic influence; instead, the adolescents who used the London forms most consistently were those viewers who also actively participated in *EastEnders* parasocially. As a narrative television series, the language used by the characters on *EastEnders* must be understood as essentially stylized, created specifically as a means toward concrete interaction with the viewing audience.

Another way in which narrative media may stylize language variation as a means of connecting to the viewing audiences arises when characters quote or otherwise reference lines or characters from other films or television. For example, in the television series *Suits* (2011–), characters frequently quote famous lines from films and television to one another. Different dyads of characters engage in the stylized quotation, and it can function both competitively and cooperatively among the characters. The television show is a law firm procedural with an interesting twist in that one of the characters (Mike, a junior associate) has faked a Harvard law degree. Mike was hired anyway by a partner (Harvey) with full knowledge that he doesn't actually have a degree. Harvey also hired Katarina as part of a bargain on a particular case, and she and Mike compete with one another for Harvey's attention.

In Example 8.5, Katrina and Mike have been forced by Harvey to work together to solve a puzzle. If they solve it, their firm and the firm's client will gain a distinct advantage in an ongoing legal dispute.

Example 8.5   *Suits*, "Conflict of Interest," Season 3, Episode 4, Aaron Korsch (creator), USA Network, August 6, 2013.

```
Katrina and Mike looking for a way to catch a
corporate raider doing something problematic

 1  Katrina:   Huh, do you wanna go down the same road
               and have another fight or do you wanna
               figure out a way that we can]
 2  Mike:                                   [Shit
 3  Katrina:   What?
```

4 Mike: [points at her and then back to looking
              at papers] We've been looking in the
              wrong place
5 [Katrina comes around to same side of table while
   Mike finds something and chuckles. He pins a post
   it to the whiteboard while Katrina looks at what
   he found.]
6 Katrina: Shi[
7 Mike: [looks at board sitting down]
              [Shit
8 Katrina: [finds another relevant post it and puts
              it on the whiteboard] shitty
              shit
9 Mike: Shi:::t<strong creaky voice>
10 Katrina: You're in ta the Wire?
11 [Mike puts celery in his mouth reminiscent of
   Bunk with a cigar, they both sit on table
   looking at their solution]
12 Together: Shi:::t
13 [Several scenes later]
14 Katrina: For what it's worth, I suggested Louis
              take you with him
15 Mike: [looks at papers] Shit @@@
16 Katrina: As Sal would say, "Just when I thought
              I was out, they pull me back in"<gruff
              voice>
17 Mike: O.k., so you watch the Sopranos,
              too?
18 Katrina: Nobody watches the Wire without starting
              with the Sopranos
19 [They smile at each other]
20 Mike: you, uh, did you really suggest that to
              Louis?
21 Katrina: It was your idea. [..] You deserve the
              credit
22 Mike: [purses lips; puts out hand to shake
              with her] Truce?
23 [Shaking hands]
24 Katrina: Truce
25 Together: Shi:::t

In lines 2–9, the scene is directly reminiscent of the scene in *The Wire* detailed at the end of Chapter 7 in which two characters solve a crime uttering only variations on the word 'fuck.' In this case, something very similar happens but with the word 'shit.' Katrina and Mike figure out how to catch the corporate raider in problematic practices that will force him to deal differently with their client. In line 9, Mike utters 'shit' in a very specific way, mimicking the character Clay Davis from *The Wire*. This prompts Katrina to ask Mike if he watches *The Wire* and he responds by visually mimicking Bunk, the character in the 'fuck' scene we discussed in Chapter 7. Then, the two of them together repeat the stylized Clay Davis.

This stylized media code performance continues later in the episode when Katrina gives Mike the credit for solving the puzzle to one of the senior partners, Louis Litt, represented in lines 14–25. When Katrina says she gave Mike the credit, he responds (line 15) with 'shit,' though this time in his own voice rather than the stylized voice of *The Wire*. Katrina then responds by mimicking a character from *The Sopranos* (1999–2007), a well-known crime drama focused on organized crime figures that itself frequently quotes *The Godfather* (1972), the famous Francis Ford Coppola film about organized crime. Katrina says she is quoting Sal and shifts her voice to stylize him. Sal, however, was quoting Michael Corleone from *The Godfather*.

Her reference to this character prompts Mike to acknowledge the stylized media code being used in a reference with which the audience can connect more or less directly, noting with some surprise that Katrina also watches *The Sopranos*. Her response offers a clearly recursive index to other media when she says that no one watches *The Wire* without first watching *The Sopranos*. Both series were widely acclaimed critical and commercial successes for HBO, which created them as part of its move to providing original programming. In many ways, *The Sopranos* solidified a road largely paved by another hit HBO series, *The Larry Sanders Show* (1992–1998). *The Sopranos*, though, brought a new kind of grit and realism to cable television that allowed it to compete head to head with network television for the first time. The comment places Katrina in the company of audience members who share the same opinion and reverence for the two shows.

Once Katrina and Mike declare a truce with one another (lines 20–24), they repeat the quotation of Clay Davis that they did in line 12, indicating their own surprise and satisfaction at the turn their relationship has taken (although they will continue to be highly competitive with one another). This is a complex piece of performance, connecting the two characters who are solving a crime and connecting those audience members familiar with the 'fuck' scene in *The Wire* to the characters in *Suits*. The complexity in these relationships, which arises in part because the interactions are taking place within the scene as well as outside of it, illustrate a concept known as *intertextuality*. Basically, intertextuality signals how one text can help construct the meaning of another. Intertextuality recalls the idea of citation that we discussed in Chapter 7 as one of the ways that a speech event is recognized as such. In the case of stylization and stylized media codes, intertextuality provides a means for the viewing audience to see the characters in a show or film as embedded in a similar social world to that of the viewers themselves. Intertextuality thus helps create the context for parasocial activity while allowing the audience to remain fully aware that their interactions with the characters, as real as they may be, are with fictional characters.

The USA Network, which airs *Suits*, facilitates this very type of interaction with its series *Suits Recruits* (http://classaction.usanetwork.com), which is made available online for fans. *Suits Recruits* offers interactive games, bonus scenes, and links to Twitter accounts for the major characters (and these are separate from the Twitter accounts maintained by the actors, who often retweet what the characters tweet in a highly stylized performance). As described by Broadway World,

> This season, USA broke new digital ground as it rolled out innovative social and digital engagements including second screen syncs for every episode. Leading into the premiere, USA was the first network to partner with Tinder, a social discovery app, which introduced SUITS characters into people's match stream. This generated a record-setting half a million matches in four weeks. The network also rolled out a new chapter of the award-winning Suits Recruits, an interactive, multi-platform social game. Suitors engaged in record numbers with the legal sequel Suits Recruits: Class Action, which showed an increase of 76% in uniques and 81% in visits from last year. (Broadway World 2013)

One of the *Suits Recruits* bonus episodes, "Quote for Quote," takes the stylized media code even further with a scene between Mike and Harvey made up entirely of famous quotes from famous movies, most from the 1970s, 1980s, and 1990s.

Example 8.6 *Suits*, "Quote for Quote," Aaron Korsch (creator), USA Network, released online June, 2012

```
1 Mike:    Uh, Houston we have a problem.
2 Harvey:  Did you order the Code Red
```

3 Mike: You can't handle the truth.
4 Harvey: You talkin' to me?
5 Mike: Say hello [.] to my little friend. [Harvey
          looks at the file.] The greatest trick the
          Devil ever pulled was convincing the world
          he didn't exist.
6 Harvey: Surely you can't be serious
7 Mike: I am serious... and don't call me Shirley.
          I'm as mad as hell, and I'm not going to
          take this anymore.
8 Harvey: He pulls a knife, you pull a gun. He sends
          one of yours to the hospital, you send one
          of his to the morgue! That´s the Chicago
          way!
9 Mike: Im'a make him an offer he can´t refuse!
10 Harvey: Release the Kraken!
11 Mike: I see dead people.
12 Harvey: Have fun storming the castle!
13 Mike: I´ll be back.
14 Harvey: May the force be with you.
15 Mike: Yippie kay yay motherfucker

This scene does little to develop the characters or further the plot. It exists primarily to connect the audience to the show, but not through parasocial activity specifically. Rather, here the entertainment comes from recognizing what is being quoted and delighting in the creativity involved in this kind of recursive and reflexive stylization of a media code.[1]

In this self-conscious, postmodern, stylized performance, the scene captures the essence of connecting an audience with a media product. Here, the scene is extraneous to the series' plot; however, its connection to an interactive game on the *Suits* website offers fans a way to distinguish themselves from those who simply watch the show. The scene links iconic films and lines from films that the audience is likely to recognize and, as such, the choices point to the target audience for the show (namely, 18- to 34-year-old men). The show *Suits* also connects audiovisual narrative media together, as we saw in the scene referencing *The Wire* and *The Sopranos*, and in so doing creates an opportunity for a variety of types of interaction between the producers of the show, its characters, and its audience.

The End

Throughout this book we have navigated a delicate tension between looking at language through the lens of the media and looking at media through the lens of language. In this final chapter, we have seen this tension as it circles around the question of the viewing audience and the various ways that language helps link the audience to audiovisual narrative media. This linkage occurs through the design of language variation with an audience in mind, through the various means we have of categorizing linguistic variation, and through the relationships that develop between the emergence of those categories and the narrative media themselves. By examining whole systems, we come full circle to where we started, namely, with the idea that language functions as more than just a representation of a story or a character. Language functions in its own right as a foundational part of the engine that drives the mass media.

While the mass media may not define us as human beings, no other species on our planet has developed anything remotely like it as a channel for sharing information, entertainment, and the contents of our deepest imaginations. The mass media make it possible to be a part of communities that are dispersed in time and space, and to capture both important and mundane moments in social and cultural time. They can expand our understanding of the world we live in and the people who are among this world's inhabitants. They can, of course, also serve as a tool of tyranny, of the oppression of voices deemed problematic, and of raw struggles over social, political, economic, and cultural power. In and of themselves, the mass media are a neutral force, imbued with various meanings by virtue of their users. Surprisingly, language is rather similar.

It's that similarity that has brought me back to thinking about language in the mass media again and again since the late 1990s, at a time when my own discipline was wholly uninterested in the media, and media studies scholars saw language as little more than a vehicle of representation. Language and mass media are very different channels, designed to do vastly different sets of things. They share, however, the role of serving as a conduit or connection between people. Language exists as one of the most critical aspects of being human and facilitates both the most basic of functions, such as sharing what's on our minds with one another, and the most complex, such as putting together a long-running television series. I hope to have convinced you that there is vastly more to language than media scholars (and others) may have considered and vastly more to the media than linguists (and others) may have considered. I take great delight in the creativity with which so many narrative media products play with language. My wish for readers who have come to this point in the book is that a path to your delight has been opened as well.

Figure 8.1   Iconic ending for *Looney Tunes* (© Warner Home Video).

Note

1   For those interested in which movies the quotes come from, a simple Google search of "Suits Recruits: Quote for Quote" will result in many hits of fansites where the scene has been deconstructed for the relevant movies. Or, of course, in another recursive move, readers of this book may find playing the game of interest as well.

References

Abzug, Robyn. 2011. *The Future of Television Audience Research: Changes and Challenges.* The Normal Lear Center: USC Annenberg School for Communication and Journalism.

Agha, A. 2007. *Language and Social Relations.* Cambridge: Cambridge University Press.

Ain't It Cool News. 2012. Mr. Beaks and Paul Rudd Talk WANDERLUST, Erections and Elvin Bishop! Retrieved August 17, 2013, from http://www.aintitcool.com/node/53826.

Auter, P.J., and P. Palmgreen. 2000. Development and Validation of a New Parasocial Interaction Measure: The Audience-Persona Interaction Scale. *Communication Research Reports* 17: 79–89.

Babel, Anna. 2010. *Contact and Contrast in Valley Spanish.* Ann Arbor: University of Michigan.

Bakhtin, Mikhail. 1986. *Speech Genres and Other Late Essays.* Austin: University of Texas Press.

Bauman, Richard. 2011a. Commentary: Foundations in Performance. *Journal of Sociolingiustics* 15(5): 707–720.

Bauman, Richard. 2011b. The Remediation of Storytelling: Narrative Performance on Early Commercial Sound Recordings. In *Telling Stories: Language, Narrative and Social Life,* ed. D. Schiffrin, a. de Fina, and A. Nylund, 23–42. Washington, D.C.: Georgetown University Press.

Beal, J.C. 2009. You're Not from New York City, You're from Rotherham. *Journal of English Linguistics* 37(3): 223–240.

Bell, Allan. 1984. Language Style as Audience Design. *Language in Society* 13: 145–204.

Bell, Allan. 1999. Styling the Other to Define the Self: A Study of New Zealand Identity Making. *Journal of Sociolinguistics* 3(4): 523–541.

Bell, Allan, and Andy Gibson. 2011. Staging Language: An Introduction to the Sociolinguistics of Performance. *Journal of Sociolingiustics* 15(5): 555–572.

Boyd, Betsy. 2009. Sedgwick Perfects Southern Accent. Retrieved August 19, 2013, from http://variety.com/2009/scene/news/sedgwick-perfects-southern-accent-1118004602/.

Briggs, Charles, and Richard Bauman. 1992. Genre, Intertextuality and Social Power. *Journal of Linguistic Anthropology* 2(2): 131–172.

Broadway World. 2013. USA Greenlights Fourth Season of Hit Drama SUITS. Retrieved December 3, 2013, from http://www.broadwayworld.com/bwwtv/article/USA-Greenlights-Fourth-Season-of-Hit-Drama-SUITS-20131024.

Bucholtz, M., and Q. Lopez. 2011. Performing Blackness, Forming Whiteness: Linguistic Minstrelsy in Hollywood Film. *Journal of Sociolinguistics* 15(5): 680–706.

Chun, Elaine. 2009. Speaking Like Asian Immigrants: Intersections of Accommodation and Mocking at a US High School. *Pragmatics* 19(1): 17–38.

Coupland, N. 2007. *Style: Language Variation and Identity.* Cambridge: Cambridge University Press.

Coupland, Nikolas. 1980. Style-Shifting in a Cardiff Work Setting. *Language in Society* 9(1): 1–12.

Eckert, Penelope. 2008. Variation and the Indexical Field. *Journal of Sociolinguistics* 12(4): 453–476.

Eckert, Penelope, and Etienne Wenger. 2005. Communities of Practice in Sociolinguistics. *Journal of Sociolinguistics* 9(4): 582–589.

Errington, Joseph. 1988. *Structure and Style in Javanese: A Semiotic View of Linguistic Etiquette.* Philadelphia: Univeristy of Pennsylvania Press.

Giles, David. 2012. Parasocial Relationships: Current Directions in Theory and Method. In *The Social Uses of Media*, ed. H. Bilandzic, G. Patriarche, and P.J. Traudt, 161–176. Chicago: Intellect.

Goode, Jayne, and James Robinson. 2013. Linguistic Synchrony in Parasocial Interaction. *Communication Studies* 64(4): 453–466.

Halliday, Michael A.K. 1964. Comparison and Translation. In *The Linguistic Sciences and Language Teaching*, ed. M.A.K. Halliday, A. McIntosh, and P. Strevens, 224–265. London: Longman.

Halliday, Michael A.K. 1978. *Language as Social Semiotic: The Social Interpretation of Language and Meaning.* London: Arnold.

Irvine, Judith. 2001. Style as Distinctiveness: The Culture and Ideology of Linguistic Differentiation. In *Style and Sociolinguistic Variation*, ed. P. Eckert and J. Rickford, 21–43. Cambridge: Cambridge University Press.

Irvine, Judith, and Susan Gal. 2000. Language Ideology and Linguistic Differentiation. In *Regimes of Language*, ed. P. Kroskrity, 35–83. Santa Fe, N.M.: School of American Research Press.

Joos, Martin. 1961. *The Five Clocks.* New York: Harcourt.

Kim, Sangkyun. 2012. Audience Involvement and Film Tourism Experiences: Emotional Places, Emotional Experiences. *Tourism Management* 33: 387–396.

Kozloff, Sarah. 2000. *Overhearing Dialogue.* Berkeley: University of California Press.

Kroskrity, Paul. 2000. Regimenting Languages: Language Ideological Perspectives. In *Regimes of Language: Ideologies, Polities, and Identities*, ed. P. Kroskrity, 1–34. Santa Fe, N.M.: School of American Research Press.

Labov, William. 1972. *Sociolinguistic Patterns.* Philadelphia: University of Pennsylvania Press.

Mertz, Elizabeth. 1998. Linguistic Ideology and Praxis in U.S. Law School Classrooms. In *Language Ideologies: Practice and Theory*, ed. B. Schieffelin, K. Woolard, and P. Kroskrity, 149–162. Oxford: Oxford University Press.

Orange, B. Alan. 2012. Elizabeth Banks Talks Effie Trinket in the "Hunger Games." Retrieved November 30, 2013, from http://www.movieweb.com/news/elizabeth-banks-talks-effie-trinket-in-the-hunger-games.

Perse, E.M., and R.B. Rubin. 1989. Attribution in Social and Parasocial Relationships. *Communication Research* 16: 59–77.

Queen, Robin. 2004. "Du hast jar keene Ahnung": African American English Dubbed into German. *Journal of Sociolinguistics* 8(4): 515–537.

Semigran, Aly. 2011. LIFE Names "The Worst Accents in Movie History." Rough week, in'nit Anne Hathaway. Retrieved August 19, 2013, from http://popwatch.ew.com/2011/08/23/life-worst-accents-in-movie-history/.

Silverstein, Michael. 1979. Language Structure and Linguistic Ideology. In *The Elements: A Para-session on Linguistic Units and Levels*, ed. P.R. Clyne, W.F. Hanks, and C.L. Hofbauer, 193–247. Chicago: Chicago Linguistic Society.

Squires, L. 2011. Enregistering Internet Language. *Language in Society* 39(4): 457–492.

Stuart-Smith, Jane, Gwilym Pryce, Claire Timmins, and Barrie Gunter. 2013. Television Can Also Be a Factor in Language Change: Evidence from an Urban Dialect. *Language* 89(3): 501–536.

Trudgill, Peter. 1983. Acts of Conflicting Identity: The Sociolinguistics of British Pop-Song Pronunciation. In *On Dialect: Social and Geographic Perspectives*, ed. P. Trudgill, 141–160. Oxford: Blackwell.

Weldon, Tracey L. 2013. Vignette 13a. Working with Scripted Data: A Focus on African American English. In *Data Collection in Sociolinguistics: Methods and Applications*, ed. C. Mallinson, B. Childs, and G. Van Herk, 228–231. New York: Routledge.

Woolard, Kathryn A. 1998. Simultaneity and Bivalency as Strategies in Bilingualism. *Journal of Linguistic Anthropology* 8(1): 3–29.

Zubair, Cala. 2011. Stylization and the Boundaries of Genre: A Case Study of *The Daily Show* with Jon Stewart. *eVox* 5: 1–15.

Index

Page numbers in *italics* refer to illustrations